Seventh SIGHAN Workshop on Chinese Language Processing 2013

Held at the 6th International Joint Conference on Natural Language Processing (IJCNLP 2013)

Nagoya, Japan
14-18 October 2013

ISBN: 978-1-62993-544-7

Printed from e-media with permission by:

Curran Associates, Inc.
57 Morehouse Lane
Red Hook, NY 12571

CURRAN ASSOCIATES INC. proceedings.com

Some format issues inherent in the e-media version may also appear in this print version.

Printed by Curran Associates, Inc. (2014)

Association for Computational Linguistics
209 N. Eighth Street
Stroudsburg, Pennsylvania 18360

Phone: 1-570-476-8006
Fax: 1-570-476-0860

acl@aclweb.org

Additional copies of this publication are available from:

Curran Associates, Inc.
57 Morehouse Lane
Red Hook, NY 12571 USA
Phone: 845-758-0400
Fax: 845-758-2634
Email: curran@proceedings.com
Web: www.proceedings.com

We wish to thank our sponsors and supporters!

Platinum Sponsors

www.anlp.jp

Silver Sponsors

www.google.com

Bronze Sponsors

www.rakuten.com

Supporters

Nagoya Convention & Visitors Bureau

Organizers

Asian Federation of Natural Language Processing (AFNLP)

Toyohashi University of Technology

Preface

Welcome to the Seventh SIGHAN Workshop on Chinese Language Processing! Sponsored by the Association for Computational Linguistics (ACL) Special Interest Group on Chinese Language Processing (SIGHAN), this year's SIGHAN-7 workshop is being held in Nagoya, Japan, on October 14, 2013, and is co-located with IJCNLP 2013. The workshop program includes a keynote speech, research paper presentations and a Chinese Spelling Check Bake-off. We hope that these events will encourage the participation of researchers and bring them together to share ideas and developments in various aspects of Chinese language processing.

We are honored to welcome as our distinguished speaker Dr. Keh-Jiann Chen (Research Fellow, Academia Sinica, Taiwan). Dr. Chen will be speaking on "Lexical Semantics of Chinese Language". We would also like to thank Shih-Hung Wu, Chao-Lin Liu and Lung-Hao Lee for their great efforts in organizing the Chinese Spelling Check Bake-off which will feature seventeen teams from China, Japan, Singapore, Taiwan and United Kingdom, and is expected to further the development of more accurate Chinese spelling checkers.

Finally, we would like to thank all authors for their submissions. We appreciate your active participation and support to ensure a smooth and successful conference. The publication of these papers represents the joint effort of many researchers, and we are grateful to the efforts of the review committee for their work, and to the SIGHAN committee for their continuing support.

We wish all a rewarding and eye-opening time at the workshop.

Liang-Chih Yu
Yuen-Hsien Tseng
Jingbo Zhu
Fuji Ren
SIGHAN-7 Workshop Co-Chairs

Organizers

SIGHAN Committee:

Hsin-Hsi Chen, National Taiwan University
Chengqing Zhong, Chinese Academy of Science
Gina-Anne Levow, University of Washington
Ming Zhou, Microsoft Research Asia

Workshop Co-Organizers:

Liang-Chih Yu, Yuan Ze University
Yuen-Hsien Tseng, National Taiwan Normal University
Jingbo Zhu, Northeastern University
Fuji Ren, The University of Tokoshima

Bake-off Co-Organizers:

Shih-Hung Wu, Chaoyang University of Technology
Chao-Lin Liu, National Chengchi University
Lung-Hao Lee, National Taiwan University

Steering Committee:

Berlin Chen, National Taiwan Normal University
Keh-Jiann Chen, Academia Sinica
Sin-Horng Chen, National Chiao Tung University
Eduard Hovy, Carnegie Mellon University
Haizhou Li, Institute for Infocomm Research
Chao-Lin Liu, National Chengchi University
Hwee Tou Ng, National University of Singapore
Jianyun Nie, University of Montreal
Wen-Lian Hsu, Academia Sinica
Martha Palmer, University of Colorado Boulder
Jian Su, Institute for Infocomm Research
Keh-Yih Su, Behavior Design Corporation
Hsin-Min Wang, Academia Sinica
Kam Fai Wong, Chinese University of Hong Kong
Chung-Hsien Wu, National Chen Kung University
Guodong Zhou, Soochow University

Program Committee:

Chia-Hui Chang, National Central University
Chien-Liang Chen, Academia Sinica
Kuan-hua Chen, National Taiwan University
Minghui Dong, Institute of Infocomm Research
Donghui Feng, Google Inc.
Zhao-Ming Gao, National Taiwan University
Xungjing Huang, Fudan University
Chunyu Kit, City University of Hong Kong

Olivia Kwong, City University of Hong Kong
Lung-Hao Lee, National Taiwan University
Jun-Lin Lin, Yuan-Ze University
Chao-Hong Liu, National Chen Kung University
Cheng-Jye Luh, Yuan-Ze University
Weiyun Ma, Columbia University
Houfeng Wang, Peking University
Jia-Ching Wang, National Central University
Xiangli Wang, Japan Patent Information Organization
Derek F. Wong, University of Macau
Nianwen Xue, Brandeis University
Chin-Sheng Yang, Yuan-Ze University
Jui-Feng Yeh, National ChiaYi University
Min Zhang, Tsinghua University

Table of Contents

Workshop Program

Monday, October 14, 2013

09:30 09:40 Opening

09:40 10:30 *Keynote Speech: Lexical Semantics of Chinese Language*
Keh-Jiann Chen

10:30 10:50 Break

Oral Session 1: Chinese Language Processing

10:50 11:15 *Can MDL Improve Unsupervised Chinese Word Segmentation?*
Pierre Magistry and Benoît Sagot

11:15 11:40 *Deep Context-Free Grammar for Chinese with Broad-Coverage*
Xiangli Wang, Yi Zhang, Yusuke Miyao, Takuya Matsuzaki and Junichi Tsujii

11:40 12:05 *Lexical Representation and Classification of Eventive Verbs - Polarity and Interaction between Process and State*
Shu-Ling Huang, Yu-Ming Hsieh, Su-Chu Lin and Keh-Jiann Chen

12:05 12:30 *Response Generation Based on Hierarchical Semantic Structure with POMDP Re-ranking for Conversational Dialogue Systems*
Jui-Feng Yeh and Yuan-Cheng Chu

12:30 13:30 Lunch

Oral Session 2: Chinese Spelling Check Bake-off

13:30 13:50 *Chinese Spelling Check Evaluation at SIGHAN Bake-off 2013*
Shih-Hung Wu, Chao-Lin Liu and Lung-Hao Lee

13:50 14:10 *Chinese Word Spelling Correction Based on N-gram Ranked Inverted Index List*
Jui-Feng Yeh, Sheng-Feng Li, Mei-Rong Wu, Wen-Yi Chen and Mao-Chuan Su

14:10 14:30 *Chinese Spelling Checker Based on Statistical Machine Translation*
Hsun-wen Chiu, Jian-cheng Wu and Jason S. Chang

Monday, October 14, 2013 (continued)

14:30 14:50 *A Hybrid Chinese Spelling Correction Using Language Model and Statistical Machine Translation with Reranking*
Xiaodong Liu, Kevin Cheng, Yanyan Luo, Kevin Duh and Yuji Matsumoto

14:50 15:10 *Introduction to CKIP Chinese Spelling Check System for SIGHAN Bakeoff 2013 Evaluation*
Yu-Ming Hsieh, Ming-Hong Bai and Keh-JIann Chen

15:10 15:30 Break

15:30 16:20 **Poster Session**

Automatic Chinese Confusion Words Extraction Using Conditional Random Fields and the Web
Chun-Hung Wang, Jason S. Chang and Jian-Cheng Wu

Conditional Random Field-based Parser and Language Model for Tradi-tional Chinese Spelling Checker
Yih-Ru Wang, Yuan-Fu Liao, Yeh-Kuang Wu and Liang-Chun Chang

A Maximum Entropy Approach to Chinese Spelling Check
Dongxu Han and Baobao Chang

A Study of Language Modeling for Chinese Spelling Check
Kuan-Yu Chen, Hung-Shin Lee, Chung-Han Lee, Hsin-Min Wang and Hsin-Hsi Chen

Description of HLJU Chinese Spelling Checker for SIGHAN Bakeoff 2013
Yu He and Guohong Fu

Graph Model for Chinese Spell Checking
Zhongye Jia, Peilu Wang and Hai Zhao

Sinica-IASL Chinese spelling check system at Sighan-7
Ting-Hao Yang, Yu-Lun Hsieh, Yu-Hsuan Chen, Michael Tsang, Cheng-Wei Shih and Wen-lian Hsu

Automatic Detection and Correction for Chinese Misspelled Words Using Phonological and Orthographic Similarities
Tao-Hsing Chang, Hsueh-Chih Chen, Yuen-Hsien Tseng and Jian-Liang Zheng

NTOU Chinese Spelling Check System in SIGHAN Bake-off 2013
Chuan-Jie Lin and Wei-Cheng Chu

Keynote Speech: Lexical Semantics of Chinese Language

Dr. Keh-Jiann Chen
Institute of Information Science, Academic Sinica, Taiwan
kchen@iis.sinica.edu.tw

Abstract

In this talk, we are going to give a systematic view of lexical semantics of Chinese language. From macro perspective point of view, lexical conceptual meanings are classified into hierarchical semantic types and each type plays some particular semantic functions of Host, Attribute, and Value to form a semantic compositional system. Lexical senses and their compositional functions will be exemplified by the semantic expressions of E-HowNet. Entities and relations are two major semantic types of the compositional system. Lexical senses and phrasal senses are compositions of these two types. From micro perspective point of view, each lexical word has individual idiosyncratic semantic contents, focuses and features. Hence words of same semantic type may have various different syntactic properties which make automatic language processing very difficult. On the other hand lexical syntactic properties are strongly influenced by lexical semantic structures. Morpho-semantic structures may systematically lead the way to derive lexical senses and syntactic behaviors of lexemes. It was observed that allowable alternations of sentence-patterns for verbs are mainly determined by their lexical semantic structures. It follows that senses and syntactic properties of out-of-vocabulary words become predictable and lexical compositional properties do shed light on automatic Chinese language understanding. Supporting evidences and logical interpretations of semantic and syntactic interactions will be presented in this talk.

Vita

Keh-Jiann Chen obtained a B.S. in mathematics from National Cheng Kung University in 1972. He received a Ph.D. in computer science from the State University of New York at Buffalo in 1981. Since then he joined the Institute of Information Science as an associate research fellow and became a research fellow in 1989. He was the deputy director of the institute from August 1991 to July 1994. His research interests include Chinese language processing, lexical semantics, lexical knowledge representation, and corpus linguistics. He had been and continued in developing the research environments for Chinese natural language processing including Chinese lexical databases, corpora, Treebank, lexical analyzer and parsers. Dr. Chen is one of the founding members of the Association of Computational Linguistic and Chinese Language Processing Society (also known as ROCLING). He had served as 2nd term president of the society from 1991 to 1993. Currently he is the board member of the Chinese Language Computer Society, the advisory board member of the International Journal of Computational Linguistics and Chinese Language Processing, the editor of journal of Computer Processing of Oriental Language.

Can MDL Improve Unsupervised Chinese Word Segmentation?

Pierre Magistry
Alpage, INRIA & Univ. Paris 7,
75013 Paris, France
pierre.magistry@inria.fr

Benoît Sagot
Alpage, INRIA & Univ. Paris 7,
75013 Paris, France
benoit.sagot@inria.fr

Abstract

It is often assumed that Minimum Description Length (MDL) is a good criterion for unsupervised word segmentation. In this paper, we introduce a new approach to unsupervised word segmentation of Mandarin Chinese, that leads to segmentations whose Description Length is lower than what can be obtained using other algorithms previously proposed in the literature. Suprisingly, we show that this lower Description Length does not necessarily corresponds to better segmentation results. Finally, we show that we can use very basic linguistic knowledge to coerce the MDL towards a linguistically plausible hypothesis and obtain better results than any previously proposed method for unsupervised Chinese word segmentation with minimal human effort.

1 Introduction

In Chinese script, very few symbols can be considered as word boundary markers. The only easily identifiable boundaries are sentence beginnings and endings, as well as positions before and after punctuation marks. Although the script doesn't rely on typography to define (orthographic) “words”, a word-level segmentation is often required for further natural language processing. This level corresponds to minimal syntactic units that can be POS-tagged or used as input for parsing.

Without word-boundary characters, like whitespace in Latin script, there is no trivial tokenization method that can yield a good enough approximation for further processing. Therefore, the first step of many NLP systems for written Chinese is the Chinese word segmentation task.

A great variety of methods have been proposed in the literature, mostly in supervised machine learning settings. Our work addresses the question of unsupervised segmentation, i.e., without any manually segmented training data. Although supervised learning typically performs better than unsupervised learning, we believe that unsupervised systems are worth investigating as they require less human labour and are likely to be more easily adaptable to various genres, domains and time periods. They can also provide more valuable insight for linguistic studies.

Amongst the unsupervised segmentation systems described in the literature, two paradigms are often used: Branching Entropy (BE) and Minimum Description Length (MDL). The system we describe in this paper relies on both. We introduce a new algorithm which searches in a larger hypothesis space using the MDL criterion, thus leading to lower Description Lengths than other previously published systems. Still, this improvement concerning the Description Length does not come with better results on the Chinese word segmentation task, which raises interesting issues. However, it turns out that it is possible to add very simple constraints to our algorithm in order to adapt it to the specificities of Mandarin Chinese in a way that leads to results better than the state-of-the-art on the Chinese word segmentation task.

This paper is organized as follows. Section 2 describes the role of Branching Entropy in various previous works on Chinese word segmentation, including the algorithm we use as an initialisation step in this paper. In Section 3 we explain how the MDL paradigm is used amongst different Chinese word segmentation systems in the literature. We describe in Section 4 the way we use MDL for trying and improving the results of the initialisation step. A first evaluation and the error analysis given in Section 5 allow us to refine the algorithm and achieve our best results, as shown in Section 6. Finally, we discuss our findings and their implications for our futur work in Section 7.

2 Branching Entropy and Word Segmentation

2.1 The Harrissian hypothesis

Branching Entropy and its discrete counterpart, Accessor Variety are commonly used indicators of linguistically relevant boundaries.

Accessors Variety (hereafter AV) is simply the number of distinct contexts (right or left) in which a given string occurs in a corpus. Branching Entropy (hereafter BE) can be seen as a continuous version of AV that takes into account the probability distribution of cooccurrences. It is the entropy of the probability distribution of the contexts occurring on the right or on the left of a given string. Both measure the diversity of the contexts in which a string can occur.

The main idea behind the use of AV for unsupervised word segmentation was first introduced by Harris (1955) as a procedure from morpheme segmentation in phonemic transcription of speech. In 1955, Harris did not use a corpus to estimate the AV but asked native speakers of various languages how many phonemes they can think of that can follow or precede a given phoneme sequence. Harris made the hypothesis that linguistic boundaries relate with the *variation* of the AV and proposed algorithms to perform segmentation based on the data collected from native speakers. The underlying idea is the following: when given a prefix of a morpheme as input, we have a certain knowledge of what may be the next phoneme; the variety of possible continuations decreases as we add phonemes to the input string, but when reaching a linguistic boundary, the variety of what may come next suddenly increase.

2.2 Variation of Branching Entropy

Kempe (1999) adapted the method proposed by Harris to corpus linguistics and did the switch from variation of AV to variation of BE (hereafter VBE) which is a better estimation of uncertainty.

Branching Entropy (Right and Left) can be defined as follows: given an n-gram $x_{0..n} = x_{0..1}\, x_{1..2} \ldots x_{n-1..n}$ with a left context $\chi_{\rightarrow}$, its *Right Branching Entropy* (RBE) $h_{\rightarrow}(x_{0..n})$ writes as

$$\begin{aligned} h_{\rightarrow}(x_{0..n}) &= H(\chi_{\rightarrow} \mid x_{0..n}) \\ &= -\sum_{x \in \chi_{\rightarrow}} P(x \mid x_{0..n}) \log P(x \mid x_{0..n}). \end{aligned}$$

The *Left Branching Entropy* (LBE) is defined symetrically: if we call $\chi_{\leftarrow}$ the right context of $x_{0..n}$, its LBE is defined as:

$$h_{\leftarrow}(x_{0..n}) = H(\chi_{\leftarrow} \mid x_{0..n}).$$

From $h_{\rightarrow}(x_{0..n})$ and $h_{\rightarrow}(x_{0..n-1})$ on the one hand, and from $h_{\leftarrow}(x_{0..n})$ and $h_{\leftarrow}(x_{1..n})$ on the other hand, we can defined the *Variation of Branching Entropy* (VBE) in both directions:

$$\begin{aligned} \delta h_{\rightarrow}(x_{0..n}) &= h_{\rightarrow}(x_{0..n}) - h_{\rightarrow}(x_{0..n-1}) \\ \delta h_{\leftarrow}(x_{0..n}) &= h_{\leftarrow}(x_{0..n}) - h_{\leftarrow}(x_{1..n}). \end{aligned}$$

2.3 Previous work on VBE-based segmentation

Several unsupervised segmentation algorithms and systems in the literature are based on BE or VBE.

Cohen et al. (2002) use BE as an indicator in their Voting Experts system. They point the need for normalisation but use BE directly, not VBE.

Jin and Tanaka-Ishii (2006) propose a system for unsupervised Chinese word segmentation based on the VBE and evaluate it against a manually segmented corpus in Mandarin Chinese.

Zhikov et al. (2010) use BE to get an initial segmentation. They put a boundary at each position that exceeds a threshold. This threshold is determined by an unsupervised procedure based on MDL. They refine this initial segmentation using two different procedures, also based on BE, which aim at minimizing the Description Length (see next section).

Wang et al. (2011) propose ESA (*Evaluation, Selection, and Adjustment*), a more complex system combining two measures of cohesion and noncohesion iteratively. The Branching Entropy is also at the root of their calculations. They achieve best published results but rely on a parameter used to balance the two measures that can be difficult to set without training data.

In Magistry and Sagot (2012), we use a normalized VBE to define a measure of the *autonomy* of a string (word candidate). The autonomy of a word candidate x is defined as $a(x) = \tilde{\delta h}_{\leftarrow}(x) + \tilde{\delta h}_{\rightarrow}(x)$ where $\tilde{\delta h}(x)$ denotes VBE normalized in order to reduce the bias related to the variation of word lengths. This autonomy function is then used in a segmentation algorithm that maximize the autonomy of all the words in a sentence. The segmentation choosen for a given sentence s

is then chosen among all possible segmentations $w \in Seg(s)$ as being

$$\arg\max_{W \in Seg(s)} \sum_{w_i \in W} a(w_i) \cdot len(w_i),$$

Our results were slightly below ESA, but the system is simpler to implement and improve on; moreover, it does not rely on any parameter for which a value must be chosen.[1]

The system presented in this paper extends both the work of Zhikov et al. (2010) and of Magistry and Sagot (2012): we rely on the notion of autonomy introduced by the latter and use it both for computing an initial segmentation and for guiding the MDL in a way inspired by the former.

3 MDL and Word Segmentation

The Minimum Description Length was introduced by Rissanen (1978). It can be considered as an approximation of the Kolmogorov complexity or as the formalisation of the principle of least effort (Zipf, 1949) by a compression model. The underlying idea behind the use of MDL for Word Segmentation is the following: once a corpus is segmented, it can be recoded as a lexicon and a sequence of references to the lexicon. A good segmentation should result in a more compact representation of the data. Probability distributions of lexical items in the corpus and Shannon entropy are used to determine the theoretically optimal compression rate we could achieve with a given segmentation.

A segmented corpus is therefore considered as a sequence of words encoded using a lexicon, or word model, M_w, which represent each word using a code that depends on its frequency: a frequent word is to be represented by a shorter code. The description length $L(C)$ of a corpus C can then be computed as the length $L(M_w)$ of the lexicon plus the length $L(D|M_w)$ of the sequence of word codes:

$$L(C) = L(D, M_w) = L(M_w) + L(D|M_w).$$

[1] With the current impletation of our algorithm presented in (Magistry and Sagot, 2012), the results are not as good as those from the previous paper. This is due to a bug in normalisation which used to include values of sentence initial and final dummy tokens. This was creating a biais in favor of one-character units and yields better scores. Our latest version of the system, which is used in this paper sticks to the definitions and is thus cleaner but does not perform as well.

The content of the lexicon can be further encoded as a sequence of characters, using a model M_c accounting for characters probability distributions in the lexicon. As a result,

$$L(M_w) = L(D_w, M_c) = L(M_c) + L(D_w|M_c).$$

$L(D|M)$ is given by:

$$L(D|M) = -\sum_{i=1}^{|M|} \#w_i \log \frac{\#w_i}{N}$$

As shown for example by Zhikov et al. (2010), it is possible to decompose this formula to allow fast update of the DL value when we change the segmentation and avoid the total computation at each step of the minimization.

MDL is often used in unsupervised segmentation systems, where it mostly plays one of the two following roles: (i) it can help selecting an optimal parameter value in an unsupervised way (Hewlett and Cohen, 2011), and (ii) it can drive the search for a more compact solution in the set of all possible segmentations.

When an unsupervised segmentation model relies on parameters, one needs a way to assign them adequate values. In a fully unsupervised setup, we cannot make use of a manually segmented corpus to compute these values. Hewlett and Cohen (2011) address this issue by choosing the set of parameters that yields the segmentation associated with the smallest DL. They show that the output corresponding to the smallest DL almost always corresponds to the best segmentation in terms of word-based f-score. In the system by Zhikov et al. (2010), the initial segmentation algorithm requires to chose a threshold: for a given position in the corpus, they mark the position as a word boundary if the BE is greater than the threshold. The value of this threshold is unsupervisingly discovered with a bisection search algorithm that looks for the smallest DL.

However, the main issue with MDL is that there is no tractable search algorithm for the whole hypothesis space. One has to rely on heuristic procedures to generate hypotheses before checking their DL. (Zhikov et al., 2010) propose two distinct procedures that they combine sequentially. The first one operate on the whole corpus. They begin by ordering all possible word-boundary positions using BE and then try to add word boundaries checking each position sorted by decreasing BE, and to

remove word boundaries checking each position by increasing order of BE. They accept any modification that will result in a smaller DL. The rationale behind this strategy is simple: for a given position, the higher the BE, the more likely it is to be a word-boundary. They process the more likely cases first. The main limitation of this procedure is that it is unable to change more than one position at a time. It will miss any optimisation that would require to change many occurrences of the same string, e.g., if the same mistake is repeated in many similar places, which is likely to happen given their initial segmentation algorithm.
To overcome this limitation, Zhikov et al. (2010) propose a second procedure that focuses on the lexicon rather than on the corpus. This procedure algorithm tries (i) to split each word of the lexicon (at each position within each word type) and reproduce this split on all occurrences of the word, and (ii) to merge all occurrences of each bi-gram in the corpus provided the merge results in an already existing word type. This strategy allows them to change multiple positions at the same time but their merging procedure is unable to discover new long types that are absent from the initial lexicon.

4 A new segmentation Algorithm based on MDL and nVBE

We propose a new strategy to reduce the DL. We use the algorithm introduced in Magistry and Sagot (2012) as an initialisation procedure followed by a DL reduction step. This step relies on an *autonomy*-driven algorithm that explores a larger part of the hypothesis space, which we shall now describe.

Given an initial segmentation of the corpus, we define a scoring function for boundary positions. As our initial procedure is based on the maximization of autonomy, any change at any position will result in a lower autonomy of the sequence. Our scoring function evaluates this loss of autonomy whenever a segmentation decision is changed. This can be viewed as similar to the ordered n-best solutions from Magistry's procedure.

The context of a boundary position is defined as a triple containing:

a position state between two characters, i.e., a boolean set to *true* if the position is a word boundary,

a prefix which is the sequence of characters running from the previous word boundary to the position,

a suffix which is the sequence of characters running from the position to the next word boundary.

When scoring a position, there are two possibilities:

- the position is currently a word boundary (we evaluate a merge),
- the position is currently not a word boundary (we evaluate a split).

In order to compute the difference in autonomy scores between the current segmentation and the one which is obtained only by performing a merge at one particular position, we simply have to subtract the autonomy of the prefix and suffix and to add the autonomy of the concatenation of the two strings.

Similarly, to evaluate a splitting decision we have to add the autonomy of the prefix and suffix and to subtract the *autonomy* of the concatenation of the two strings.

Note that with this scoring method and this definition of a context as a tuple, all occurrences of a context type will have the same score, and can therefore be grouped. We can thus evaluate the effect of changing the segmentation decision for a set of identical positions in the corpus in just one step.

Like the lexicon cleaning procedure by Zhikov et al. (2010), we can evaluate the effect of a large number of changes at the same time. But contrarily to Zhikov et al. (2010), because we process the whole corpus and not the lexicon, we have a broader search space which allows for the creation of large words even if they were previously absent from the lexicon.

A remaining issue is that changing a segmentation decision at a particular position should result in a change of the scores of all the neighbouring positions inside its *prefix* and its *suffix* and require to rebuild the whole agenda, which is a costly operation. To make our algorithm faster, we use a simplified treatment that freezes the affected positions and prevent further modification (they are simply removed from the agenda). As the agenda is sorted to test the more promising positions first (in terms of autonomy), this trade-off between exhaustiveness for speed is acceptable. Indeed, it turns out

Algorithm 4.1: algorithm1($Corpus$)

```
seg ← MagistrySagot2012(Corpus)
DL ← DescriptionLength(seg)
MinDL ← ∞
Agenda ← SortBoundaries(Corpus, seg)
while DL < MinDL
  do { MinDL ← DL
       for each changes ∈ Agenda
         do { changes ← removeFrozen(changes)
              newDL = Score(changes)
              if newDL < MinDL
                then
                  do { seg ← ApplyChange(changes)
                       freeze(changes)
                       DL ← newDL
                       break
```

Figure 1: DL minimization

that we still reach lower description length than Zhikov et al. (2010).

The details of our minimization of DL algorithm using this scoring method are presented in figure 4. As we shall see, this system can be further improved. We shall therefore refer to it as the *base system*.

5 Evaluation of the base system

5.1 Reference corpora

The evaluation presented here uses the corpora from the 2005 Chinese Word Segmentation Bakeoff (Emerson, 2005). These corpora are available from the bakeoff website and many previous works use them for evaluation, results are therefore easily comparable. This dataset also has the advantage of providing corpora that are segmented manually following four different guidelines. Given the lack of consensus on the definition of the minimal segmentation unit, it is interesting to evaluate unsupervised systems against multiple guidelines and data sources: since an unsupervised system is not trained to mimic a specific guideline, its output may be closer to one or another. The dataset includes data from the Peking University Corpus (PKU), from the LIVAC Corpus by Hong-Kong City-University (City-U), from Microsoft Research (MSR) and from the Balanced Corpus of the Academia Sinica (AS). It was initially intended for supervised segmentation so each corpus is divided between a training and a test set, the latter being smaller. We retain these splits in order to provide results comparable with other studies and to have an idea of the effect of the size of the training data. All the scores we provide are computed on the test set of each corpus. As our task is unsupervised segmentation, all whitespaces were of course removed from the training sets. Details about the size of the various corpora are given in Table 1.

Corpus	Words		Characters	
	Tokens	Types	Tokens	Types
AS	5 449 698	141 340	8 368 050	6 117
CITYU	1 455 629	69 085	2 403 355	4 923
PKU	1 109 947	55 303	1 826 448	4 698
MSR	2 368 391	88 119	4 050 469	5 167

Table 1: Size of the different corpora

5.2 Evaluation Metrics

The metric used for all following evaluations is a standard f-score on words. It is the harmonic mean of the word recall

$$R_w = \frac{\text{\#correct words in the results}}{\text{\#words in the gold corpus}}$$

and the word precision

$$P_w = \frac{\text{\#correct words in the result}}{\text{\#words in the result}},$$

which leads to the following:

$$F_w = \frac{2 \times R_w \times P_w}{R_w + P_w}$$

For each corpus and method, we also present the Description Length of each segmentation.

Note that, as mentioned by several studies (Huang and Zhao, 2007; Magistry and Sagot, 2012; Sproat and Shih, 1990), the agreement between the different guidelines and even between untrained native speakers is not high. Using cross-trained supervized systems or inter-human agreement, these studies suggest that the topline for unsupervised segmentation is beetween 0.76 and 0.85. As a result, not only the output of an unsupervised system cannot be expected to perfectly mimic a given “gold” segmented corpus, but performances around 0.80 against multiple “gold” segmented corpora using different guidelines can be regarded as satisfying.

5.3 Results

The results of our base system, without and with our MDL step, are presented in Table 2. We also

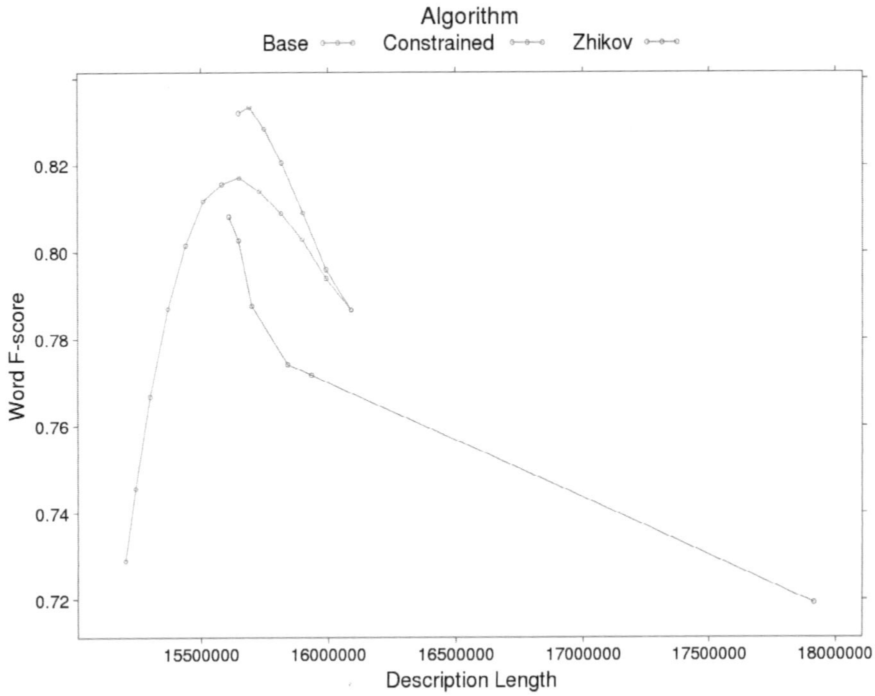

Figure 2: f-score on words as a function of description length for the three algorithms

provide results for our re-implementation of the algorithm by Zhikov et al. (2010), without and with their own MDL step. Our initialisation (without our MDL step) obtains very good results; on the MSR corpus, they are even as high as the results of Zhikov *et al.*'s full algorithm, including their MDL step. However, at a first sight, the results we get when using our MDL procedure are disappointing: it sometimes worsen the results of the initisalisation step. However, we observe that our MDL step succesfully decreases the Description Lengths obtained after the initialisation step, and leads to Description Lengths lower than Zhikov *et al.*'s system although with lower f-scores. This tackles the common idea that lower Description Length yields better segmentation, and calls for further analysis.

5.4 Step-by-step MDL results

In both systems, ours and Zhikov *et al.*'s, the MDL algorithm is iterative. We therefore decided to dump intermediary results at each iteration to observe the evolution of the segmentation quality as the DL gets smaller. Figure 5.3 shows the resulting f-scores as a function of the DL at different stages, on the PKU corpus (results on other corpora behave similarly). Each iteration of one MDL algorithm or the other reduces the DL, which means that a given curve on this graphic are followed by the corresponding system step after step from right to left. The leftmost dot on each curve corresponds to the point when the corresponding system decides to stop and produce its final output.

This graphic shows that our system produces better segmentation at some point, outperforming Zhikov *et al.*'s system. But it doesn't stop at that point and the f-score drops as the DL continue to decrease. This seems to mean that our algorithm, because it explores a larger search space, manages to find segmentations that are optimal as far as DL is concerned, but that do not constitute optimal word-level segmentation.

In order to better understand what is going on, we have added a logging functionality to our implementations, so we can check which operations are made when the f-score decreases. We shall now discuss several typical examples thereof.

5.5 Error analysis

A sample of the latest modifications made by our system while the f-score is falling is given in Table 3. We show the modification that are applied to the largest numbers of occurrences. The type of operation is either a merge (suppression of a boundary) or a split (adding a boundary). We pro-

Method	f-score	DL (Mb)
PKU corpus		
Zhikov *et al.* (no MDL)	0.719	17.9
Zhikov *et al.* (with their MDL)	**0.808**	15.6
This paper (no MDL)	0.786	16.1
This paper (with our base MDL)	0.729	**15.2**
Gold	*1.0*	*15.0*
City-U corpus		
Zhikov *et al.* (no MDL)	0.652	23.2
Zhikov *et al.* (with their MDL)	**0.787**	19.8
This paper (no MDL)	0.744	20.3
This paper (with our base MDL)	0.754	**19.3**
Gold	*1.0*	*19.0*
MSR corpus		
Zhikov *et al.* (no MDL)	0.690	37.1
Zhikov *et al.* (with their MDL)	**0.782**	31.9
This paper (no MDL)	**0.782**	33.0
This paper (with our base MDL)	0.690	**31.1**
Gold	*1.0*	*30.8*
AS Corpus		
Zhikov *et al.* (no MDL)	0.614	80.8
Zhikov *et al.* (with their MDL)	**0.762**	67.1
This paper (no MDL)	0.758	68.9
This paper (with our base MDL)	0.711	**65.7**
Gold	*1.0*	*65.3*

Table 2: Scores on different Corpora for Zhikov *et al.*'s (2010) algorithm (without and with their MDL-based improvement step) and for our base system (without MDL and with our base MDL algorithm). Final results are displayed in Table 6

vide the prefix and suffix, whether the merge or split is an error or not, as well as English glosses.

The first observation we make is that amongst highly frequent items, our system only performs merges. Splits are indeed performed on a large number of rare types for which both the prefix and the suffix exist in the lexicon. We note that for bigrams, such splits are almost always an erroneous decision.

Merge operations include valid decisions, erroneous decisions producing multi-word expression units (MWE), and erroneous decisions that merge a grammatical word to one of its collocations.

6 Description and evaluation of our constrained system

Given this error analysis, there are three main types of common mistakes that we would like to avoid:

- merging MWEs such as named entities;
- merging function words with content words when the co-occurrence is frequent;

Operation	String	Evaluation
merge	的 . 发展 DE - development	error
merge	据 . 新华社 According to - Xinhua Agency	error
merge	新华社 . 北京 Xinhua Agency - Peking	error
merge	经济 . 发展 economic - growth	error (MWE)
merge	进行 . 了 conduct - LE (-ed)	error
merge	和 . 发展 AND - development	error
merge	在 . 北京 AT - Peking	error
merge	邓小平 . 理论 Deng Xiaoping - Theories	error (MWE)
merge	领导 . 干部 leading - cadre	error (MWE)
merge	常 . 委会 standing - committee	error (MWE)
merge	改革 . 开放 reform and opening	error (MWE)
merge	反 . 腐败 anti - corruption	correct
merge	节 . 日 holi-day	correct
merge	党 . 中央 central committee	correct
merge	金融 . 危机 finance - crisis	error (MWE)
merge	新 . 世纪 new - century	error
merge	副 . 总理 vice - premier	correct
merge	国民 . 经济 national - economy	error (MWE)
merge	北京 . 市 Peking - city	no
merge	基础 . 上 basis - postposition (=basically)	error
merge	副 . 主席 vice-chairman	correct
merge	结构 . 调整 structural adjustment	error (MWE)
merge	产业 . 化 industrial - ize	correct
merge	现代化 . 建设 modernization - drive	error (MWE)
merge	人 . 大 Acronym for Renmin University	correct

Table 3: Modification made (sorted by number of occurrences)

Method	f-score	DL (Mb)
PKU corpus		
Zhikov *et al.* (with their MDL)	0.808	15.6
This paper (with constrained MDL)	**0.832**	15.6
Gold	*1.0*	*15.0*
City-U corpus		
Zhikov *et al.* (with their MDL)	0.787	19.8
This paper (with constrained MDL)	**0.801**	19.8
Gold	*1.0*	*19.0*
MSR corpus		
Zhikov *et al.* (with their MDL)	0.782	31.9
This paper (with constrained MDL)	**0.809**	32.1
Gold	*1.0*	*30.8*
AS Corpus		
Zhikov *et al.* (with their MDL)	0.762	67.1
This paper (with constrained MDL)	**0.795**	67.3
Gold	*1.0*	*65.3*

Table 4: Final results

- splitting bigrams that were correct in the initial segmentation.

If we give up on having a strictly language-independent system and focus on Mandarin Chinese segmentation, these three issues are easy to address with a fairly low amount of human work to add some basic linguistic knowledge about Chinese to the system.

The first issue can be dealt with by limiting the length of a merge's output. A MWE will be larger than a typical Chinese word that very rarely exceeds 3 characters. With the exception of phonetic loans for foreign languages, larger units typically correspond to MWE that are segmented in the various gold corpora.[2] The question whether it is a good thing to do or not will be raised in the discussion section, but for a higher f-score on word segmentation, leaving them segmented does help.

The second issue can be addressed using a closed list of function words such as aspectual markers and pre/post-positions. As those are a closed list of items, listing all of them is an easily manually tractable task. Here is the list we used in our experiments:
的、了、上、在、下、中、是、有、和、与、和、就、多、于、很、才、跟

As for the third issue, since Chinese is known to favour bigram words, we simply prevent our system to split those.

[2]A noticeable exception are the 4-characters idioms (chengyu) but they seem less frequent than 2+2 multiword expressions.

We implemented these three constraints to restrict the search space for our minimization of the Description Length an re-run the experiments. Results are presented in the next section.

6.1 Evaluation of the constrained system

The scores obtained by our second system are given in Table 6. They show a large improvement on our initial segmentation and outperform previously reported results.

7 Discussion and futur work

The results presented in this paper invite for discussion. It is well accepted in the literature that MDL is a good indicator to find better segmentation but our results show that it is possible to reach a lower description length without improving the segmentation score. However, this paper also demonstrates that MDL can still be a relevant criterion when its application is constrained using very simple and almost zero-cost linguistic information.

The constraints we use reflect two underlying linguistic phenomena. The first one is related to what would be called "multi-word expressions" (MWE) in other scripts. It is unclear whether it is a limitation of the segmentation system or a problem with the definition of the task. There is a growing interest for MWE in the NLP community. Their detection is still challenging for all languages, but has already been proven useful for deeper analysis such as parsing. It is somewhat frustrating to have to prevent the detection of multi-words expressions to achieve better segmentation results.

The second restriction concerns the distinction between content words and grammatical words. It is not so surprising that open and closed classes of words show different distributions and deserve specific treatments. From a practical point of view, it is worth noting that MDL is useful for open classes where manual annotation or rule-based processing are costly if even possible. On the other hand, rules are helpful for small closed classes and represent a task that is tractable for human, even when facing the need to process a large variety of sources, genres or topics. This division of labour is acceptable for real-world applications when no training data is available for supervised systems.

References

Paul Cohen, Brent Heeringa, and Niall Adams. 2002. An unsupervised algorithm for segmenting categorical timeseries into episodes. *Pattern Detection and Discovery*, page 117–133.

Thomas Emerson. 2005. The second international chinese word segmentation bakeoff. In *Proceedings of the Fourth SIGHAN Workshop on Chinese Language Processing*, volume 133.

Zellig S. Harris. 1955. From phoneme to morpheme. *Language*, 31(2):190–222.

Daniel Hewlett and Paul Cohen. 2011. Fully unsupervised word segmentation with bve and mdl. In *Proceedings of the 49th Annual Meeting of the Association for Computational Linguistics: Human Language Technologies: short papers*, volume 2, pages 540--545.

Changning. Huang and Hai Zhao. 2007. 中文分词十年回顾 (Chinese word segmentation: A decade review). *Journal of Chinese Information Processing*, 21(3):8–20.

Zhihui Jin and Kumiko Tanaka-Ishii. 2006. Unsupervised segmentation of Chinese text by use of branching entropy. In *Proceedings of the COLING/ACL on Main conference poster sessions*, page 428–435.

André Kempe. 1999. Experiments in unsupervised entropy-based corpus segmentation. In *Workshop of EACL in Computational Natural Language Learning*, page 7–13.

Pierre Magistry and Benoît Sagot. 2012. Unsupervized word segmentation: the case for mandarin chinese. In *Proceedings of the 50th Annual Meeting of the Association for Computational Linguistics: Short Papers-Volume 2*, pages 383--387. Association for Computational Linguistics.

Jorma Rissanen. 1978. Modeling by shortest data description. *Automatica*, 14(5):465--471.

Richard W. Sproat and Chilin Shih. 1990. A statistical method for finding word boundaries in Chinese text. *Computer Processing of Chinese and Oriental Languages*, 4(4):336–351.

Hanshi Wang, Jian Zhu, Shiping Tang, and Xiaozhong Fan. 2011. A new unsupervised approach to word segmentation. *Computational Linguistics*, 37(3): 421–454.

Valentin Zhikov, Hiroya Takamura, and Manabu Okumura. 2010. An efficient algorithm for unsupervised word segmentation with branching entropy and mdl. In *Proceedings of the 2010 Conference on Empirical Methods in Natural Language Processing*, pages 832--842. Association for Computational Linguistics.

George Kingsley Zipf. 1949. *Human Behaviour and the Principle of Least-Effort*. Addison-Wesley.

Deep Context-Free Grammar for Chinese with Broad-Coverage

Xiangli Wang
Japan Patent Information Organization, Tokyo, Japan
xiangli_wang@japio.or.jp

Yi Zhang
Dept of Computational Linguistics and DFKI GmbH, Saarland University, Saarland, Germany
yizhang@dfki.de

Yusuke Miyao
National Institute of Informatics, Tokyo, Japan
yusuke@nii.ac.jp

Takuya Matsuzaki
National Institute of Informatics, Tokyo, Japan
takuya-matsuzaki@nii.ac.jp

Junichi Tsujii
Microsoft Research Asia, Beijing, China
jtsujii@microsoft.com

Abstract

The accuracy of Chinese parsers trained on Penn Chinese Treebank is evidently lower than that of the English parsers trained on Penn Treebank. It is plausible that the essential reason is the lack of surface syntactic constraints in Chinese. In this paper, we present evidences to show that strict deep syntactic constraints exist in Chinese sentences and such constraints cannot be effectively described with context-free phrase structure rules as in the Penn Chinese Treebank annotation; we show that such constraints may be described precisely by the idea of Sentence Structure Grammar; we introduce how to develop a broad-coverage rule-based grammar for Chinese based on this idea; we evaluated the grammar and the evaluation results show that the coverage of the current grammar is 94.2%.

1 Introduction

Penn Treebank (PTB) was built based on the idea of context-free PSG (Marcus et al., 1993). It is now a common practice to develop data-driven English parsers using PTB annotation and encouraging performances have been reported (Collins, 2000; Charniak, 2000).

Following the success of PTB, Xue et al. 2000 built Penn Chinese Treebank (CTB). CTB is also based on context-free PSG. Since CTB provides training data for Chinese parsing, researchers attempted to train Chinese parsing with CTB (Bikel and Chiang, 2000; Chiang and Bikel, 2002; Levy and Manning, 2003; Bikel, 2004; Wang et al., 2006; Zhang and Clark, 2009; Huang et al., 2009). However, these works showed that the performances of Chinese parsing were significantly worse than English.

Such inferior performances can be the result of several factors. One of them being that Chinese is an isolating language. Verbs and nouns of Chinese have little morphological paradigms so that the surface syntactic constraints of Chinese sentences less than English sentences. For example, the word "process" acts as different roles in English sentences 1a), 1b) and 1c). The morphologies of the word provide constraints for the roles that it acts as. As a contrast, "处理/process" acts as different roles also in Chinese sentences 2a), 2b) and 2c), but there is no morphology change of the word. Either English PSG rules of PTB or Chinese PSG rules of CTB describe surface syntactic structures of sentences. The lack of surface syntactic constraints of Chinese causes that PSG rules of CTB for Chinese sentences are looser than PSG rules of PTB for English sentences. Therefore, we speculate that the lack of surface syntactic constraints of Chinese sentences is the essential reason why the performances of Chinese PSG parsing are lower than English obviously.

1a. Students process data
1b. Data processing system
1c. Data was processed

2a. 学生 处理 数据
Student process data
Students process data
2b. 数据 处理 系统
Data process system
Data processing system

2c. 数据 处理 了
Data process le
Data was processed

There is another question: are there strict deep syntactic constraints in Chinese sentences? If there were strict deep syntactic constraints in Chinese sentences, and there was grammar formulism capable of describing such constraints precisely, then it would be possible to further improve the performances of Chinese parsing.

In this paper, we present evidences to show that there are strict deep syntactic constraints in Chinese sentences, which are constraints of co-occurrence between deep sentence structures and predicate verbs, but such constraints cannot be described with PSG rules of CTB (section 2); we present examples to show that the idea of Sentence Structure Grammar (SSG) can describe such deep syntactic constraints so that SSG rules can analyze Chinese sentences deeper and more precisely than PSG rules of CTB (section 3);we also show how a broad-coverage Chinese grammar was developed based on SSG (section 4); we evaluate the coverage of the grammar and the results show that its coverage is satisfactory (section 5).

2 Deep Syntactic Constraints in Chinese Sentences

There are plenty of evidences showing that strict deep syntactic constraints exist in Chinese sentences. These are constraints of co-occurrence between deep sentence structures and predicate verbs. We present some examples here.

Sentences (3a-3c) and (4a-4c) can be abstracted into two deep structures: 5a) and 5b). Since the structures like 5a) and 5b) describe the relations between the predicate and its semantic-related constituents like "Agent" and "Direction", we call such structures as ***deep sentence structures***. The deep sentence structures 5a) and 5b) accept "飞/fly" as their predicates but not "吃/eat", and "喜欢/like". Therefore, 3a) and 4a) are grammatical sentences but 3b), 3c), 4b) and 4c) are ungrammatical.

3a. 鸟儿 向 南方 飞
Bird towards south fly
Birds fly towards the south
3b. *鸟儿 向 南方 吃
Bird towards south eat
Birds eat towards the south
3c. *鸟儿 向 南方 喜欢
Bird towards south like
Birds like towards the south
4a. 鸟儿 飞 向 南方
Bird fly towards south
Birds fly towards the south
4b. *鸟儿 吃 向 南方
Bird eat towards south
Birds eat towards the south
4c. *鸟儿 喜欢 向 南方
Bird like towards south
Birds like towards the south
5a. Agent Direction V
5b. Agent V xiang4 Direction

Sentences (6a-6c) and (7a-7c) can be abstracted into two deep sentence structures: 8a) and 8b). 8a) and 8b) accept "吃/eat" as their predicates but not "飞/fly" and "喜欢/like". That is why 6a) and 7a) are grammatical sentences but 6b), 6c), 7b) and 7c) are ungrammatical.

6a. 鸟儿 把 种子 吃 了
Bird ba seed eat le
Birds ate the seeds
6b. *鸟儿 把 种子 飞 了
Bird ba seed fly le
Birds fly the seeds
6c. *鸟儿 把 种子 喜欢 了
Bird ba seed like le
Birds liked the seeds
7a. 种子 被 鸟儿 吃 了
Seed bei bird eat le
Seeds were eaten by birds
7b. *种子 被 鸟儿 飞 了
Seed bei bird fly le
Seeds were flied by birds
7c. *种子 被 鸟儿 喜欢 了
Seed bei bird like le
Seeds were liked by birds

8a. Agent ba Object V le
8b. Object bei Agent V le

Sentences (9a-9c) and (10a-10c) can be abstracted into two deep sentence structures: 11a) and 11b). 11a) and 11b) accept "喜欢/like" as their predicates but not "吃/eat" and "飞/fly". For this reason, the sentences 9a) and 10a) are grammatical but 9b), 9c), 10b) and 10c) are ungrammatical sentences.

9a. 鸟儿 比 狗儿 喜欢 种子
bird than dog like seed
Birds like seeds than dogs
9b. *鸟儿 比 狗儿 飞 种子
bird than dog fly seed
Birds fly seeds than dogs
9c. *鸟儿 比 狗儿 吃 种子
bird than dog eat seed
Birds eat seeds than dogs
10a. 鸟儿 喜欢 狗儿 偷 种子
Bird like dog steal seed
Birds like that dogs steal seeds

10b. *鸟儿 飞 狗儿　偷　种子
Bird fly dogs steal seed
Birds fly that dogs steal seeds
10c. *鸟儿 吃 狗儿 偷 种子
Bird eat dog steal seed
Birds eat that dogs steal seeds

11a. Agent Comparison V Object
11b. Agent V Objects

The above examples provide evidences that deep sentence structures and predicate verbs choose each other. In another words, constraints of co-occurrence between deep sentence structures and predicate verbs exist widely in Chinese sentences.

Deep sentence structures choose predicates according to their deep syntactic properties. "飞/fly" accepts a direction constituent but not an object or a comparison constituent, so it can appear 5a) and 5b) but not 8a), 8b), 11a) and 11b). "吃/eat" accepts an object but not a direction constituent or a comparison constituent, thus it chooses 8a) and 8b) but not 5a), 5b), 11a) and 11b); "喜欢/like" accepts an object, an sentential object or a comparison constituent but not a direction constituent so that it can be predicates of 11a) and 11b) but not 5a), 5b), 8a) and 8b).

Constraints of co-occurrence between deep sentence structures and predicate verbs exist in Chinese sentences commonly. Obviously, CTB rules that describe sentences with context-free phrase structures cannot describe such deep syntactic constraints in Chinese sentences so that distinguish the grammatical sentences from ungrammatical sentences in the above sentences. The rule set of CTB are written to cover the grammatical sentences 3a), 4a), 6a), 7a), 9a), and 10a), but they also cover all ungrammatical sentences above.

12a. IP→ NP-SBJ VP
IP-OBJ→ NP-SBJ VP
VP→ BA IP-OBJ
VP→ LB IP-OBJ
VP→ PP VP
VP→ VP PP
VP→ VV
VP→ VV NP-OBJ
VP→ VV IP-OBJ
PP→ P NP

3 Describing Deep Syntactic Constraints with SSG Rules

Sentence Structure Grammar (SSG) is an idea for grammar formulism (Wang and Miyazaki, 2007; Wang et al., 2012a). SSG focus on describing constraints of co-occurrence between deep sentence structures and predicate verbs that are discussed in section 2. Deep sentence structures in section 2 are treated as rules based on SSG ideas (figure 2); predicate verbs are classified according to their deep syntactic properties (as shown in figure 3); for each type of predicate verbs, only the deep sentence structures that co-occur with them are treated as SSG rules (figure 4). SSG rules not only present deeper information but avoid effectively covering ungrammatical sentences that are covered by CTB rules.

We show how SSG rules present deeper information than CTB rules. SSG is a kind of context-free grammar, but its idea to analyze language is different from context-free PSG. Rather than PSG rules describing a sentence with phrases, SSG rules treat a sentence as a whole that consists of a predicate and its semantic-related constituents. For example, PSG rules of CTB analyze 4a) as shown in figure 1 but SSG rules analyze the same sentence as shown in figure 2. SSG rules present semantic role information like "Agent" and "Direction" besides phrase information such noun phrase, while CTB rules present phrase information and syntactic role like "SBJ".

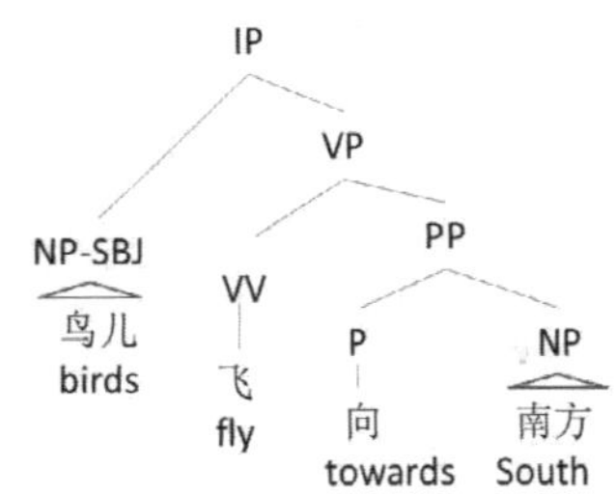

Figure 1: the CTB tree of 4a)

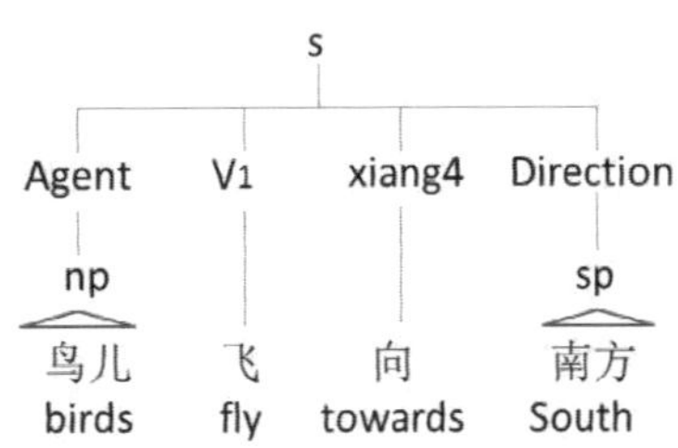

Figure 2: the SSG tree of 4a)

We show how SSG rules avoid covering ungrammatical sentences in section 2, which are covered by CTB rules. Predicate verbs would be classified according to their deep syntactic properties based on SSG ideas. The verbs "飞/fly" belongs to a type that accept an agent and a direction constituent; "吃/eat" belongs to the type that accept an agent and an object but not a direction constituent and a comparison constituent; "喜欢/like" is in a type that accept an agent, an object, a comparison constituent, and a sentential constituent (figure 3).

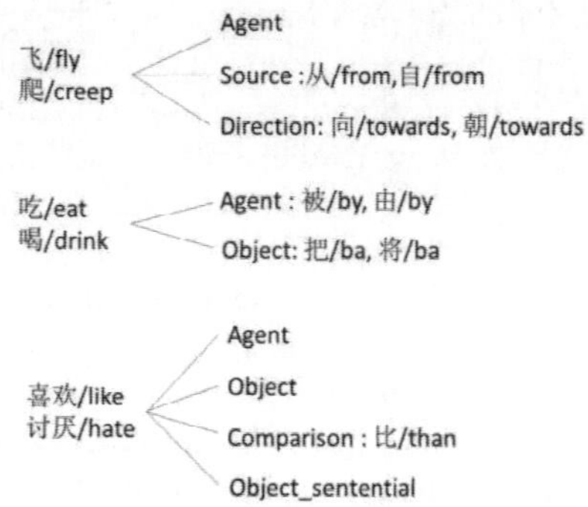

Figure 3: how to classify the predicate verbs based on SSG

For each type of predicate verbs, only deep sentence structures that co-occur with them are treated as rules. As shown in figure 4, for the verbs like "飞/fly", only 5a) and 5b) are the deep sentence structures that co-occur with them, but 8a), 8b), 11a) and 11b) are not, so only 5a) and 5b) are described as the SSG rules 13a) and 13b) for this type of predicate verbs. In the same way, the deep sentence structures 8a) and 8b) are treated as the SSG rules 14a) and 14b) for the type of predicate verbs like "吃/eat"; the deep sentence structures 11a) and 11b) are written as the SSG rules 15a) and 15b) for the type of predicate verbs like "喜欢/like". In this way, the SSG rules 13a) and 13b) only cover the grammatical sentences 3a) and 4a) but not cover the ungrammatical sentences 3b), 3c), 4b) and 4c); the SSG rules 14a) and 14b) cover the grammatical sentences 6a) and 7a) but not cover ungrammatical sentences 6b, 6c), 7b) and 7c); the SSG rules 15a) and 15b) cover the grammatical sentences 9a) and 10a) but not cover the ungrammatical sentences 9b), 9c), 10b) and 10c). The constraints of co-occurrence between deep sentence structures and predicate verbs are described precisely by SSG rules by this way.

13a. s→ Agent V1 xiang4 Direction
Agent→ np
Direction→ sp

13b. s → Agent Direction V1
Agent→ np
Direction→ xiang4 sp

14a. s→ Agent ba Object V2 le
Agent→ np
Object→ np

14b. s→ Object bei Agent V2 le
Agent→ np
Object→ np

15a. s→ Agent Comparison V3 Object
Agent→ np
Object→ np
Comparison→ bi3 np

15b. s→ Agent V3 Objects
Agent→ np
Objects→ s
s→ Agent V2 Object

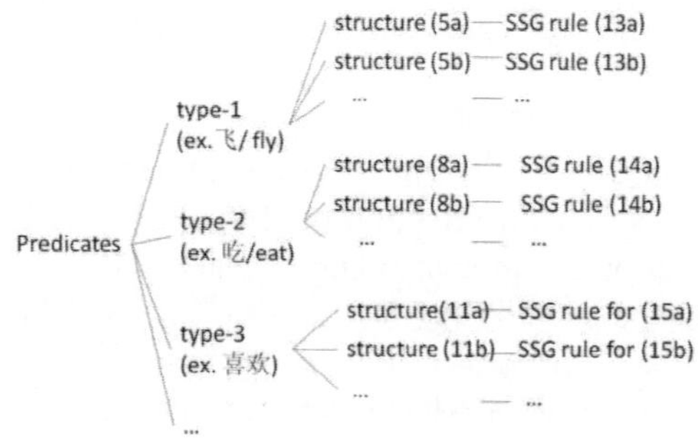

Figure 4: how to develop the SSG rules

4 Grammar Development for Chinese Based on SSG

A broad-coverage grammar for Chinese, named Chinese Sentence Structure Grammar (CSSG), had been developed based on SSG (Wang et al., 2012b).

The idea of SSG is helpful for developing broad-coverage grammar. The predicate verbs of Chinese are classified into 52 types according to their deep syntactic properties. Such classification of predicate verbs provides a clear goal for the developer to develop a broad-coverage grammar. It is to cover all deep sentence structures that co-occur with each type of predicate verbs (shown in fig. 4). For example, for the type of predicate verbs like "吃/eat", the deep sentence structures (16a-16l) are covered by the SSG rules (17a-17l) in CSSG. (16a-16l) include various constructions wide-discussed in linguistic literatures like ba-construction, bei-construction, topic-construction and so on. Figure 5 shows the SSG trees of (16a-16l).

16a. 约翰 吃 苹果 皮
John eat apple skin
John eats apple skin
16b. 约翰 把 苹果 皮 吃 了
John ba apple skin eat le
John ate the apple skin
16c. 苹果 皮 被 约翰 吃 了
apple skin bei John eat le

The apple skin was eaten by John
16d. 苹果 皮 约翰 吃 了
apple skin John eat le
The apple skin was eaten by John
16e. 约翰 把 苹果 吃 了 皮
John ba apple eat le skin
John eats the skin of the apple
16f. 苹果 被 约翰 吃 了 皮
Apple bei John eat le skin
The skin of the apple was eaten by John
16g. 苹果 约翰 吃 了 皮
apple John eat le skin
The skin of the apple was eaten by John
16h. 苹果 被 约翰 把 皮 吃 了
Apple bei John ba skin eat le
The apple skin was eaten by John
16i. 苹果 约翰 把 皮 吃 了
Apple John ba skin eat le
The apples, John ate their skin
16j. 苹果 皮 被 吃 了
Apple skin bei eat le
The apple skin was eaten
16k. 苹果 被 吃 了 皮
Apple bei eat le skin
The apples, their skin was eaten
16l. 苹果 被 把 皮 吃 了
Apple bei ba skin eat le
The apples, their skin was eaten

17a. s→ Agent V2 Object
17b. s→ Agent ba Object V2 le
17c. s→ Object bei Agent V2 le
17d. s→ Object Agent V2 le
17e. s→ Agent ba Object-of0 V2 le Object-of1
17f. s→ Object-of0 bei Agent V2 le Object-of1
17g. s→ Object-of0 Agent V2 le Object-of1
17h. s→ Object-of0 bei Agent ba Object-of1 V2 le
17i. s→ Object-of0 Agent ba Object-of1 V2 le
17j. s→ Object bei V2 le
17k. s→ Object-of0 bei V2 le Object-of1
17l. s→ Object-of0 bei ba Object-of1 V2 le

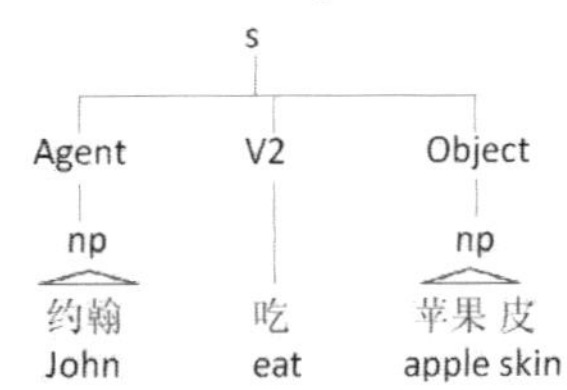

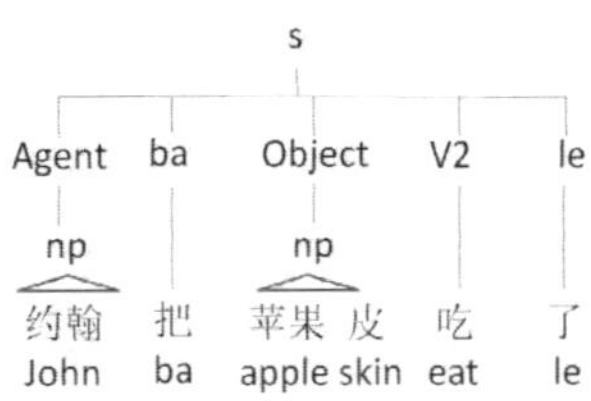

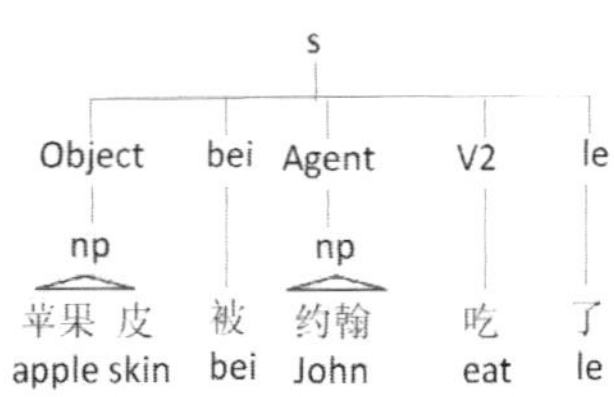

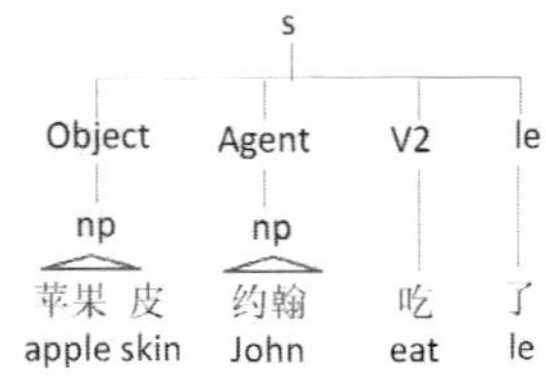

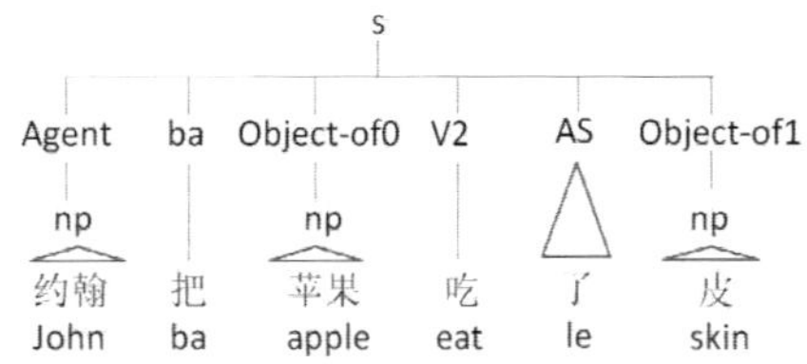

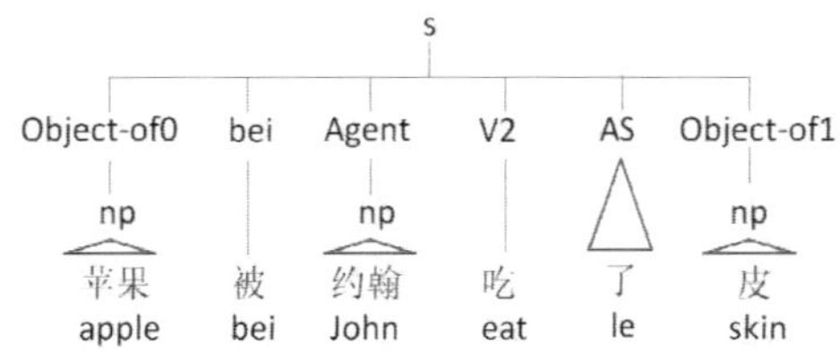

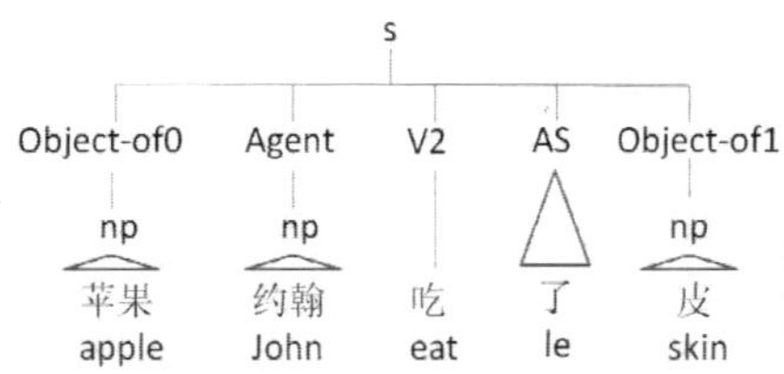

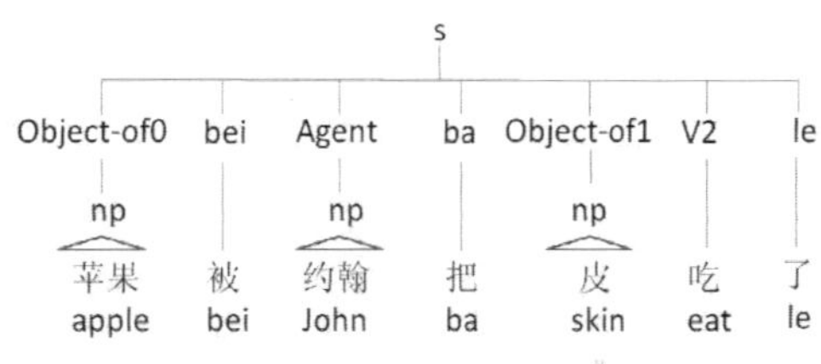

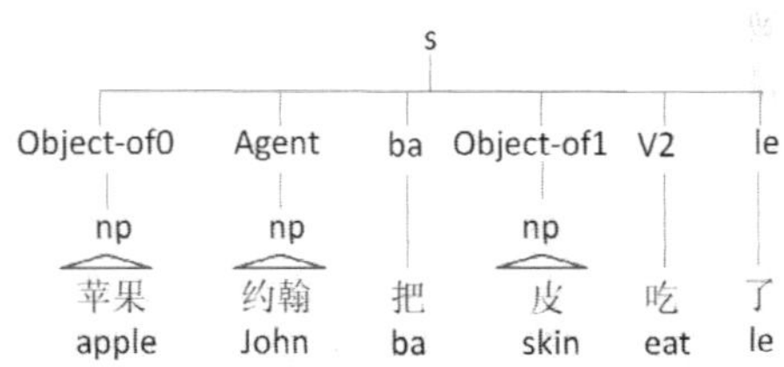

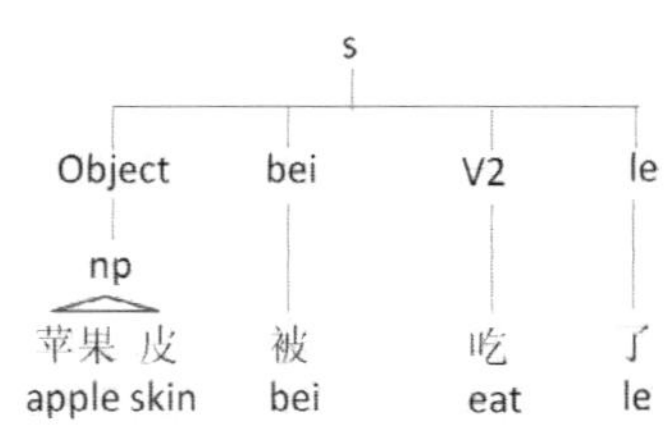

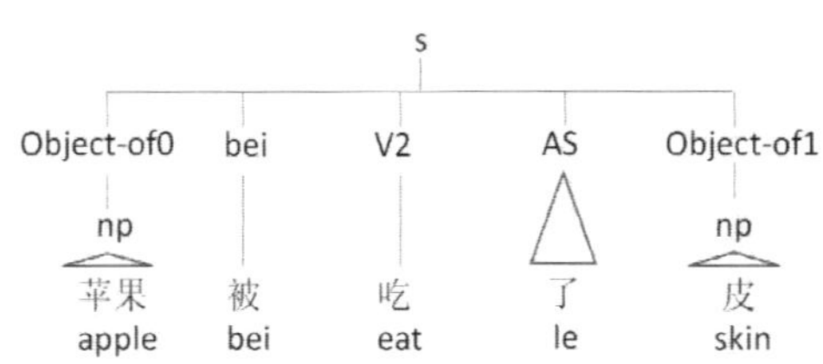

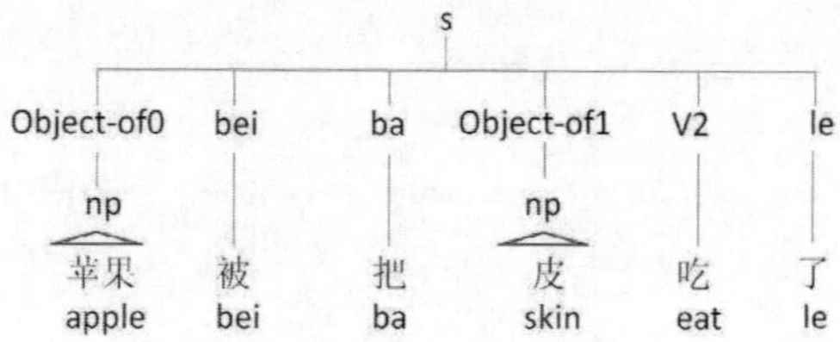

Figure 5: the SSG trees for (16a-16l)

There is a practical issue when developing a broad-coverage grammar based on the SSG idea. It is that the number of SSG rules covering a kind of language would be huge. Wang and Miyazaki 2007 proposed a method to avoid developing a huge number of rules. They divide constituents of a sentence into indispensable parts and dispensable parts. Indispensable constituents must appear while dispensable constituents may or may not appear in a sentence. For example, in the SSG rule set 18a), the asterisked constituents "advp", "AS" and "y" are dispensable constituents, while "Agent", "Object" and "V2" are indispensable constituents. By this way, one SSG rule set 18a) can cover a lot of structures, like (19a-19i) (shown in figure 6).

18a. s→ advp* Agent advp* V_2 AS* Object y*
Agent→ np
Object→ np
AS→ le
AS→ zhe
AS→ guo
advp→ tp
advp→ pp-loc

19a. 约翰 吃 了 苹果 皮
John eat le apple skin
John ate the apple skin

19b. 约翰 吃 过 苹果 皮
John eat guo apple skin
John has ever eaten apple skin

19c. 约翰 也 吃 苹果 皮
John also eat apple skin
John eats apple skin also

19d. 约翰 吃 苹果 皮 吗
John eat apple skin ma
Does John eat apple skin

19e. 今天 约翰 吃 苹果 皮
Today John eat apple skin
John eat apple skin today

19f. 约翰 在 家 吃 苹果 皮
Johan at home eat apple skin
John eats apple skin at home

19g. 今天 约翰 在 家 吃 苹果 皮
Today John at home eat apple skin
John eats apple skin at home today

19h. 今天 约翰 也 在 家 吃 苹果 皮
Today John also at home eat apple skin
John also eats apple skin at home today

19i. 今天 约翰 也 在 家 吃 苹果 皮 吗
Today John also at home eat apple skin ma
Does John also eat apple skin at home today

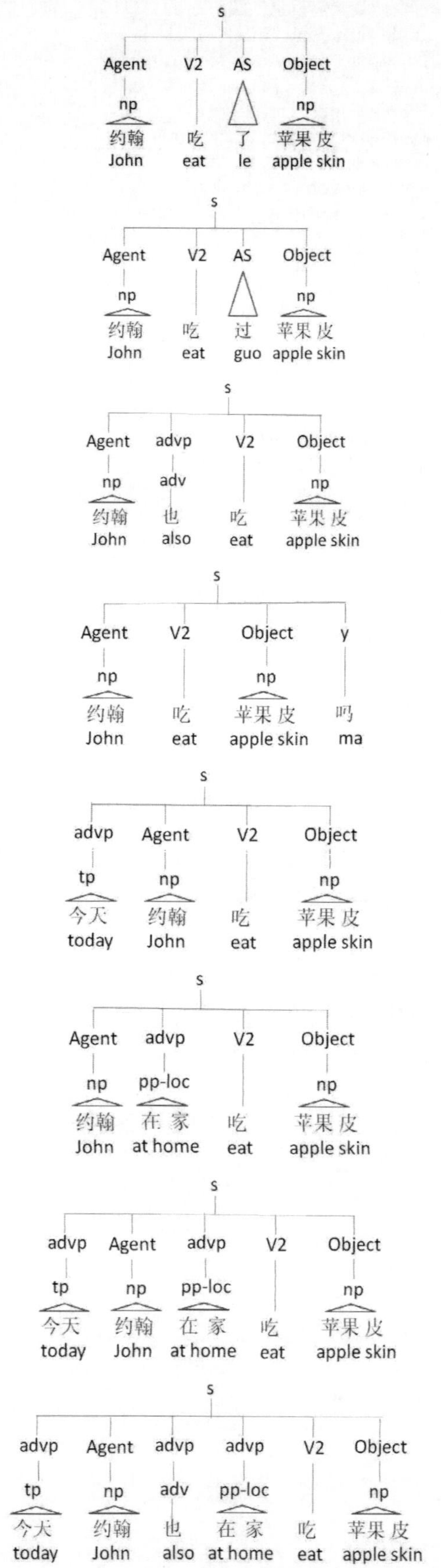

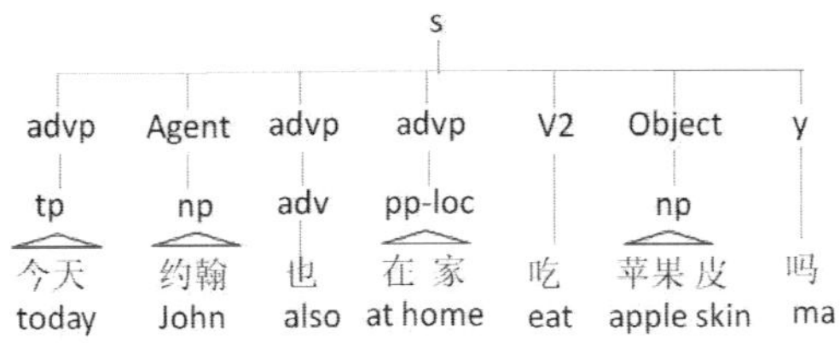

Figure 6: the SSG trees for (19a-19i)

5 Evaluation and Discussion

5.1 Evaluation Results

We evaluated the coverage of CSSG. We chose the first 200 sentences from CTB development data as the test set. We convert the CTB trees of the test data into the CSSG trees semi-automatically with heuristics and some manual correction. Then we evaluate how many constructions of the test data are covered by the CSSG rules.

5,333 construction instances are exacted from the test data (table 1). These may be divided into 3 types:

1) Sentential constructions: the constructions of simple sentences and complex sentences;
2) Semantic roles: the constructions of semantic roles like “Agent”, “Object” and “Direction”;
3) Phrase constructions: the constructions of phrase like “np”, “advp” and “tp”.

Among these constructions, 19.1% are the sentential constructions; 14.4% are the semantic roles; 62.9% are the phrase constructions.

Sen. Constr.	Sem. Role	Phr. Constr.	Total
1,014(19.1%)	770(14.4%)	3549(66.5%)	5,333(100%)

Table 1: the contents of the constructions of the test data

	Total	Matched	Unmatched
Sen. Constr.	1014(100%)	905(89.3%)	109(10.7%)
Sem. Role	770(100%)	764(99.2%)	6(0.8%)
Phr. Constr.	3549(100%)	3355(94.5%)	194(5.5%)
Total	5333(100%)	5024(94.2%)	309(5.8%)

Table 2: coverage of the CSSG

Table 2 shows that the coverage of CSSG. 94.2% of the total constructions of the test data are covered by CSSG: 89.3% of sentences constructions; 99.2% of semantic roles; 94.5% of phrase constructions.

Unmatched Sen. Constr.	Unmatched for simple Sen.	Unmatched for complex Sen.
109(100%)	13(11.9%)	96(88.1%)

Table 3: contents of unmatched sentential constructions

Since the coverage of the sentential constructions of the CSSG is lower than the other types, we analyze the unmatched sentential constructions further. As shown in table 3, 88.1% of unmatched sentential constructions are for complex sentences, only 11.9% for simple sentences. 90.5% of the sentential constructions are for simple sentences (table 4) and 98.6% of the constructions for simple sentences are covered by the CSSG (table 5).

Sen. Constr.	Constr. for simple Sen.	Constr. for complex Sen.
1014(100%)	918(90.5%)	96(9.5%)

Table 4: contents of sentential constructions of the test data

Constr. for simple Sen.	Matched	Unmatched
918(100%)	905(98.6%)	13(1.4%)

Table 5: coverage of the simple sentential constructions of CSSG

We analyzed the type of the unmatched constructions for simple sentences. These may be divided into 3 types:

1) The constructions for special structures;
2) The constructions for common structures;
3) The constructions for new types of predicate verbs.

Table 6 summarizes the contents of the unmatched constructions for simple sentences.

the type of unmatched constr.	Number
Special structure	2
Common structure	9
New type of verbs	2
	13

Table 6: analysis of the unmatched constructions for simple sentence

5.2 Discussion

The evaluation results show that the coverage of the sentential constructions of the CSSG is lower than the coverage of the total rules (table 2), but 88.1% of the unmatched constructions are for complex sentences (table 3). As the discussion in section 2 and section 3, the CSSG rules focus on covering the deep sentence structures of simple sentences. The rules for complex sentences are still not included by the current version of the CSSG.

Table 4 shows that 90.5% of the sentential constructions are for simple sentences, and the coverage of the constructions of simple sentences of CSSG is 98.6% (table 5). The results verified that the CSSG rules cover the deep sentence structures of Chinese widely.

There are 13 deep sentence structures that failed to be covered by CSSG (table 5). As shown in table 6, most of them appear commonly but CSSG failed to cover these constructions; two of them are special structures like 20a) and 20b), these structures need to be described with special rules; two of them are not covered because their predicate verbs are not covered by the current version of the CSSG. The two verbs are "获悉/know from" and "符合/be in accord with". "获悉/know from" accept a sentential object and a source constituent; "符合/be in accord with" accept a nominal subject, a sentential subject and an object (figure 7). These two types of verbs are still not included by the predicate classification of CSSG. It is possible to improve the coverage of CSSG by adding such new types of verbs to the predicate classification of CSSG and describing the SSG rules for them. For example, the predicate verb of 21a) is "获悉/know from", and 22a) is the deep sentence structure of 21a); the predicate verbs of 23a) and 23b) are "符合/be in accord with". 24a) and 24b) are the deep sentence structures of 23a) and 23b). We can add the new types of predicates like "获悉/know from" and "符合/be in accord with" to the predicate classification of CSSG, then describe SSG rules for the deep sentence structures 22a), 24a) and 24b). In this way, the coverage of CSSG can be further improved.

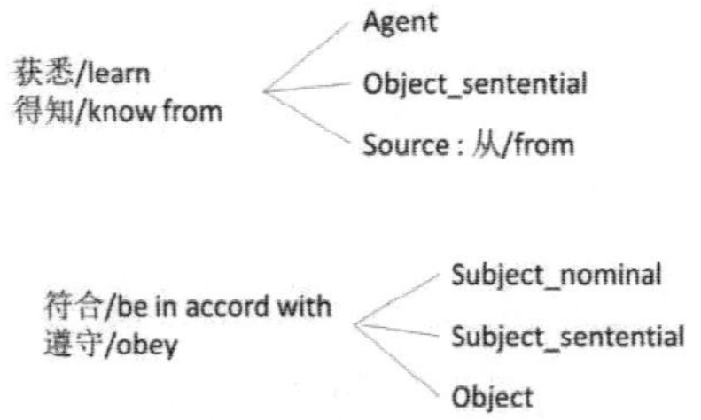

Figure 7: the new types of predicate verbs

20a. 中国 的 友好城市 以 日本 为 最 多
China de sister city yi3 Japan wei2 most few
Japan has most of the sister cities of China

20b. 他 给 人 以 挑战者 的 印象
He give people yi3 challenger de impression
He gives people an impression of a challenger

21a. 他 从 记者 获悉 日本 发生 地震
He from reporter learn Japan happen earthquake
He learned from reporters that there was an earthquake in Japan

22a. Agent Source Vi Object_sentential

23a. 他 符合 雇用条件
He be in accord with employment condition
He is in accord with the employment condition

23b. 减少 工资 符合 公司利益
Decrease salary be in accord with company's benefit
It is in accord with company's benefit to decrease salaries

24a. Subject _nominal Vj Object
24b. Subject_ sentential Vj Object

6 Conclusion and Future Work

In this paper, we argued that the lack of surface syntactic constraints of Chinese is the essential reason of the lower performances of the Chinese parsing trained on CTB than the English parsing trained on PTB. We gave examples to show that surface syntactic constraints of Chinese are less than English. We presented evidences to show that there exist strict deep syntactic constraints in Chinese sentences but CTB rules cannot effectively describe such constraints. We showed how to describe such deep syntactic constraints precisely based on SSG and how to develop a broad-coverage SSG-based Chinese grammar. The evaluating experiment was done and the results showed that the coverage of the Chinese grammar is 94.2%.

The CSSG rules analyze Chinese sentences deeper and more precisely than the CTB rules, so we will attempt to use it for Chinese parsing in the future.

References

Daniel M. Bikel and David Chiang. 2000. Two statistical parsing models applied to the Chinese Treebank. In Second workshop on Chinese language processing, volume 12, pages 1-6. Morristown, NJ, USA.

David Chiang and Daniel M. Bikel. 2002. Recovering latent information in treebanks. In Proceedings of the 19th international conference on Computational linguistics, volume 1, pages 1-7. Association for Computatical Linguistics.

Daniel M. Bikel. 2004. On the parmeter space of generative lexicalized statistical parsing models. Ph.D. thesis, Citeseer.

Eugene Charniak. 2000. Amaximum-entropy-inspired parser. In Proceedings of NAACL.

Liang Huang, Wenbin Jiang, and Qun Liu. 2009. Bilingually-constrained (monolingual) shift-reduce parsing. In Proceedings of the 2009 conference on Empirical Methods in Natural Language Processing, volume 3, pages 1222-1231. Association for Computational Linguistics.

Mengqiu Wang, Kenji Sagae, and Teruko Mitamura. 2006. A fast, accurate deterministic parser for Chinese. In Proceedings of the 21st International Conference on Computational Linguistics, pages 425-432. Association for Computational Linguistics.

M. Marcus, B. Santorini, M.A. Marcinkiewicz. Building a large annotated corpus of English: the Penn TreeBank. Computational linguistics. Vol 19, 1993.

Michael Collins. 2000. Discriminative reranking for natural language parsing In Proceedings of ICML, pages 175-182. Morgan Kaufmann, San Francisco, CA.

Nianwen Xue and Fei Xia. 2000. The bracketing Guidelines for the Penn Chinese Treebank.

Roger Levy and Christopher Manning. 2003. It is harder to parse Chinese, or the Chinese Treebank? In Annual Meeting of the Association for Computational Linguistics, volume 1, pages 439-446. Morristown, NJ, USA.

Xiangli Wang, Masahiro Miyazaki. 2007. *Chinese Syntactic Analysis Using Sentence Structure Grammar(in Japanese).* Journal of Natural Language Processing. vol.14, No.2. April 2007

Xiangli Wang, Yusuke Miyao and Yuan Li. 2012a. *Chinese Grammatical resources based on Sentence Structure Grammar and its application on patent field (in Japanese).* Proceeding of Japan Natural Language Processing. 2012.

Xiangli Wang, Terumasa Ehara and Yuan Li. 2012b. Parsing Simplified Chinese and Traditional Chinese with Sentence Structure Grammar. In proceedings of the Second CIPS-SIGHAN Joint Conference on Chinese Language Processing, Pages 179-187.

Yue Zhang and Stephen Clark. 2009. Transition-based parsing of the Chinese Treebank using a global discriminative model. In Proceedings of the 11th International Conference on Parsing Technologies, pages 162-171. Association for Computational Linguistics.

Lexical Representation and Classification of Eventive Verbs

— Polarity and Interaction between Process and State

Shu-Ling Huang[1] **Yu-Ming Hsieh**[1, 2] **Su-Chu Lin**[1] **Keh-Jiann Chen**[1]

[1] Institute of Information Science, Academia Sinica, Taiwan

[2] Department of Computer Science, National Tsing-Hua University, Taiwan

{josieh,morris,jess,kchen}@iis.sinica.edu.tw

Abstract

Event classification is one of the most crucial tasks in lexical semantic representation. Traditionally, researchers regarded process and state as two top level events and discriminated them by semantic and syntactic characteristics. In this paper, we add cause-result relativity as an auxiliary criterion to discriminate between process and state by structuring about 40,000 Chinese verbs to the two correspondent event hierarchies in E-HowNet. All verbs are classified according to their semantic similarity with the corresponding conceptual types of the ontology. As a consequence, we discover deficiencies of the dichotomy approach and point out that any discrete event classification system is insufficient to make a clear cut classification for synonyms with slightly different semantic focuses. We then propose a solution to remedy the deficiencies of the dichotomy approach. For the process or state type mismatched verbs, their inherited semantic properties will be adjusted according to their POS and semantic expressions to preserve their true semantic and syntactic information. Furthermore, cause-result relations will be linked between corresponding processes and states to bridge the gaps of the dichotomy approach.

1 Introduction

Clarifying the nature of verb classes is a crucial issue in lexical semantic research, being of great interest to both theoretical and computational linguistics. Many classification and representation theories have already been presented including the widely cited theories proposed by Vendler (1967), Dowty (1979), Bach (1986), Parsons (1990), Levin (1993), Pustejovsky (1995) and Rosen (2003). Additionally, several online verb classification systems, such as WordNet (Fellbaum 1998), VerbNet (Kipper-Schuler 2006), FrameNet (Fillmore et al. 2003) and Levin's verb classification are also available. Each approach views events from a different perspective, and each approach clarifies a different part of the overall problem of understanding the linguistic representation of events. Overall, they can be divided into two main schools, one is semantic classification, such as Vendler's approach; and the other is syntactic classification, such as Levin's approach.

Since different event classifications pinpoint the basic features of events that need to be represented, we need to clarify the goal we want to achieve before adopting or proposing an event classification. In this paper, we aim to achieve a better lexical semantic representation framework for E-HowNet (Chen et al. 2003), and we adopt the typologies of process and state as the two top level event types. However, since verbs may express different aspects or viewpoints of conceptual events, is difficult in some cases to make a clear-cut difference between process and state verbs. Verb-result compounds, such as 購妥 gou-tuo 'to complete procurement', are obvious examples which are either pure process or state. Furthermore their semantic interactions also need to be clarified. Consider, for example, the synonym words (strictly speaking near synonyms and hyponyms) of 記得 ji-de 'remember' in Mandarin Chinese: (a) 想起 xiang-qi 'call to mind', 記取 ji-qu 'keep in mind', 背起來 bei-qi-lai 'memorize', (b) 念念不忘 nian-nian-bu-wang 'memorable', 刻骨銘心 ke-gu-ming-xin 'be remembered with deep gratitude'; although these words are near synonyms, their senses shift slightly according to different semantic focuses and often resulting in different grammatical behavior. If we classify group (a) as a process type, and group (b) as a state type by their fine-grained semantic focuses, we may lose the important information of they are actually near synonyms and denote the same event type. Therefore, in order to design a better semantic and syntactic representational framework for verbs, we try to clarify the polarity and interaction between process and state.

The remainder of this article is organized as follows. In the next section, we begin with a review of past research. Section 3 clarifies the polarity between process and state, and then difficulties of the dichotomy approach will be addressed. In Section 4 we describe the interaction between process and state, and propose solutions to overcome the difficulties mentioned in the previous section. Finally, we conclude our findings and possible future research in Section 5.

2 Backgrounds

Over 2300 years ago, Aristotle (1984) proposed the first event-based classification of verbs. His main insight was the distinction between states and events (called 'processes' in this paper). From the late 1960's, a large number of event classifications, variously based on temporal criteria (such as tense, aspect, time point, time interval), syntactic behavior (such as transitivity, object case, event structure), or event arguments (such as thematic role mapping, agent type, verb valence) have been suggested and have aroused many heated discussions. These representations can be roughly divided into the two main schools of semantic classification and syntactic classification. In the following discussion, we take Vendler and Levin as representatives for the two respective schools, and we will find that both schools treat process and state as two obviously different event types.

2.1 Vendler's Classification

Vendler's classification (1967) is the most influential and representative system in terms of the semantic classification approach. He classified verbs into four categories "to describe the most common time schemata implied by the use of English verbs" (pp. 98-99). The four categories are given in (1):

(1) a. *States*: non-actions that hold for some period of time but lack continuous tenses.
b. *Activities*: events that go on for a time, but do not necessarily terminate at any given point.
c. *Accomplishments*: events that proceed toward a logically necessary terminus.
d. *Achievements*: events that occur at a single moment, and therefore lack continuous tenses (e.g., the progressive).

Distinctly, states denote a non-action condition and are irrelevant to temporal properties, while the other three denote an event process or a time point in an event process. Vendler's successors, such as Verkuyl (1993), Carlson (1981), Moens (1987), Hoeksema (1983), extended this discussion without changing Vendler's basic framework. According to Rosen (2003), the successors all pointed out that state and process are two major event types. Ter Meulen (1983, 1995) thus suggested a redefinition of the Vendler classes. She defined states have no internal structure or change, while events, i.e., the processes dealt with in our paper and consisting in Vendler's other three event types, are defined on the basis of their parts.

2.2 Levin's Classification

Levin (1993) believes that identifying verbs with similar syntactic behavior provides an effective means of distinguishing semantically coherent verb classes. She proposed a coarse-grained classification for verbs based on two observations: the first is many result verbs lexicalize results that are conventionally associated with particular manners, and vice versa, many manner verbs lexicalize manners that are conventionally associated with particular results. The examples she gave are listed in (2):

(2) The pervasiveness of the dichotomy (Levin 2011)

	Manner verbs	**vs.**	**Result verbs**
Verbs of damaging:	*hit*	vs.	*break*
Verbs of putting–2-dim	*smear*	vs.	*cover*
Verbs of putting–3-dim	*pour*	vs.	*fill*
Verbs of removal	*shovel*	vs.	*empty*
Verbs of combining	*shake*	vs.	*combine*
Verbs of killing	*stab*	vs.	*kill*

Levin argued the origins of the dichotomy arises from a lexicalization constraint that restricts manner and result meaning components to fit in a complementary distribution: a verb lexicalizes only one type; and those components of a verb's meaning are specified and entailed in all uses of the verb, regardless of context. Further, not only do manner and result verbs differ systematically in meaning, but they differ in their argument realization options (Rappaport and Levin 1998, 2005). For example, result verbs show a causative alternation, but manner verbs

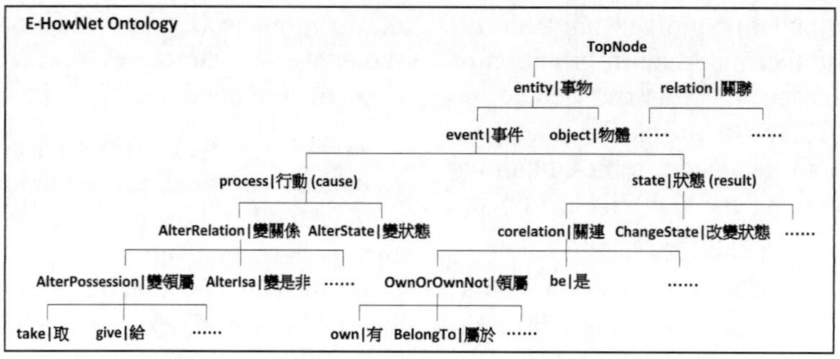

Figure 1. The Architecture of E-HowNet

do not, as shown in example (3); and, manner verbs show considerably more and different argument realization options than result verbs (Rappaport and Levin 1998), such as those described in (4).

(3) a. Kim broke the window./The window broke.
b. Kim wiped the window./*The window wiped.

(4) a. Terry wiped. (activity)
b. Terry wiped the table. (activity)
c. Terry wiped the crumbs off the table. (removing)
d. Terry wiped the crumbs into the sink. (putting)
e. Terry wiped the slate clean. (change of state)
f. Terry wiped the crumbs into a pile. (creation)

Levin's manner verb and result verb dichotomy characterizes semantic and syntactic interactions between verbs. Specifically, this syntactic dichotomy is caused by the semantic characteristics of the language. We consider a similar semantic relation of cause-result between process verbs and state verbs to show the dichotomy and interactions between them. In fact, Levin's result verbs are verb-result compounds in Chinese and our result verbs refer to pure states. The above cited verbs pairs, such as *stab* and *kill* in (2), are both process verbs. By our notion of process and state dichotomy *wounded* and *die* are result states of *stab* and *kill,* respectively.

2.3 E-HowNet's Classification

E-HowNet (Chen et al. 2005) is a frame-based entity-relation model that constructs events, objects and relations in a hierarchically-structured ontology. By following the conventional event classification theories, verbs are partitioned into process and state first, which is a higher priority dichotomous classification criterion than the syntactic classification in E-HowNet, since E-HowNet is a primarily semantic classification system. Furthermore, semantic classification is more intuitive, and more in line with the general view of the real world. Based on this criterion, the top-level E-HowNet ontology is established as depicted in Figure 1.

3 The Polarity and Interaction between Process and State

Process and state have long been treated as two top classes of events. Semantically, their distinctions are evident and intuitive, such as the obvious difference between the process verb 取悅 qu-yue 'please' and the state verb 喜悅 xi-yue 'joyful'. With respect to syntax, process and state verbs also have their own individual characteristics; for example, 取悅 qu-yue 'please' must have a patient object but 喜悅 xi-yue 'joyful' does not. Differentiating them is considered obvious in theoretic and practical linguistic research areas. However, from the perspective of a fine-grained lexical analysis, researchers have also found that it is difficult to make clear cut differences between process and state. Take the following as examples. The state verb 生氣 sheng-qi 'angry' may accept an object goal in Mandarin and can be hardly differentiated from the process verb 發脾氣 fa-pi-qi 'get angry' in semantics. In this paper, we do not aim to strictly partition 生氣 sheng-qi 'angry' and 發脾氣 fa-pi-qi 'get angry' into state and process type. Instead, our objective is to discriminate processes from states with an emphasis on why we encounter difficulties of discriminating them, and what are better representations that may preserve as much semantic and syntactic information as possible. For example, the verb 遇害 yu-hai 'be murdered' can be either classified as a process of *kill* or a state of *die*, with neither classification being absolute. A better solution might be that even if the verb is misclassified into either type, we can still recognize that the experiencer of 遇害 yu-hai 'be murdered' is killed and dead. In this section, we emphasize the general distinction between process and state, and then in the next section, we introduce several approaches we adopted while encountering difficulties of process-state dichotomy.

The differentiating characteristics between process and state verbs, other than semantic differences, are not obvious. Summarizing the previously mentioned theories in Section 2, the polarities between process and state can be generalized as below:

(5) The polarities and interactions between process and state
Processes: cause of states, dynamism (i.e., relevant to temporal properties), object domination
States: result of processes, stasis (i.e., irrelevant to temporal properties), object modification

The polarity of dynamism and stasis is a semantic-based distinction, whereas the domination of objects or their modification is a syntax-based distinction. They are both common but coarse-grained event classification criteria and most verbs can be distinguished by these coarse-grained classification criteria. However some verbs like 發脾氣 fa-pi-qi 'get angry' and 遇害 yu-hai 'be murdered' are not easily classified. In our study, we propose an interaction between cause and result as an auxiliary criterion, which asserts that *processes* are the cause of states and they denote an event process or a time point on an event process. On the other hand, *states* are the result of processes and they denote a non-action condition and are thus irrelevant to temporal properties, i.e., they have no internal structure or change. Although it would appear that cause-result is a natural differentiation criterion between processes and states, it may not be a one-to-one relation and some of verb types may not have obvious cause-result counterparts. For instance, the concept of causative process {earn|賺} may achieve several resultant states such as {obtain|得到} and {rich|富}, though the process of {swim|游} does not have an obvious result state. Nonetheless if we can use the characteristics of (5) to differentiate all verbs into process and state types, which may help us achieve the first step towards a lexical semantic classification for verbs. We then use semantic expressions, part-of-speech (POS) features, and relational links such as cause-result relationship between process types and state types to make a better lexical semantic representation. Regarding the verb type classification, the following questions may be raised. Is the process-state dichotomy approach feasible? How are the verbs denoting complex event structures, such as verb-result compounds, classified? Is it true that all states have causing processes and all processes have result states? The following observations will provide the answers to these questions.

3.1 Observations and Difficulties of the Process-State Dichotomy in E-HowNet

In order to develop the lexical semantic representation system E-HowNet, we classified all Chinese verbs into a process and state type-hierarchy, as illustrated in Figure 1. We use the characteristics (5) of dynamism and stasis as a semantic-based distinction; the domination and modification of objects as a syntax-based supporting criterion; as well as the cause-result relation as a complementary criterion to distinguish process from state. It is interesting that with the exception of general acts, almost all top-level Chinese verb types; whether of process or state types, necessarily have their cause-result counterpart. However for the fine-grained lower level types or lexical level verbs, there are three different cases of lexical realizations of cause-result dichotomy, which are listed in the following.

Case 1: Process types have result states and vice versa. An example of cause-result mapping between process and state is given in (6).

(6) Causative process type {brighten|使亮}: e.g., 磨光 mo-guang 'burnish', 擦亮 ca-liang 'polish' etc. ←→
Resultant state type {bright|明}: e.g., 水亮 shui-liang 'bright as water', 光燦 guang-can 'shining' etc.

For this case, the process and state are two different types and can be differentiated by the fundamental differences between dynamic and static types or by the cause-result relation. However, lexemes may shift their senses due to different compounding, resulting in a classification dilemma of semantic similarity first or dichotomy of process and state first. As was mentioned in the above example, the causative process type {kill|殺害}, e.g., 弔死 diao-si 'hang by the neck', has a resultant state type {die|死}, e.g., 往生 wang-sheng 'pass away'. Then, how about the result-state verb 遇害 yu-hai 'be murdered'? Should we classify 遇害 yu-hai 'be murdered' as a process type {kill|殺害}? Or, as a state type {die|死}? The verb 遇害 yu-hai 'be murdered' seems to be the resultant state {die|死} in terms

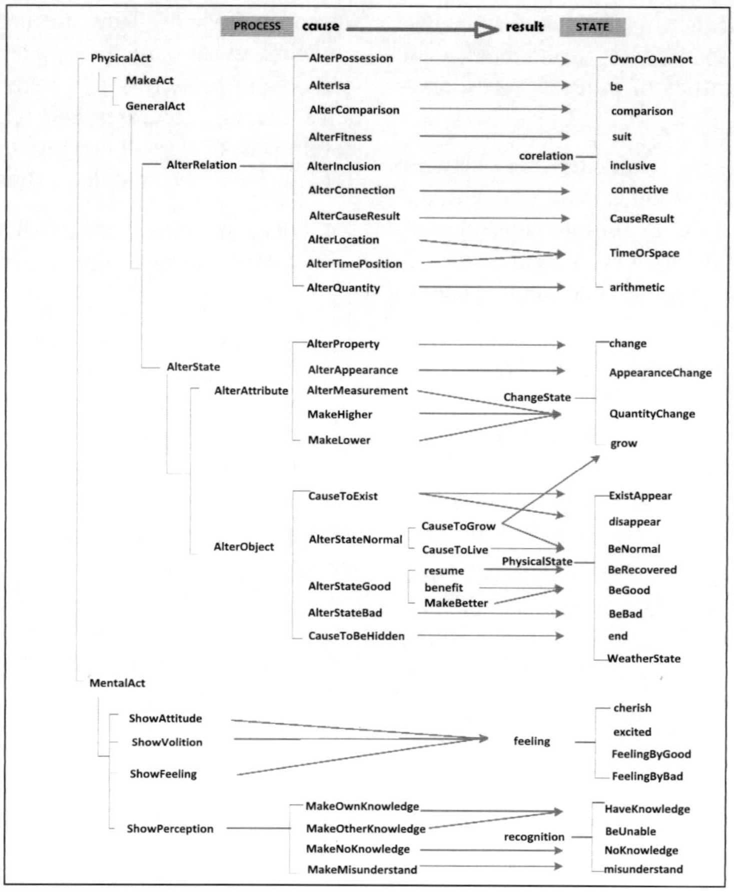

Figure 2. The Matching between Processes and Result States in E-HowNet

of stativity, but from the perspective of a semantic focus, it is more akin to a causative process {kill|殺害}. This classification difficulty always occurs when we analyze verbs denoting different aspect situations, such as passive or achieved situations. As a result, near synonyms of same event type could be separated apart for denoting different aspectual situations.

In terms of the E-HowNet ontology, the cause-result matching between processes and states almost reaches 100% respecting hypernymy concepts as shown in Figure 2. However, at the hyponym or lexical level, we found that the correspondent rate was not as high as in top-level concepts. This results in Case 2 below.

Case 2: Process types neither have nodes of result states nor do state types have nodes of causing processes in the E-HowNet ontology, which means the result states or causal processes are either vague or they are not lexicalized common concepts. (7), (8) are typical examples.

(7) The causative process type {punish|處罰}, such as 行刑 xing-xing 'execute' or 處決 chu-jue 'put to death', have the corresponding aspectual resultant states, such as 受刑 shou-xing 'be put to torture' and 伏法 fu-fa 'be executed', but no lexicalized concept in common to denote *being punished* or *being tortured* in Chinese. Therefore, there is no proper node of state type to which the above two stative verbs belong in E-HowNet.

(8) There is no lexicalized concept in common to denote causative processes, such as 板起(臉) ban-qu-(lian) 'put on a stern expression' and 正色 zheng-se 'with a stern countenance' in Chinese, and which are the cause of the resultant state type {austere|冷峻}, e.g., 凝重 ning-zhong 'serious', 不苟言笑 bu-gou-yan-xiao 'serious in speech and manner'. That is, there is no proper node of the process type to which the above two process verbs 板起臉 ban-qu-lian 'put on a stern expression' and 正色 zheng-se 'with a stern countenance' belong.

For lexemes of Case 2, the characteristics of process and state of (5) can still differentiate the lexemes on the process and state types, but there are no actual corresponding conceptual nodes in the ontology. This means that some stative verbs must be attached to the process type node and some of process verbs should be attached to stative type node in the ontology for the sake of keeping reasonable semantic consistency.

Case 3: Some processes and respective states co-exist concurrently and are not in the cause-result temporal sequence. We call such concurrent process and state a dual process-state. There are 26 dual process-state type primitives in the E-HowNet ontology, with example (9) describing one of them.

(9) the dual process-state {living|生活} includes: (a) 求生 qiu-sheng 'seek to survive', 度日 du-ri 'subsist', and (b) 生存 sheng-cun 'exist', 在世 zai-shi 'be living', 一息尚存 yi-xi-shang-cun 'be still alive'. The semantic focus of group (a) indicates a process of *making a living* or *to live*, while group (b) indicates the state of *being alive* or *be living*. The two types of process and state coexist and they are not cause-result relation.

For the dual process-state type, we encounter the similar dilemma of the previous two cases. If we choose the bipartite process and state approach, near synonyms will belong to two nodes far apart in the ontology. If we adopt the approach of a unified conceptual node for each dual process-state type, the result will be the same problem as in Case 2, i.e., stative verbs and process verbs are of the same type.

Furthermore, in Mandarin Chinese we have many verb-result compounds (VR), such as 累病 lei-bing 'sick from overwork', 驚退 jing-tui 'frighten off' and 購妥 gou-tuo 'to complete procurement'. Since causative process and resultant state are contained in the same verb, how should we classify them?

4 Knowledge Representation for Process and State Verbs

The difficulties of the dichotomous approach are caused by the semantic interaction between state and process. We thus propose the classification criterion (5) and a representational scheme according to the above observations, and try to solve the corresponding difficulties without changing the framework of the dichotomy structure. The idea is that all verbs are classified according to their semantic similarity with the conceptual types of the ontology. The process or state type mismatched verbs will have their types adjusted by their POS or semantic expressions. Such an approach is functional insofar as, for example, using the feature of *'don't fly'* to adjust the flying property for penguins as bird type and still maintaining the inherent properties. Furthermore, cause-result relations will be linked between corresponding processes and states to bridge the gaps of the dichotomy approach. This proposal is put forward to interpret the semantic and syntactic consistency and differences of verbs with respect to lexical representation.

4.1 Lexical Semantic Representation for Verbs that are Attached to Process or State Primitives

For the Case 1 verbs, every process has the corresponding result state, and every state has the corresponding causal processes. For synonym verbs with a process and state dichotomy, each verb is placed under its corresponding conceptual nodes. In addition, cause-result relation links will be established between corresponding process types and state types, as exemplified in the Figures 2 and 4. In real implementation, there are 310 corresponding cause-result pairs established. However from a practical point of view, all semantic representation systems are discrete systems. Given that they use a limited number of primitive concepts to express complex concepts, the result is that some words are forced to be classified to the most similar concept node but with a mismatched major type, such as 遇害 yu-hai 'be murdered' possibly being classified as the process type {kill|殺害} instead of the state type {die|死}. We will resolve such kind of problem by the following method for Case 2.

As shown in the observation of Case 2, some of the cause-result corresponding concepts are vague and some are not lexicalized, neither of which occur as conceptual type nodes in the ontology. As a result, for verbs whose potential hypernyms are missing, we will classify these verbs to their cause-result counterpart conceptual nodes instead. After this, we use the part-of-speech to distinguish the state or process, as illustrated in (10).

(10) causative process: {FondOf|喜歡}←→ there is no corresponding resultant state
lexicons: 看中 kan-zhong 'take fancy to', 喜愛 xi-ai 'love', 酷愛 ku-ai 'ardently love', 熱衷 re-zhong 'be addicted to'. Since these verbs in E-HowNet are tagged with active POS, they are classified to {FondOf|喜歡}.

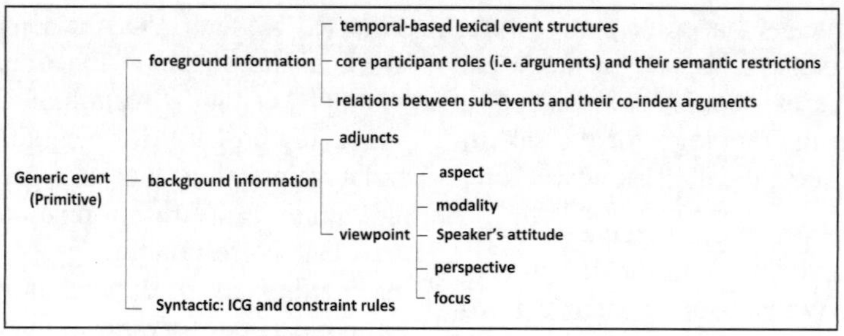

Figure 3. The Content and Formation of LESRE

The verbs of 癡情 chi-qing 'be infatuated', 興致盎然 xing-zhi-ang-ran 'full of interest' in E-HowNet are tagged with stative POS, but there is no lexicalized state primitive to place these verbs, and as such, they are classified to the corresponding existing hypernym process node, i.e., {FondOf|喜歡}.

With part-of-speech tags, we have no problem discriminating state verbs that are attached to a process primitive. In fact, we can define state verbs in {result(process)} format; or process verbs in {cause(state)} format in order to make both semantic distinctions and link relations. Example (11) lists the expressions of verbs in (10).

(11) 看中 kan-zhong 'take fancy to', 喜愛 xi-ai 'love', 酷愛 ku-ai 'ardently love', 熱衷 re-zhong 'be addicted to' are defined as {FondOf|喜歡}; 癡情 chi-qing 'be infatuated', 興致盎然 xing-zhi-ang-ran 'full of interest' are defined as {result({FondOf|喜歡})}.

Moreover, fine-grained part-of-speech tags also provide syntactic constraint information for each verb; this solves the difficulty in Case 2 and effectively makes a semantic and syntactic distinction for synonyms.

4.2 Lexical Representation for Verbs that are Attached to Dual Process-State Primitives

For Case 3 dual process-state verbs, the bipartite nodes for state and process are not needed for two reasons. Firstly, it is hard to make distinction between process and state for the dual types, and secondly, state and process are just two different viewpoints of same events. A single dual process-state conceptual type may contain both process and stative verbs of same event type of different viewpoints. We use part-of-speech tags to tell the difference between semantic focus and the syntactic behavior of each verb. In addition, the dual process-state type also indicates that the process and state coexist at the same time.

4.3 Lexical Semantic Representation for Verb-Result Compounds

In addition to the verbs belonging to Cases 1-3, we also wanted to address the solution for classification difficulty of VR compounds. Take as examples the verbs with VR structure in example (12); no matter which event type we classified them to, no difference was caused with respect to lexical representation.

(12) 累病 lei-bing 'sick from overwork' def:{ill|病態: cause={tired|疲乏}}
驚退 jing-tui 'frighten off' def:{frighten|嚇唬: patient={x}, result={leave|離開:theme={x}}}
購妥 gou-tuo 'to complete procurement' def:{buy|買: aspect={Vachieve|達成}}

The semantic expressions provide information to clarify the accurate word meaning and relation between V1 and V2, as well as to constrain the syntactic behaviors in the Verb-Result structure. Although it is controversial to recognize the semantic focus of these verbs, i.e., to determine whether they are more state-like or more process-like, it is not an important issue in making a semantic and syntactic distinction in lexical representation. We built explicit links of cause-result relations between sub-events in the LESRE framework of E-HowNet (Chen et al. 2013), such as {ill|病態} and {tired|疲乏} of the verb 累病 lei-bing 'sick from overwork'. We also encoded the co-indexed arguments for all related event pairs, e.g., the patient of {frighten|嚇唬} is the agent of {leave|離開} in (12).

5 Discussion and Conclusion

Levin (2010) had pointed out that different studies support positing verb classes of varying grain-sizes, including (a) coarse-grained classification discriminating *manner verb*, *result verb*;

Figure 4. Three Grain-sizes of Event Classification in E-HowNet Construction

(b) medium-grained classification discriminating *motion verbs*, *speaking verbs* etc., with Fillmore's verb classification being regarded as a representative of medium-grained classification; and (c) fine-grained classification discriminating *run,* which lexicalizes a manner of motion that causes directed displacement towards a goal. Nevertheless, while these classifications are different in grain-size, they are not contradictory for the classification criteria.

In E-HowNet, we carry this viewpoint through the whole construction by firstly classifying events into causative processes and their corresponding resultant states, i.e., the top two levels of events we mainly discussed in this paper; we then further subdivided more than 1200 generic events (i.e., primitives) into a semantic hierarchy framework as a medium-grained event classification. Finally, the near synonyms were attached to each primitive and discriminated by fine-grained features that were integrated in the lexical event structure representation of E-HowNet (abbreviated as LESRE; see Chen et al. 2013). The content and formation of LESRE is shown in Figure 3.

We believe the varying grain-sizes classifications provide different semantic and syntactic realization options, such as the coarse-grained classification in which process verbs show considerably more and different argument options than state verbs; further, the idiosyncrasy of each grain-size classification, as well as their interaction, will provide us with advanced knowledge in lexical representation. We will, therefore, continue to complete the LESRE theory in the near future, with the ultimate objective being to establish a completed event classification system which can be applied to both theoretical and computational linguistics. The sketch of different grain-sized event classification in the E-HowNet construction is detailed in Figure 4.

Event classification is one of the most crucial tasks in lexical semantic representation. Traditionally, researchers have regarded process and state as two top level events and defined them by counter temporal features and syntactic rules. In this paper, we added cause-result relativity as an auxiliary criterion to discriminate between process and state, and structured about 40,000 Chinese verbs to the two correspondent event classes. All verbs were classified according to their semantic similarity with the conceptual types of the ontology. The process or state type mismatched verbs would have their types be adjusted by their POS or semantic expressions. Furthermore cause-result relations would be linked between corresponding processes and states to bridge the gaps of the dichotomy approach.

We not only aimed to claim the deficiency of dichotomy approach, but also to point out that any discrete event classification system is insufficient to make a clear cut classification for all verbs, such as synonyms with slightly different semantic focuses. Although misclassification maybe unavoidable, under our framework of event classification, we proposed the remedy of using fine-grained feature expressions to recover erroneous information inherited from the mismatched classification and differentiated the fine-grained semantic differences for near synonyms. The E-HowNet feature expression system is an incremental system, i.e., fine-grain features can be added gradually without side effects. Currently we have resolved the medium-grained classification among 1200 generic event types for about 40,000 Chinese verbs. In the future, we will improve their fine-grained feature expressions to achieve better lexical semantic and syntactic representations.

References

Aristotle, 1984, Metaphysics. In Jonathan Barnes (eds.), The Complete Works of Aristotle: *The Revised Oxford Translation*, Volume 2. Princeton, NJ: Princeton University Press.

Chen Keh-Jiann, et al., 2003, *E-HowNet*, CKIP Group, Academia Sinica, http://ehownet.iis.sinica.edu.tw /ehownet.php.

Chen, Keh-Jiann, Shu-Ling Huang, Yueh-Yin Shih, Yi-Jun Chen, 2005, *Extended-HowNet- A Representational Framework for Concepts*, OntoLex 2005 - Ontologies and Lexical Resources IJCNLP-05 Workshop, Jeju Island, South Korea.

Chen Keh-Jiann, Shu-Ling Huang and Suchu Lin, 2013, *The Lexical Event Structure Representation of E-HowNet*, technical report, CKIP Group, Academia Sinica. (In preparation).

Levin, B., 1993, *English Verb Classes and Alternations: A Preliminary Investigation*. Chicago: University of Chicago Press. http://www-personal.umich.edu/~jlawler/levin.verbs.

Levin, B., 2010, *What is the best grain-size for defining verb classes?* Conference on Word Classes: Nature, Typology, Computational Representations, Second TRIPLE International Conference, Università Roma Tre, Rome, pp.24-26.

Levin, B., 2011, *Verb Classes Within and Across Languages*, Valency Classes Conference, Max Planck Institute for Evolutionary Anthropology, Leipzig, pp.14-17.

Meulen Alice G.B. ter, 1983, The Representation of Time in Natural Language. In A.G.B. ter Meulen (ed.), *Studies in Modaltheoretic Semantics*. Dordrecht: Foris.

Meulen Alice G.B. ter, 1995, *Representing Time in Natural Language: The Dynamic Interpretation of Tense and Aspect*. Cambridge, MA: MIT Press.

Rappaport Hovav, M. and B. Levin, 1998, *Building Verb Meanings*, in M. Butt and W. Geuder, eds., The Projection of Arguments, CSLI Publications, Stanford, CA, pp.97-134.

Rappaport Hovav, M. and B. Levin, 2005, Change of State Verbs: Implications for Theories of Argument Projection, in N. Erteschik-Shir and T. Rapoport, eds., *The Syntax of Aspect*, Oxford: Oxford University Press, pp.274-286.

Rosen, S. T., 2003, The Syntactic Representation of Linguistic Events, In L. Cheng & R. Sybesma (eds.), *The 2nd State of the Article Book*. Mouton de Gruyter, Berlin, pp. 323-365. Reprinted from Glot International, 4, 3-10.

Vendler, Z., 1967, *Linguistics in Philosophy*, Ithaca, New York: Cornell University Press, pp.97-121.

Response Generation Based on Hierarchical Semantic Structure with POMDP Re-ranking for Conversational Dialogue Systems

Jui-Feng Yeh **Yuan-Cheng Chu**
Department of Computer Science and Information Engineering,
National Chiayi University,
No.300 Syuefu Rd., Chiayi City 60004, Taiwan (R.O.C.).
Ralph@mail.ncyu.edu.tw s1000444@mail.ncyu.edu.tw

Abstract

Conversational spoken dialogue systems can assist individuals to communicate with machine to obtain relevant information to their problems efficiently and effectively. By referring to relevant response, individuals can understand how to interact with an intelligent system according to recommendations of dialogue systems. This work presents a response generation based on hierarchical semantic structure with POMDP Re-ranking for conversational dialogue systems to achieve this aim. The hierarchical semantic structure incorporates the historical information according to dialogue discourse to keep more than one possible values for each slot. According to the status of concept graph, the candidate sentences are generated. The near optimal response selected by POMDP Re-ranking strategy to achieve human-like communication. The MOS and recall/precision rates are considered as the criterion for evaluations. Finally, the proposed method is adopted for dialogue system in travel domain, and indicates its superiority in information retrieval over traditional approaches.

1 Introduction

Intelligent space is one of the new trends about computing environment construction. From providing the natural intelligent human machine interaction, conversational dialogue systems play an essential role in iterative communication. Let us now attempt to extend the observation into the frameworks of spoken dialogue systems, in viewpoints of input and output aspects, speech recognition and speech synthesis provide the main acoustic interfaces between users and dialogue management. However, the semantic extraction and generating of natural language processing plays more essential roles for human machine interactions. As shown in Figure 1, a spoken dialogue system is composed of three components: speech recognition and natural language processing, dialogue management, and response generating and text to speech. Actually, we should now look more carefully into the results obtained in speech recognition and natural language processing. Since the accuracy of speech recognition is not near to perfect, it will cause the natural language misunderstanding.

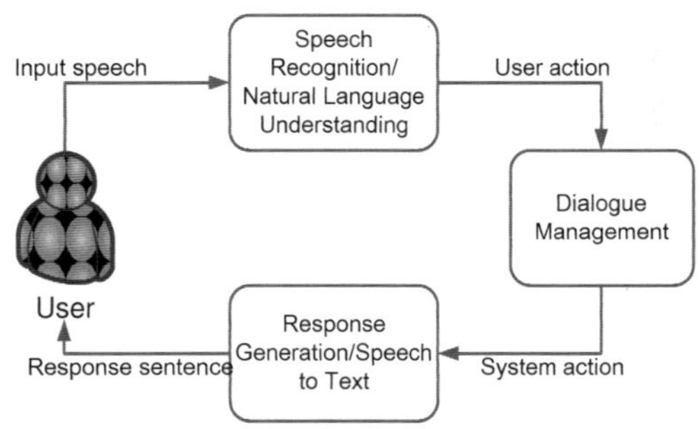

Figure 1. Overview of spoken dialogue systems.

That is to say, it is hard for conversational dialogue systems to fill the values in the semantic slots perfectly. Dialogue management with only limited information about semantic slots is unable to decide the correct system actions. Based on the incorrect system actions, the indisposed response generated by the system will make the system unfriendly. In the latest decades, some research efforts on response generating are invested for improving the quality of conversational dialogue systems.

The goal of natural language generating is aimed at obtaining the sentence that is suitable to understand for users. Herein, there are three categories of sentence generating: template-based, rule-based and statistics-based approaches. Template-based approaches were first developed for generating the sentence in natural language processing (Lemon 2011; Bauer 2009; Zhan 2010). Fang et al. used the mixed template for constructing the declarative sentences. The declarative sentences were further converted into interrogative sentences by changing the word order and verb forms (Fang et al. 2006). Compared to template-based approaches, rule-based approaches were designed to provide more flexibility and desired sentences (Reiter and Dale 2000; Reiter 1996). Three main modules are included here in rule-based approaches: content determination and text planning, sentence planning and surface realization. Content determination and text planning are designed to decide the on the information communicated in a generated text. Dialogue management plays essential roles in content determination in conversational dialogue systems. According to the results of content determination, sentence planning selects and organizes the propositions, events and states to generating the sentence which usually contain one issue. Its main function is to select and adapt linguistic forms so that the generated sentences are suitable for the local context in which they are to appear. Surface realization is designed to create a syntactic representation in the form of a generated sentence given the semantic concepts. The overall flow of the rule-based approach is illustrated in Figure 2.

The third category about sentence generation is statistics-based approaches. The statistics-based approaches are also called as trainable generation. Instead of the predefined templates and rules, trainable approaches build the models and the corresponding parameters using the gathered corpus. Branavan et al. used the reinforcement learning to predict causal relationship between content and event, the causal relationship was further adapted to derive the higher level content determination (Branavan et al. 2012). Walker et al. proposed trainable sentence planner, DSyntS, to enhance the variousness of generated sentences (Walker et al. 2001; Walker et al. 2002; Melcuk 1988). Stent et al. added the rhetorical knowledge into the sentence planner to form the system, SPaRKy (Stent et al. 2004).
Since the response generating plays an essential role in conversational dialogue systems, the excellent response generating will cause the system more practical. For avoiding the limitation of human labeling, this paper invests a statistical approach based on hierarchical semantic structure with partially observable Markov decision process (POMDP) re-ranking strategy to produce the more spontaneous speaking style output.

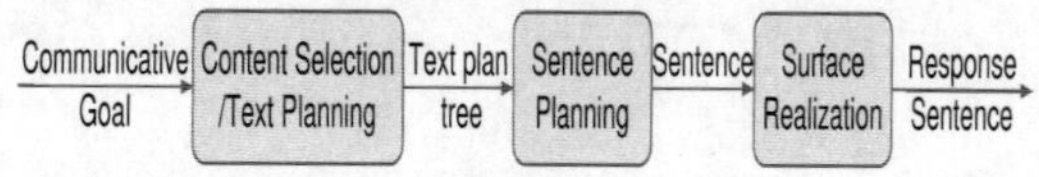

Figure 2. The flow chart of rule-based sentence generation that composed three modules.

The rest of this paper is organized as follows. Section 2 describes the proposed method and the related important modules in conversational dialogue system. Next, Section 3 presents the detail description about the proposed method especially in hierarchical semantic structure and partial observable Markov decision process (POMDP) re-ranking strategy. Experiments to evaluate the proposed approach and the related discussion are presented in Section 4. Concluding remarks are finally made in Section 5.

2 The proposed system framework

With this investment, we want to generate the human-like response of conversational dialogue systems by statistical approach. Herein, the system framework is divided into two phases: training and generation as described in Section 2.1 and 2.2 respectively.

2.1 Training phase

Human to human conversations are gathered as the training corpus. The utterance obtained from the corpus is first as the seed sentence for equivalent utterance expansion. The keywords and corresponding sentence pattern are extracted from the utterance and are fed into a web search engine by API to gather the expanding utterances. Basically, the utterance with the near-meaning will be recalled as the candidates for further processing. For each candidate utterance, the semantic objects embedded here will be extracted as the values and filled into semantic slots defined in conceptual graph. Due to the hypernym (superordinate) plays an essential role in information retrieval and dialogue management, eHownet, developed by academia Sinica, Taiwan, is used as the knowledge based to provide relative information. The expanded utterances and the original one are all ranked. The ranking can be composed of system pre-ranking and human adjustment. According the results of ranking and the status of concept graph, the POMDP parameters are estimated for generation phase. One of the most important issues is the reward function training.

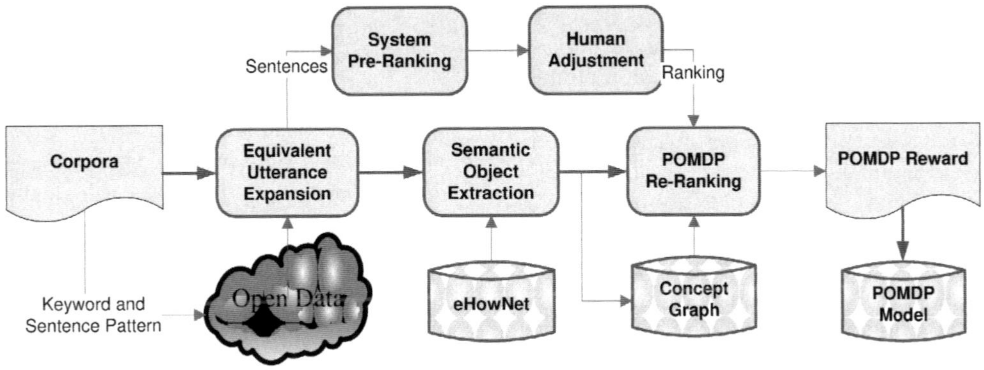

Figure 3. The system flow of training phase in proposed approach

2.2 Generation phase

As described in previous sections, response generation can be divided into content determination, sentence planning and surface realization. Herein, we combined the sentence planning and surface realization. That is to say, the proposed generation phase consists of two models: content selection and sentence planning and surface realization.

Semantic objects are first extracted from user's input utterance and fed into corresponding semantic slots defined in concept graph. According to the absent information in concept graph, the proposed method will decide the response contents. The results of the response content decision will be further fed into sentence planning and equivalent utterance expansion. Sentence planning will form the basic word set and sentence patterns for surface realization. The equivalent utterance expansion will gather the relevant sentence from the internet and the select candidate sentence with potential for surface realization. Open data contain many sentences is fit for the response generation. After the surface realization, the acceptable spoken utterances are obtained. A POMDP reward function is used to rank the spoken utterances according the POMDP model obtained in the training phase. According to the result of POMDP re-ranking, the generated response is obtained.

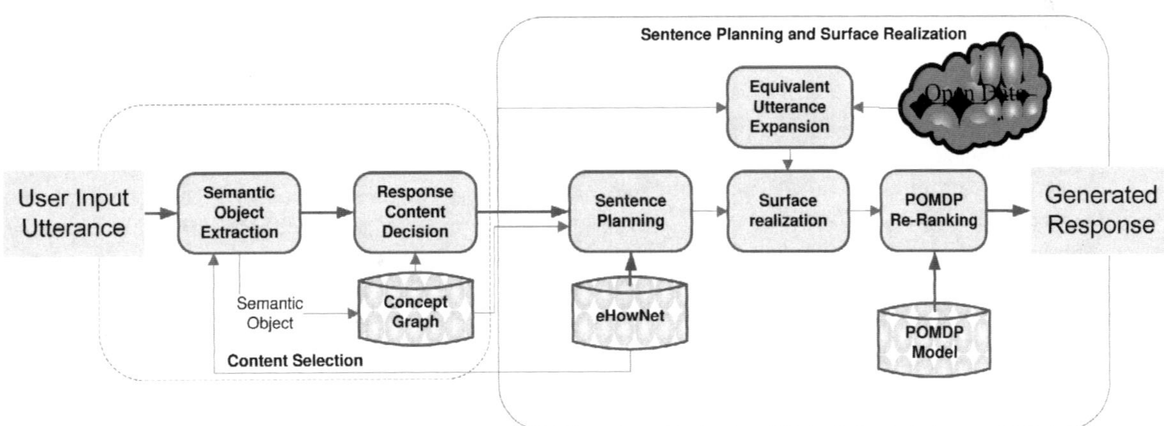

Figure 4. The system flow of generation phase in proposed approach

3 The proposed hierarchical semantic structure with POMDP re-ranking

This investment proposed a various response generation method for conversational dialogue systems. Actually, it is important for the practicability of spoken conversation interface how to increase adoption in response generation. Context determination decides which meaning would be carried in response. Realization strategies for dialogue responses depend on communicative confidence levels and interaction management goals. However, the only one value kept for each semantic slot in traditional dialogue management makes some information lost resulting in the persecution of users. Enrich the number of the response utterances and their sentence will increase users' delight. Some sentence patterns and linguistics material will enrich the natural language generation significantly. In fact, these issues connect to the conversational dialogue system practice or not. In this section, we may consider the subject under the following heads: conceptual graph and hierarchical semantic structure and POMDP re-ranking strategy. It seems reasonable to consider response generation through two types of organization.

3.1 Hierarchical semantic structure

Thinking ways about speech is very essential because it provides insight into the utility of human communication. In other words, that human uses communication as a tool to further their own ends not merely in human to human communication but also in human machine interactions. Ignoring semantic relations among semantic objects causes the exactly extracting the values from spoken utterance hard in traditional spoken dialogue systems. Conceptual graph is adopted as the knowledge representation for describing the semantic relations in this paper. Compared to the semantic slot with only one value, this investment proposed a hierarchical semantic structure to store the potential values for corresponding semantic slot by a linked list.

Concept graph is one of formalisms for knowledge representation. Herein, we used them to represent the conceptual schemas used in conversational dialogue systems. An example of conceptual graph for speech act, 訂票 (booking ticket for the train), is illustrated in Figure 5. Speech act "訂票 (booking ticket for the train)" is the centre in the conceptual graph. Some non-terminal nodes denote the concepts. Here, the item concept refers to the relationship between certain symbols and signifiers such as semantic objects. Semantic objects are regarded as the possible values for some semantic slots. For example, the non-terminal concept "旅程 (journey)", in the top left of Figure 5, is composed of two semantic slots "起點(departure)" and "終點(destination)" and their relation. When talking about the "終點(destination)," users say "台北(Taipei)" and the dialogue management imagines "台北(Taipei)" is the potential value of the semantic slot "終點(destination)". Then you have just used a signifier (the word "台北(Taipei)") to indicate a semantic slot "終點(destination). A large part of semantics is language, which uses words to symbolize things. Signifiers may be ideas, nouns, places, objects or feelings corresponding to semantic slots defined in conversational dialogue system.

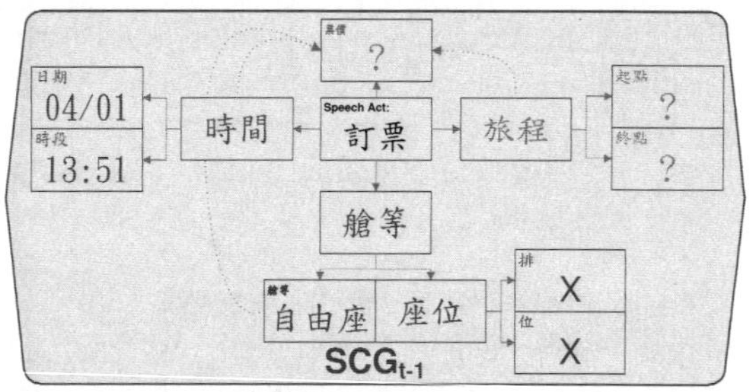

Figure 5. An example of conceptual graph for the speech act "booking train tickets"

This paper proposed a linked list based semantic slot for keeping more than one possible values for each semantic slot. In other word, the proposed system will extract all possible semantic objects from discourse. This structure provides more flexible combinations for the response generation. According to these combinations, the response utterances will be re-ranked by POMDP strategy.

3.2 POMDP re-ranking strategy

Response utterances can be further divided into two source categories. The first category comes from sentence planning and surface realization by the system according to the concept graph and eHownet. The second category comes from internet data from the equivalent utterance expansion. Finally, POMDP is adopted as the re-ranking process to select the near optimal utterance to be the generated response.

Due to the conversational dialogue is an interactive process. Considering the current user utterance and predicting the next user utterance, generated responses are re-ranked by POMDP. The POMDP adopted as the response generation operates as follows. At each time-step, that is to say, one turn in dialogue the state on the discourse record is in some unobserved state s_t. Due to the values in semantic slot is not exactly sure, the concept graph is partially observable. Since s_t is not known exactly, a distribution over possible states called a belief state b_t is maintained where $b_t(s_t)$ indicates the probability of being in a particular state s_t. Based on *both*, the dialogue management selects an action a_t, generating the response to user, receives a reward *Rt*, and transitions to next unobserved state, the corresponding concept graph at *t+1*. Here, syntactic and semantic scores are used to calculate the reward. We call it as s_{t+1}, where s_{t+1} depends only on s_t and a_t. The dialogue system then receives an observation o_{t+1}, which is dependent on s_{t+1} and a_t. Herein, o_{t+1} means the speech act and the semantic object carried in user utterance at turn *t+1*.This process is represented graphically as an influence diagram in Figure 6.

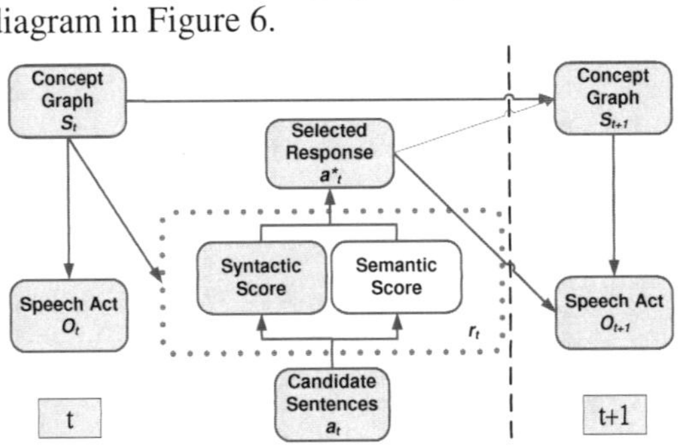

Figure 6. Illustration about the proposed POMDP re-ranking strategy

Given an existing belief state b_t, the last system action a_t, and a new observation o_{t+1}, the new updated belief state b_{t+1} is given by

$$b_{t+1}(s_{t+1}) = \eta P(o_{t+1}|b_{t+1}, a_t) \sum_{s_t} P(s_{t+1}|s_t, a_t) b(s_t) \quad (1)$$

Where η denotes the normalization factor. It can be calculated as equation (2).

$$\eta = P(o_{t+1}|b_t, a_t) \quad (2)$$

The standard optimizing process of POMDP is used for estimating of the action policy.

4 Experimental results

For evaluating the performance of the proposed method, a corpus contains 243 dialogues with 7,445 sentences are used for training. A conversational dialogue system using mandarin in travel domain is developed for assessing dynamically. Ignore of the error resulted from speech recognition engine, five dialogues for each individual to obtain the statistics.

To evaluate the performance of the proposed method, the subjective evaluation, the mean opinion score (MOS), is used to measure the qualities of the voice transformation approaches. The opinion score was r is expressed in one number, from 1 to 5 (1 means bad and 5 denotes excellent). MOS is quite subjective, as it is based figures that results from what is perceived by people during tests. Twenty two individuals are asked to be the users using the conversation dialogue system developed in travel domain in this paper. Five dialogues with MOS scores for each individual during two weeks are recorded for further evaluation. Another system based on template response generation is also developed for comparison (Lee et al. 2009). Four aspects, variety, naturalness, suitability, intelligibility, are used to appraise the response systems. The experimental results are shown in Figure 7.

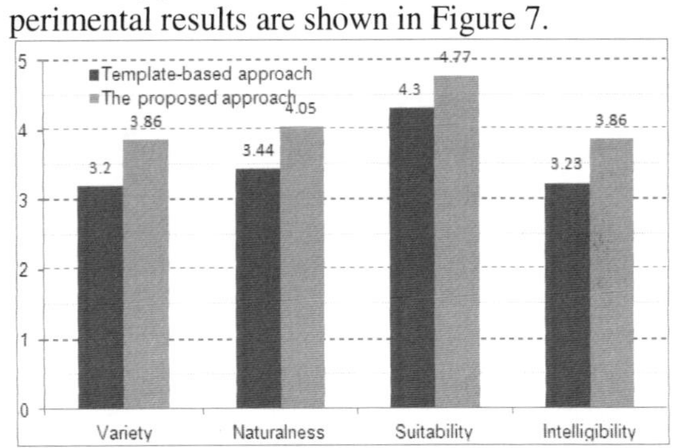

Figure 7. Evaluation results about template-based and the proposed approaches

According to the results, the suitability of these two approaches is high enough. Due to either template approach or the proposed approach are both able to provide the right information for users. The proposed approach outperforms the template approach significantly in variety and naturalness. These results show the concept graph and POMDP re-ranking ability to obtain improvement.

5 Conclusions

A new approach to generate responses for conversational dialogue systems has been presented in this study. The algorithm is based on the idea of hierarchical semantic structure of concept graph and POMDP re-ranking strategy. Linked list based semantic slot is applied to extract the values of semantic objects from input utterance. The two sentence generation sources: natural language generation and gathering open data from the internet are used to keep the variety of generated responses. POMDP re-ranking further selects near optimal utterance considering of the status of concept graph. The experimental results verified that the proposed approach results in keeping more information in concept graph and various responses generated especially in variation and naturalness. The future works include applying more precise estimation for POMDP.

Acknowledgments

The author would like to acknowledge National Science Council (NSC) of Taiwan for financial support to this research (project number: NSC 102-2221-E-415-006-MY3).

References

Lemon, O. 2011. Learning What to Say and How to Say it: Joint Optimization of Spoken Dialogue Management and Natural Language Generation. *Journal Computer Speech and Language.* 25(2): 210-221.

Bauer, D. 2009. Statistical Natural Language Generation as Planning. *Master's thesis of Department of Computational Linguistics, Saarland University*, Saarbrucken, Germany.

Zhan, W.D. 2010. A Brief Introduction to Natural Language Understanding and Generation. *Terminology Standardization & Information Technology* 4.

Fang, Z.-W., Du, L.-M., Yu, S.-Y. 2006. A Chinese Sentence Generator Based on Hybrid-Template for Spoken Dialogue System. *Journal of the Graduate School of the Chinese Academy of Sciences*, 23(1): 23-30.

Reiter, E., and Dale, R. 2000. *Building Natural Language Generation Systems.* Cambridge University Press.

Reiter, E. 1996. *Building Natural-Language Generation Systems.* In Alison Cawsey, ed., Proceedings of the AI and Patient Education Workshop, Glasgow, GIST Technical Report G95.3, Department of Computing Science, University of Glasgow.

Branavan, S.R.K., Kushman, N., Lei, T., Barzilay, R. 2012. Learning High-Level Planning from Text. *Proceeding ACL '12 Proceedings of the 50th Annual Meeting of the Association for Computational Linguistics*: Vol. 1: 126-135.

Walker, M. A. Rambow, O., Rogati, M. 2001. SPoT: A Trainable Sentence Planner. *Proceedings of the 2nd Annual Meeting of the North American Chapter of the Associataion for Computational Linguistics.*

Walker, M. A. O. Rambow, O., Rogati, M. 2002. Training a Sentence Planner for Spoken Dialogue using Boosting. *Computer Speech and Language*: Special Issue on Spoken Language Generation, 2002.

Melcuk, I. A. 1988. *Dependency Syntax: Theory and Practice*, SUNY, Albany, New York.

Stent, A., Prasad, R., and Walker, M. 2004. Trainable Sentence Planning for Complex Information Presentation in Spoken Dialog Systems. *Proceedings of ACL.*

Lee, C., Jung, S., Kim, S., Lee, G. G. 2009. Example-based Dialog Modeling for Practical Multi-domain Dialog System. *Speech Communication* 51(5): 466–484.

Chinese Spelling Check Evaluation at SIGHAN Bake-off 2013

Shih-Hung Wu
Chaoyang Univ. of Technology
Taichung, Taiwan
shwu@cyut.edu.tw

Chao-Lin Liu
National Chengchi Univ.
Taipei, Taiwan
chaolin@nccu.edu.tw

Lung-Hao Lee
National Taiwan Univ.
Taipei, Taiwan
lhlee@ntnu.edu.tw

Abstract

This paper introduces an overview of Chinese Spelling Check task at SIGHAN Bake-off 2013. We describe all aspects of the task for Chinese spelling check, consisting of task description, data preparation, performance metrics, and evaluation results. This bake-off contains two subtasks, *i.e.*, error detection and error correction. We evaluate the systems that can automatically point out the spelling errors and provide the corresponding corrections in students' essays, summarize the performance of all participants' submitted results, and discuss some advanced issues. The hope is that through such evaluation campaigns, more advanced Chinese spelling check techniques will be emerged.

1 Introduction

Spelling check is a common task in every written language, which is an automatic mechanism to detect and correct human errors. A spelling checker should have both capabilities consisting of error detection and error correction. Spelling error detection is to indicate the various types of spelling errors in the text. Spelling error correction is further to suggest the correct characters of detected errors. Spelling check must be done within a context, say a sentence or a long phrase with a certain meaning, and cannot be done within one word (Mays et al., 1991).

However, spelling check in Chinese is very different from that in English or other alphabetic languages. There are no word delimiters between words and the length of each word is very short. There are several previous studies addressing the Chinese spelling check problem. Chang (1995) has proposed a bi-gram language model to substitute the confusing character for error detection and correction. Zhang et al. (2000) have presented an approximate word-matching algorithm to detect and correct Chinese spelling errors using operations of character substitution, insertion, and deletion. Ren et al. (2001) have proposed a hybrid approach that combines a rule-based method and a probability-based method to automatic Chinese spelling checking. Huang et al. (2007) have proposed a learning model based on Chinese phonemic alphabet for spelling check. Most of the Chinese spelling errors were originated from phonologically similar, visually similar, and semantically confusing characters (Liu et al., 2011). Empirically, there were only 2 errors per student essay on average in a learners' corpus (Chen et al., 2011). How to evaluate the false-alarm rate of a spelling check system with normal corpus was also a hard task (Wu et al., 2010). Up to date, there are no commonly available data sets for spelling check for Chinese. This motivates us to develop such data sets as benchmarks for fairly evaluating the performance of state-of-the-art Chinese spelling checkers.

At SIGHAN Bake-off 2013, we organize the Chinese Spelling Check task that provides an evaluation platform for developing and implementing automatic Chinese spelling checkers. Two subtasks, *i.e.*, error detection and error correction, are designed to evaluate complete function of a spelling checker. The first subtask focuses on the ability of error detection. Given a complete sentence, the checker should detect if there are errors in the input, and point out the error locations of incorrect characters. The second subtask aims at the quality of error correction. In addition to indicating the error locations, the checker should suggest the correct characters. The hope is that, through such evaluation campaigns, more advanced Chinese spelling check techniques will be emerged.

We give an overview of Chinese Spelling task at SIGHAN Bake-off 2013. The rest of this article is organized as the follows. Section 2 details the designed task, consisting of two subtasks, *i.e.*, error detection and error correction. Section 3 introduces the data sets provided in this evaluation. Section 4 proposes the evaluation metrics for both subtasks. Section 5 presents the results of participants' approaches for performance comparison. Section 6 elaborates on the semantic and pragmatic aspects of automatic correction of Chinese text. Finally, we conclude this paper with the findings and future research direction in the Section 7.

2 Task Description

The goal of this task is to evaluate the ability of a system on Chinese spelling check. The task can be further divided into two subtasks: error detection and error correction. We detail as the follows.

2.1 Subtask 1: Error Detection

For the error detection subtask, complete Chinese sentences with/without spelling errors will be given as the input, the system should return the locations of the incorrect characters. Each character or punctuation occupies 1 spot for counting location. The error detection problem is a yes/no question plus the locations of errors. If the input sentence (each given a serial number *NID*) contains no spelling errors, the system should return: *NID*, 0. If the input contains at least one spelling errors, the output format is: *NID, location [, location]**, where the symbol "*" indicates there is zero or more of the predicting element "[, location]". We give the following example for more information. In this example, the 27th character is wrong, the correct one should be "挫".

- Input: (*NID*=99999) 在我的人生中沒有風災大浪，但我看過許多勇敢的人，不怕措折的奮鬥，這種精神值得我們學習。
- Output: 99999, 27

2.2 Subtask 2: Error Correction

For the error correction subtask, the input texts are complete Chinese sentences with spelling errors. The system should return the locations of the incorrect characters, and must point out the correct characters. The error correction problem is a follow-up problem of error detection for checking spelling errors. Since the input sentence contains at least one spelling error, the output format is: *NID [, location, correction]+*, where "+" sign indicates there is one or more of the predicting element "[, location, correction]". Take the following example as instance, the 16th and 29th characters are wrong, the correct ones are "徵" and "間", respectively.

- Input: (NID=88888) 擁有六百一十年歷史的崇禮門，象微著南韓人的精神，在一夕之門，被火燒得精光。
- Output: 88888, 16, 徵 29, 間

```
<DOC Nid="00018">
<p>有些人會拿這次的教訓來勉勵自己，好讓自己在打混摸魚時警悌，使自己比以前更好、更進步。
</p>
<TEXT>
<MISTAKE wrong_position=28>
<wrong>警悌</wrong>
<correct>警惕</correct>
</MISTAKE>
</TEXT>
</DOC>
```

Figure 1. A sample set in terms of XML format

3 Data Preparation

3.1 Sample Set and Similar Character Set

We provided the Sample Set and Similar Character Set as the linguistic resources for this evaluation. The policy of our evaluation is an open test. Participants can employ any linguistic and computational resources to do identification and corrections.

In Sample Set, there are 700 samples selected from students' essays, which are represented in XML format shown in Figure 1. A half of these samples contain at least one error and the remaining samples do not contain any errors.

The set of Chinese characters with similar shapes, same pronunciations, and similar pronunciations is especially useful for this task. Details about these sets are described in the previous work (Liu et al., 2011). For example, the set of similar shape of the character "可" and the set of similar pronunciation of the character "隔" are listed as follows:

- Similar Shape: 可, 何呵坷奇河柯苛阿倚寄崎荷蚵軻.
- Similar Pronunciation: 隔, 郃革格咯骼閤膈閣葛鬲鎘蛤.

Test Set	Subtask1	Subtask2
# of sentences	1,000	1,000
# of sentences with errors	300	1,000
# of error characters	376	1265
Average # of errors in sentences with errors	1.253	1.265
Average length of sentences	68.711	74.328
Sentence-level error percentage (%)	30%	100%
Character-level error percentage (%) (with punctuation)	0.547%	1.702%
Character-level error percentage (%) (without punctuation)	0.611%	1.902%

Table 1. Descriptive statistics of the test sets

3.2 Test Set

Table 1 shows the statistics of our prepared test sets. The sentences were collected from 13 to 14-year-old students' essays in formal written tests. The average length of sentences is about 70 characters, which is a compromise to the writing style of the students. Most of the students cannot break their sentences into short and clear ones. To preserve the context, we kept the whole long sentences as they were written on the examination paper. The character-level error percentage is about 0.5% and 2% for subtask 1 and subtask 2, respectively. The error rate is higher than it was in the original corpus, since we deleted most sentences without any error to reduce the test set size.

There were 1,000 Chinese texts selected from students' essays that covered various common errors for each subtask, respectively. The teachers manually identified the errors embedded in Chinese sentences. There is some inconsistency between teachers on the standard of whether it is an error or not. There is no authority on the standard, which is an implicit consensus of the teachers. In our prepared test data set, 300 out of 1,000 test sentences contain errors in subtask 1. In subtask 2, each of the 1,000 test sentences contains one or more errors.

We found that there were some controversial cases, especially about the usage of Chinese idioms. There are many ways to express an idiom and some of them might be considered as errors. We did our best to reduce the inconsistency manually during the preparation of the test set by deleting the controversial cases. On the other hand, we preserved as many errors as possible in the test set, such that system developers could find the kinds of errors that students actually produced. There are some common errors that occur with high frequencies, but we did not delete them so that the distribution of errors can be kept and might be used for educational purposes.

We met some difficult issues during test set preparation. The first difficulty is to ensure that there is no more error other than the pointed out ones. There is almost no question that errors pointed out by the teachers are errors. However, there are errors we detected but not pointed out by teachers. Maybe they are minor errors that some teachers omitted or did not think they are errors. We manually deleted several sentences with such cases. The second difficulty is not to modify the sentences too much while preserving the original context. Since the test set is selected from students' essays, there are some ungrammatical sentences. We modified them such that the only errors are spelling errors not other syntactical errors or improper co-occurrences.

4 Performance Metrics

4.1 Metrics of Error Detection

For error detection subtask, we adopt sentence-level metrics for performance evaluation. Since the number of error characters is very small comparing to all the characters. It is not suitable to use the number of character to calculate accuracy. Therefore, in this bake-off, we adopt the numbers of sentences as the unit of performance metrics. The computation formulas are listed as follows:

- False-Alarm Rate (**FAR**)= # of sentences with false positive errors / # of testing sentences without errors
- Detection Accuracy (**DA**)= # of sentences with correctly detected results / # of all testing sentences
- Detection Precision (**DP**)= # of sentences with correctly detected errors / # of sentences the evaluated system reported to have errors
- Detection Recall (**DR**)= # of sentences with correctly detected errors / # of testing sentences with errors
- Detection F1 (**DF1**)= 2*DP*DR / (DP+DR)
- Error Location Accuracy (**ELA**)= # of sentences with correct location detection / # of all testing sentences
- Error Location Precision (**ELP**)= # of sentences with correct error locations / # of sentences the evaluated system reported to have errors

- Error Location Recall (**ELR**)= # of sentences with correct error locations / # of testing sentences with errors
- Error Location F1 (**ELF1**)= 2*ELP*ELR / (ELP+ELR)

The criterion for judging corrections is that the output should be completely identical with the gold standard. For example, give 5 testing inputs with gold standard shown as "0022, 43, 76", "0023, 0", "0024, 0", "0025, 72, 79", and "0026, 103". The system may output the results shown as "0022, 43, 55, 80", "0023, 10", "0024, 0", "0025, 72, 79", and "0026, 103". The evaluated tool will yield the following performance metrics:

- FAR=0.5 (=1/2)
  Notes: #{"0023"}/ #{"0023", "0024"}
- DA=0.75 (=4/5)
  Notes: #{"0022", "0024", "0025", "0026"}/ #{"0022", "0023", "0024", "0025", "0026"}
- DP=0.75 (=3/4)
  Notes: #{"0022", "0025", "0026"}/ #{"0022", "0023", "0025", "0026"}
- DR=1 (=3/3)
  Notes: #{"0022", "0025", "0026"}/ #{"0022", "0025", "0026"}
- DF1= 0.8571 (=2*0.75*1/(0.75+1))
- ELA=0.6 (=3/5)
  Notes: #{"0024, 0", "0025, 72, 79", "0026, 103"}/ #{"0022, 43, 76", "0023, 0", "0024, 0", "0025, 72, 79", "0026, 103"}
- ELP=0.5 (=2/4)
  Notes: #{"0025, 72, 79", "0026, 103"}/ #{"0022, 43, 55, 80", "0023, 10", "0025, 72, 79", "0026, 103"}
- ELR= 0.6667 (2/3)
  Notes: #{"0025, 72, 79", "0026, 103"}/ #{"0022, 43, 76", "0025, 72, 79", "0026, 103"}
- ELF1=0.5714 (=2*0.5*0.6667/(0.5+0.6667))

4.2 Metrics of Error Correction

For error correction subtask, we adopt the similar metrics. The computations are formulated as follows:

- Location Accuracy (**LA**)= # of sentences correctly detected the error location / # of all testing sentences
- Correction Accuracy (**CA**)= # of sentences correctly corrected the error / # of all testing sentences
- Correction Precision (**CP**)= # of sentences correctly corrected the error / # of sentences the system returns corrections.

The criterion for judging corrections is the same with subtask 1. Take a set of gold standard shown as {"00366, 1, 倘", "00367, 10, 的", "00368, 39, 嘩, 63, 葉, 89, 嫩", "00369, 16, 炭, 48, 作", "00370, 49, 已"} for example, if the system output the results: {"00366, 1, 趟", "00367, 10, 的", "00368, 39, 嘩, 63, 葉", "00369, 16, 炭, 48, 作"} , the evaluated tool will yield the follows:

- LA=0.6 (=3/5)
  Notes: #{"00366, 1", "00367, 10", "00369,

Participant (Ordered by abbreviations of names)	**Subtask 1**	**Subtask2**
Agency for Science, Technology and Research (**A*STAR**)	0	0
Heilongjiang University (**HLJU**)	3	3
National Kaohsiung University of Applied Sciences & National Taiwan Normal University (**KUAS & NTNU**)	1	1
Nara Institute of Science and Technology (**NAIST**)	3	3
National Chiao Tung University & National Taipei University of Technology (**NCTU & NTUT**)	2	2
National Chiayi University (**NCYU**)	3	3
Nanjing University of Posts and Telecommunications (**NJUPT**)	0	0
National Tsing Hua University (**NTHU**)	3	3
National Taiwan Ocean University (**NTOU**)	3	3
University of Oxford (**OX**)	0	0
Peking University (**PKU**)	3	0
Chinese Knowledge and Information Processing Group, IIS, Academia Sinica (**SinicaCKIP**)	3	3
Intelligent Agent Systems Lab, IIS, Academia Sinica (**SinicaIASL**)	2	2
Speech, Language and Music Processing Lab, IIS, Academia Sinica & National Taiwan University (**SinicaSLMP & NTU**)	3	3
Shanghai Jiao Tong University (**SJTU**)	3	3
University of Macau (**UMAC**)	0	0
Yuan Ze University & National Cheng Kung University (**YZU & NCKU**)	1	1
Total	33	30

Table 2. Result submission statistics of all participants

Participant	Approach	Usage of Provided Corpus	Additional Resources
HLJU	N-gram Model	Both	Sinica Corpus
KUAS & NTNU	Phonological similarity, Orthographic similarity, Bi-gram Linear Regression, Rule base Model	None	Sinica Corpus, Sinica Treebank, Chinese Electronic Dictionary, and Chinese Orthography Database
NAIST	Language Model + SVM, Language Model + Statistical Machine Translation Model + SVM	Both	Chinese Gigaword, Sinica Corpus of SIGHAN Bake-off 2005, and CC-CEDICT
NCTU & NTUT	CRF-based Chinese Parser, Trigram Language Model	Both	Sinica Corpus, CIRB030, the Taiwan Panorama Magazine 4 and the Wikipedia
NCYU	N-gram + Inverted Index	Both	E-HowNet, and Gathered corpus for training n-gram
NTHU	Machine Translation Language Model, Rule based model	Both	TWWaC, Sinica Corpus, Chinese dictionary, and Chinese Idioms
NTOU	Language Model + Heuristic Rules	Both	Sinica Corpus
PKU	Maximum Entropy Model	Both	Chinese Gigaword
SinicaCKIP	Unknown Word Detection, Word Segmentation, Language Model	Similar Character Set	CKIP lexicon, Sinica Corpus, and Google 1T n-gram
SinicaIASL	Reliable Phonological Sequence Matcher, Word Segmentation, Homophone Dictionary + N-gram Model, Shape Correction Module, Language Model	Both	Revised Chinese Dictionary, Xiaoxuetang Philology Database, LDC news corpus, Chinese Information Retrieval Benchmark (CIRB), Frequent Errors List from the Web, and Google 1T n-gram
SinicaSLMP & NTU	N-gram model, Topic model	Both	Chinese Gigaword, Sinica Corpus, and Search Engine (Baidu)
SJTU	Shortest Path Word Segmentation Algorithm, Language Model, Mutual Information	Both	SogouW Dictionary, Sinica corpus of SIGHAN Bake-off 2005, IRSTLM, and OpenCC
YZU & NCKU	Web-based Score	Similar Character Set	Chinese Gigaword, and Search Engine (Google)

Table 3. A summary of participants' developed systems

16, 48"}/ #{"00366, 1", "00367, 10", "00368, 39, 63, 89", "00369, 16, 48", "00370, 49"}

- CA=0.4 (=2/5)
  Notes: #{"00367, 10, 的", "00369, 16, 炭, 48, 作"}/ #{"00366, 1, 倘", "00367, 10, 的", "00368, 39, 嘩, 63, 葉, 89, 嫩", "00369, 16, 炭, 48, 作", "00370, 49, 已"}
- CP=0.5 (=2/4)
  Notes: #{ "00367, 10, 的", "00369, 16, 炭, 48, 作"}/ #{"00366, 1, 趟", "00367, 10, 的", "00368, 39, 嘩, 63, 葉", "00369, 16, 炭, 48, 作"}

5 Evaluation Results

Table 2 shows the participant teams and their testing submission statistics. This task of bake-off 2013 attracted 17 research teams. There are 9 teams that come from Taiwan, *i.e.*, KUAS & NTNU, NCTU & NTUT, NCYU, NTHU, NTOU, SinicaCKIP, SinicaIASL, SinicaSLMP & NTU, and YZU & NCKU. The other 5 teams originate from China, *i.e.*, HLJU, NJUPT, PKU, SJTU, and UMAC. The remaining 3 ones are A*STAR from Singapore, NAIST from Japan, and OX from United Kingdom.

Among 17 registered teams, 13 teams submitted their testing results. For formal testing, each participant can submit at most three runs that use different models or parameter settings. Table 3 summarizes the participants' developed approaches and the usage of linguistic resources for this bake-off evaluation. We can observe that most of participants adopt statistical approaches such as n-gram model, language model, machine translation model, and topic model. In addition to the Sample Set and the Similar Character Set,

Submission	FAR	DA	DP	DR	DF1	ELA	ELP	ELR	ELF1
HLJU-Run1	0.6857	0.5140	0.3798	0.98	0.5474	0.3010	0.1047	0.2700	0.1509
HLJU-Run2	0.6529	0.5290	0.3849	0.9533	0.5484	0.3390	0.1292	0.3200	0.1841
HLJU-Run3	0.6929	0.5100	0.3782	0.9833	0.5463	0.2960	0.1038	0.2700	0.1500
KUAS & NTNU-Run1	0.2257	0.7890	0.6099	0.8233	0.7007	0.6940	0.3753	0.5067	0.4312
NAIST-Run1	0.2929	0.7460	0.5504	0.8367	0.664	0.6450	0.3289	0.5000	0.3968
NAIST-Run2	0.0543	0.8120	0.7979	0.5000	0.6148	0.7640	0.5426	0.3400	0.4180
NAIST-Run3	0.2243	0.7770	0.5985	0.7800	0.6773	0.6980	0.3964	0.5167	0.4486
NCTU & NTUT-Run1	0.0243	0.7220	0.6964	0.1300	0.2191	0.7110	0.5000	0.0933	0.1573
NCTU & NTUT-Run2	0.8329	0.4110	0.3352	0.9800	0.4995	0.2570	0.1596	0.4667	0.2379
NCYU-Run1	0.2371	0.7380	0.5514	0.6800	0.609	0.6230	0.2405	0.2967	0.2657
NCYU-Run2	0.2129	0.7610	0.5850	0.7000	0.6374	0.6520	0.2813	0.3367	0.3065
NCYU-Run3	0.0929	0.8250	0.7451	0.6333	0.6847	0.7480	0.4431	0.3767	0.4072
NTHU-Run1	0.0386	0.8480	0.8663	0.5833	0.6972	0.8090	0.6733	0.4533	0.5418
NTHU-Run2	0.0471	0.8570	0.8520	0.6333	0.7265	0.8150	0.6637	0.4933	0.5660
NTHU-Run3	0.0514	0.8610	0.8455	0.6567	0.7392	0.8200	0.6695	0.5200	0.5854
NTOU-Run1	0.9800	0.3140	0.3043	1.0000	0.4666	0.1090	0.0963	0.3167	0.1477
NTOU-Run2	0.9429	0.3380	0.3111	0.9933	0.4738	0.1490	0.1138	0.3633	0.1733
NTOU-Run3	0.9257	0.3500	0.3150	0.9933	0.4783	0.1350	0.0877	0.2767	0.1332
PKU-Run1	0.1486	0.7020	0.5048	0.3533	0.4157	0.6380	0.2000	0.1400	0.1647
PKU-Run2	0.5286	0.5830	0.4061	0.8433	0.5482	0.3760	0.0738	0.1533	0.0996
PKU-Run3	0.3986	0.6780	0.4795	0.8567	0.6149	0.5000	0.1474	0.2633	0.1890
SinicaCKIP-Run1	0.1300	0.8400	0.7174	0.7700	0.7428	0.7730	0.5093	0.5467	0.5273
SinicaCKIP-Run2	0.2257	0.8040	0.6238	0.8733	0.7278	0.7030	0.3833	0.5367	0.4472
SinicaCKIP-Run3	0.1629	0.8420	0.6919	0.8533	0.7642	0.7710	0.5000	0.6167	0.5523
SinicaIASL-Run1	0.3000	0.7130	0.5161	0.7467	0.6103	0.6050	0.2673	0.3867	0.3161
SinicaIASL-Run2	0.1857	0.7540	0.5873	0.6167	0.6016	0.6860	0.3714	0.3900	0.3805
SinicaSLMP & NTU-Run1	0.4471	0.6540	0.4603	0.8900	0.6068	0.5490	0.2793	0.5400	0.3682
SinicaSLMP & NTU-Run2	0.1414	0.8350	0.7027	0.7800	0.7393	0.7460	0.4354	0.4833	0.4581
SinicaSLMP & NTU-Run3	0.1414	0.8360	0.7036	0.7833	0.7413	0.7490	0.4431	0.4933	0.4669
SJTU-Run1	0.4400	0.6620	0.4671	0.9000	0.6150	0.522	0.2249	0.4333	0.2961
SJTU-Run2	0.0957	0.8560	0.7690	0.7433	0.7559	0.8050	0.5931	0.5733	0.5830
SJTU-Run3	0.0229	0.8440	0.9091	0.5333	0.6722	0.8090	0.7102	0.4167	0.5252
YZU & NCKU-Run1	0.0500	0.7290	0.6500	0.2167	0.3250	0.7050	0.4100	0.1367	0.2050

Table 4. Testing results of error detection subtask

some linguistic resources are used popularly for this bake-off evaluation such as Chinese Gigaword and Sinica Corpus.

5.1 Results of Error Detection

The goals of this subtask are to detect whether a sentence contains errors or not and to identify the locations of the errors in the input sentences. Table 4 shows the testing results of subtask 1. In addition to achieving promising detection effects of error character, reducing the false-alarm rate, which is percentage of the correct sentences that are incorrectly reported containing error characters, is also important. The research teams, NTHU and SJTU, achieved very low false alarm rates, *i.e.*, less than 0.05, while maintaining relatively high detection recall rates, *i.e.*, more than 0.5. These results are what most of the previous studies did not accomplish.

Accuracy is usually adopted to evaluate the performance, but it is affected by the distribution of testing instance. The baseline can be achieved easily by always guessing without errors. That is accuracy of 0.7 in this evaluation. Some systems achieved promising effects of more than 0.8, regardless of detection accuracy or error location accuracy.

Since each participated teams can submit up to three runs, several teams sent different runs that aimed at optimizing the recall or precision rates. These phenomena guide us to adopt F1 score to reflect the tradeoff between precision and recall. In the testing results, SinicaCKIP achieved the best error detection results, if Detection F1 was concerned. NTHU accomplished the best detection effects of indicating error locations, which resulted the best Error Location F1.

In summary, different evaluation metrics were proposed to measure the performance of Chinese spelling checkers. It is difficult to find a perfect system that usually performs better than others, when different metrics are considered. In general, the systems implemented by NTHU, SJTU, and SinicaCKIP relatively outperform the others' developed systems in subtask1 evaluation.

Submission	LA	CA	CR
HLJU-Run1	0.2650	0.2250	0.2432
HLJU-Run2	0.3230	0.2770	0.3081
HLJU-Run3	0.2640	0.2220	0.2403
KUAS & NTNU-Run1	0.4440	0.3940	0.5058
NAIST-Run1	0.5080	0.4670	0.5765
NAIST-Run2	0.2610	0.2540	0.6530
NAIST-Run3	0.4870	0.4530	0.6155
NCTU & NTUT-Run1	0.0700	0.0650	0.5118
NCTU & NTUT-Run2	0.4850	0.4040	0.4040
NCYU-Run1	0.3690	0.3070	0.4850
NCYU-Run2	**0.6630**	**0.6250**	0.7030
NCYU-Run3	**0.6630**	**0.6250**	0.7030
NTHU-Run1	0.4180	0.4090	0.6956
NTHU-Run2	0.4420	0.4310	0.7020
NTHU-Run3	0.4540	0.4430	0.6998
SinicaCKIP-Run1	0.4820	0.4420	0.5854
SinicaCKIP-Run2	0.4990	0.4620	0.5416
SinicaCKIP-Run3	0.5590	0.5160	0.6158
SinicaIASL-Run1	0.4680	0.4290	0.4286
SinicaIASL-Run2	0.4900	0.4480	0.4476
SinicaSLMP & NTU-Run1	0.5070	0.4670	0.4670
SinicaSLMP & NTU-Run2	0.4890	0.4450	0.4450
SinicaSLMP & NTU-Run3	0.4940	0.4500	0.4500
SJTU-Run1	0.3720	0.3380	0.3828
SJTU-Run2	0.4750	0.4420	0.6360
SJTU-Run3	0.3700	0.3560	**0.7050**
YZU & NCKU-Run1	0.1170	0.1090	0.4658

Table 5. Results of error correction subtask

5.2 Results of Error Correction

For subtask 2, the systems need to identify the locations of the errors in the sentences and indicate the corresponding correct characters. Table 5 shows the testing results. For indicating the locations of errors, the research team came from NCYU accomplished the best Location Accuracy. Its achievement of 0.6630 significantly outperformed than the other teams. To further consider correction effects, NCYU also achieved the best Correction Accuracy of 0.6250. However, if the Correction Precision is concerned, the spelling checker developed by SJTU is the best one, which accomplished the effect of 0.7050.

In summary, it is difficult to make the correction on all errors embedded in the input sentences, since there are many sentences that contain more than one error. The achievements of systems implemented by NCYU and SJTU are relatively satisfactory for this subtask.

6 Discussion

The errors observed in everyday writings can be categorized into three different sources. The incorrect words are similar to the correct words either in sound, shape, and/or meaning. Characters of similar pronunciations are the most common source of errors. Characters of similar shapes are not as frequent, but still exist with a significant proportion (Liu et al., 2011).

The most challenging errors to detect and correct are those caused by semantically possible and contextually permissible words. This is a main cause for inter-annotator disagreement in preparing data sets. When a writer wrote "我用槌子處理這一份中藥" (I used a wood hammer to handle this set of Chinese medicine.), a spelling checker cannot tell whether the write might want to use "鎚子" (a metal hammer) or "錘子" (a pendulum) in the place of "槌子" (a wood hammer). As a consequence, it may be difficult for the spelling checker to detect all errors in a text without false alarms. It might be a good strategy to just issue a reminder to the writers these possible alternatives and to ask for confirmations from the writers.

There are confusing word pairs existing in everyday writings, *e.g.*, "紀錄" (record) and "記錄" (record). The basic principle is very clear: the former is a noun and the latter is a verb. However, not all contexts are clear as to which one should be used, e.g., the person who writes down the minutes of a meeting is a "記錄". Other equally confusing word pairs are ["需要" (need, verb), "須要"(need, noun)] and ["計畫" (plan, noun), "計劃"(plan, verb)].

Sometimes the incorrect characters are very competitive for replacing the correct characters due to their similarity at the lexical level, e.g., ["蔓延" (spread), "漫延" (an incorrect spelling of "蔓延")] and ["璀璨" (bright), "璀燦" (an incorrect spelling of "璀璨")]. Some of these incorrect spellings are becoming so popular among the younger generations such that it might be controversial to define "correctness" in the first place, e.g., ["伎倆" (trick), "技倆" (an incorrect spelling of "伎倆")].

7 Conclusions and Future Work

This paper describes the overview of Chinese spelling check evaluation at SIGHAN Bake-off 2013. We introduce the task designing ideas, data preparation details, evaluation metrics, and the results of performance evaluation.

This bake-off motivates us to build more Chinese language resources for reuse in the future to possibly improve the state-of-the-art techniques for Chinese spelling checking. It also encourages researchers to bravely propose various ideas and implementations for possible breakthrough. No matter how well their implementations would perform, they contribute to the community by enriching the experience that some ideas or approaches are promising or impractical, as verified in this bake-off. Their reports in this proceeding will reveal the details of these various approaches and contribute to our knowledge and experience about Chinese language processing.

We hope our prepared data sets in this bake-off can serve as a benchmark to help developing better Chinese spelling checkers. More data sets that come from different Chinese learners will be investigated in the future to enrich this research topic for natural language processing and computer-aided Chinese language learning.

Acknowledgments

We thank Liang-Pu Chen and Ping-Che Yang, the research engineers of the institute for information industry, Taiwan, for their contribution of students' essays used in this Chinese Spelling Check task. We would like to thank Hsien-You Hsieh, Pei-Kai Liao, Li-Jen Hsu, and Hua-Wei Lin for their hard work to prepare the data sets for this evaluation.

This study was partially supported by the International Research-Intensive Center of Excellence Program of National Taiwan Normal University and National Science Council, Taiwan under grant 101WFA0300229.

References

Chao-huang Chang. 1995. *A New Approach for Automatic Chinese Spelling Correction.* In: Proceedings of Natural Language Processing Pacific Rim Symposium, pp. 278–283.

Yong-Zhi Chen, Shih-Hung Wu, Ping-che Yang, Tsun Ku, and Gwo-Dong Chen. 2011. *Improve the detection of improperly used Chinese characters in students' essays with error model*, Int. J. Cont. Engineering Education and Life-Long Learning, vol. 21, no. 1, pp.103-116.

Chuen-Min Huang, Mei-Chen Wu, and Ching-Che Chang. 2007. *Error Detection and Correction Based on Chinese Phonemic Alphabet in Chinese Text.* In: Proceedings of the Fourth Conference on Modeling Decisions for Artificial Intelligence, pp. 463-476.

Chao-Lin Liu, Min-Hua Lai, Kan-Wen Tien, Yi-Hsuan Chuang, Shih-Hung Wu, and Chia-Ying Lee. 2011. *Visually and phonologically similar characters in incorrect Chinese words: Analyses, identification, and applications*, ACM Transaction on Asian Language Information Processing, vol. 10, no. 2, Article 10, 39 pages.

Eric Mays, Fred J. Damerau and Robert. L. Mercer. 1991. *Context based spelling correction.* Information Processing and Management, vol. 27, no. 5, pp. 517–522.

Fuji Ren, Hongchi Shi, and Qiang Zhou. 2001. *A hybrid approach to automatic Chinese text checking and error correction.* In: Proceedings of the 2001 IEEE International Conference on Systems, Man, and Cybernetics, pp. 1693-1698.

Lei Zhang, Changning Huang, Ming Zhou, and Haihua Pan. 2000. *Automatic detecting/correcting errors in Chinese text by an approximate word-matching algorithm.* In: Proceedings of the 38th Annual Meeting of the Association for Computational Linguistics, pp.248–254.

Chinese Word Spelling Correction Based on N-gram Ranked Inverted Index List

Jui-Feng Yeh*, Sheng-Feng Li, Mei-Rong Wu, Wen-Yi Chen, Mao-Chuan Su
Department of Computer Science and Information Engineering,
National Chiayi University,
No.300 Syuefu Rd., Chiayi City 60004, Taiwan (R.O.C.).
{Ralph, s1010431, s1010432, s0992962, s0992974}@mail.ncyu.edu.tw

Abstract

Spelling correction can assist individuals to input text data with machine using written language to obtain relevant information efficiently and effectively in. By referring to relevant applications such as web search, writing systems, recommend systems, document mining, typos checking before printing is very close to spelling correction. Individuals can input text, keyword, sentence how to interact with an intelligent system according to recommendations of spelling correction. This work presents a novel spelling error detection and correction method based on N-gram ranked inverted index is proposed to achieve this aim, spelling correction. According to the pronunciation and the shape similarity pattern, a dictionary is developed to help detect the possible spelling error detection. The inverted index is used to map the potential spelling error character to the possible corresponding characters either in character or word level. According to the N-gram score, the ranking in the list corresponding to possible character is illustrated. Herein, E-How net is used to be the knowledge representation of tradition Chinese words. The data sets provided by SigHan 7 bakeoff are used to evaluate the proposed method. Experimental results show the proposed methods can achieve accepted performance in subtask one, and outperform other approaches in subtask two.

1 Introduction

Language is one of the most important capabilities of human for communication. Natural language cannot be absent in human communication either spoken communication or written text. As we known, word is the fundamental semantic unit in the most languages; it plays an essential role in natural language processing. Since the word is the building block for natural language processing, the spelling error or typos usually cause negative effects in word for computer applications.

Intelligent communication is one of the new trends about computing environment construction. In providing the natural intelligent human machine interaction, natural language expressions play an essential role. Let us now attempt to extend the observation into the frameworks of natural language processing, in viewpoints of input and output aspects, text input and sentence generation provide the main natural language interfaces between users and machines. Therefore, the semantic extraction and generating of natural language processing plays more essential roles for human machine interactions. Actually, we should now look more carefully into the results obtained in text input and natural language generating. Since the accuracy of text input is not near to perfect, it will cause the natural language misunderstanding. The spelling correction is one of the most important modules for natural language processing. The related applications including web search query, writing systems, recommend systems, document mining and typos checking before printing are very close to spelling correction.

There are many research effort developed for spelling error detection and correction recently. Sun et al. (2010) explore the phrase-based spelling error models from the clickthrough data by measuring the edit distance between an input query and the optimal spelling correction. Ahmad and Kondrak (2005) also have learned a spelling error model from search query logs to improve the quality of query. Li et al. (2006) applied distributional similarity based models for query spelling correction. Gao et al. (2010) Employed the ranker-based approach that contains a surface-form similarity, phonetic-form similarity, entity, dictionary, and frequency features for large scale web search. Besides, Ahmad and Kondrak (2005) adopted EM algorithm to enhance the performance of spelling error detection. There are some works tried to build a transformation model like machine translation, the noisy channel model was one of the selected to describe the spelling error correction. Hidden Markov Models (HMMs) are used to correct Spelling errors for search queries and developed a system called as CloudSpeller (Li et al. 2011). Considering of the domain specific domain, Bao et al. (2011) employed graph theory to correct the error in word and query levels. Cucerzan and Brill (2004) used domain knowledge to exploit the spelling correction as an iterative process. For single word, context-sensitive spelling correction and rich morphology are proposed by Ingason et al. (2009). Mitton (2010) survey the spelling checking algorithm and systems developed for writing systems in the past five decades. Huang et al. (2010) proposed a system framework integrating n-gram models and internet knowledge resources to detect spelling errors in printer driver module. Actually, some application interface (API), tools and knowledge bases are useful for spelling error detection and correction. Google (2010) has developed a Java API for Google spelling check service. Microsoft (2010) also provides Microsoft web n-gram services. An online keyword typo generates tool, Seobook (2010), was developed for generating the corpus. Considering of lexicon and ontology, WordNet and FrameNet are both the main knowledge representations for English (Christiane 1998)). Correspondingly, HowNet and E-Hownet are lexicon ontologies for simple and traditional Chinese separately (Li et al. 2011;Dong and Dong 2006). According to the word expression in E-Hownet, lexical senses are described as two aspects: entities and relations. Thus, all the taxonomic relations of lexical senses can be identified according to their definitions in E-Hownet.

Since Word spelling is the essential for natural language processing, spelling correction is a common an essential task in written language automatically to detect and correct human errors. However, spelling check in Chinese is very different from that in English or other alphabetic languages. Therefore, a novel spelling error detection and correction method based on N-gram ranked inverted index is proposed in this paper. Considering of context information such as those in a sentence or long phrase with a certain meaning, N-gram scores are used to arrange the rank of nodes in the inverted index linked list. Besides word N-gram, character frequencies are also used herein first for errors result phonologically similar or visually similar characters (Liu et al. 2011). Both character and word information are used in the proposed approach to achieve the performance of spelling correction.

The rest of this paper is organized as follows. Section 2 describes the proposed method and the related important modules in spelling correction in system framework. Next, we also present the detail description about the proposed method especially in N-gram ranked inverted index list. Experiments to evaluate the proposed approach and the related discussion are presented in Section 3. Concluding remarks and findings are finally made in Section 4.

2 The proposed system framework

In this section, we want to illustrate the proposed system framework to detect and correct the spelling errors. Our goal is to find the locations and correct the corresponding error character in input Chinese sentences. For more clear presentation, herein, the system framework is divided into two parts: training and generation phases as described in Section 2.1 and 2.2 respectively. Actually, similar pronunciation and shape dictionary and N-gram ranked inverted index list are constructed in the training phase and adopted in test phase.

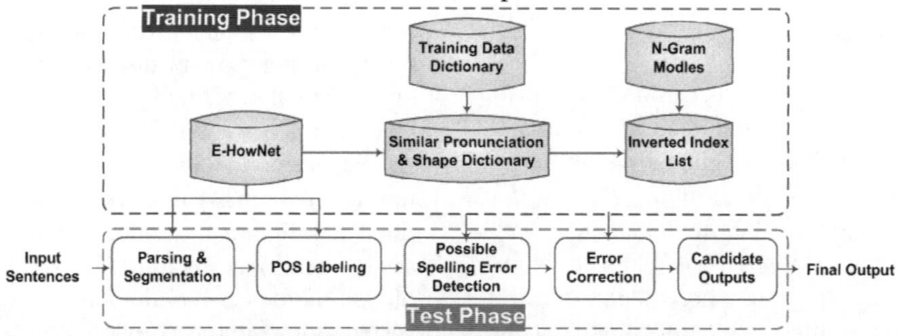

Figure 1. The proposed system framework

2.1 Training phase

The aim of training phase is to construct the dictionary containing similar pronunciation and shape information for each Chinese character. E-Hownet and pre-trained N-gram models are further used to be the ranking score construct the inverted index list. Finally, the candidate outputs are generated according to the N-gram ranked inverted index list. More detail illustration is described in the follows.

As shown in Figure 1. First, we are going to preprocess the sentences we got from the SIGHAN-7 organizer. In this step, we have to remove each sentence NID number in the input file. Then we will have the sentences that without the NID number as our output according to the traditional Chinese parser that was developed by academia Sinica, Taiwan. The results are further fed into the tool, CKIP Autotag, to do word segmentation and part-of-speech tagging based on E-Hownet. Since the corresponding part-of-speech (POS) of each word is obtained in the sentences. Each word is given a part of speech at the end of a word in parentheses. In the second step, for convenience, we are going to remove unessential blank spaces and parentheses. This way will let us more conveniently in the following file operations. In fact, these processes are also adopted in test phase.

For obtaining the correction of each possible spelling error, the similar pronunciation and shape dictionary are constructed here. Since typos usually resulted from similar pronunciation or character shape, we constructed the index for each work from its confusing set including similar pronunciation and character shape. Since the pronunciation of each Chinese character is composed of syllable and tone. Four categories of pronunciation similar confusing set those are potential correction in pronunciation, are gathered: same pronunciation, the same syllable with a different tone, similar syllable with the same tone and similar syllable with a different tone. The corresponding posterior probability is obtained by the confusing matrix used in speech recognition engine constructed by HTK. Considering of the corresponding characters, are called as potential correction in shape, those shapes are similar to that of possible spelling error character. Length based Cangjie code similarity measure is used to estimate the posterior probability for the shape confusing character set.

Since the potential correction either in pronunciation or shape are gathered and defined in the dictionary described in the previous paragraph, the competing candidates are obtained by replacing the possible spelling error using potential correction. One inverted index list for each possible spelling error is constructed according to the corresponding potential correction. Considering of efficiency, the node order is arranged according to the character frequency in initial state. Word based N-gram scoring is further used for re-sorting the node in the inverted index list. Herein, back off base tri-gram models are used to estimate the probability of the contextual information.

2.2 Test phase

As described in previous sections, the inverted index lists with N-gram ranking are built in the training phase. The spelling correction problem is formulated as the ranking of the potential corrections and original possible spelling error in the contextual score in the test phase. Since the word segmentation and part-of-speech (POS) labeling is the same as those in the training phase. Here, we begin the processes with the third step. Third, we are going to find the wrong word from the sentences. After we have the POS parsing result, we choose the word that consists of two characters from the POS result and find it with the words in E-HowNet. If we cannot find it in E-HowNet, then we regarded it as possible suspicious word and enumerate it in suspicious list. We saved its word and POS in a text file named find_wrong. E-HowNet is a lexical knowledge based evolved from HowNet and created by the CKIP group. Then we filter some words in this step in order to remove some words by mistake. Those filtered out words may be words consist of more than four characters with POS of VH ...etc., words consist of more than three characters with POS of 'Nb', 'VA', 'Nc', 'VE' ...etc and POS of 'Neu', 'Neqa', 'Nf', 'VB', 'Ncd', 'VK', 'Nh', 'P' ...etc. And we also filter out the following words contain "到"(to), "過"(through), "亂"(disorder) and "年級"(grade) ...etc. We show some of the suspicious word list.

The fourth step, we are going to do the error correction on those incorrect words. We choose one of a character in the word that to the suspicious list and refer to the similar pronunciation and similar shape dictionaries provided by the SIGHAN-7 organizer. For example, '挫' 折 (setback) and 挫 '折' (setback). We want to find out the pronunciation of the character. It may be same pronunciation with the same tone, same pronunciation without same tone, similar pronunciation with the same tone, similar pronunciation without same tone and same radical with same strokes. And we combine the character with a similar shape character into a new word. Then we find each new word in E-HowNet to verify if there is exist or not. If the new word was not found in E-HowNet, then we will save it into wrong dictionary. After fixing the error, we saved it into the correct dictionary. If the new word was found in E-HowNet, then we will skip to the next character combination word. And so on.... After finishing the word pronunciation part, then we do the same way in word shape part. Fifth, we have to remove the duplicate words in the wrong dictionary. And remove it in wrong and correct dictionary synchronously. As a result, we can prevent doing the same thing twice. Sixth, we use the words in the wrong dictionary to find in the sentences. If we found it, that is to say, the sentence contains this error. Then we replace the error with the corresponding correct word in the correct dictionary and calculate the error location in the output. Seventh, we have several different potential corrections and original possible spelling error, then re-ranking the order according to the N-gram language models in the optimization step. Finally, we can output the best result with the highest N-gram score to the output file.

3 Experimental results

This goal of this study is spelling error detection and correction according Chinese spelling check competition in SigHan. The aim of the subtask 1 is to find out the location of the spelling error in the sentences. On the other hand, the subtask 2 aims at finding out the error location and do the error correction. All sentences at least contain more than one error. In this bake-off, the evaluation includes two sub-tasks: error detection and error correction. The errors are collected from students' written essays. Since there are less than 2 errors per essay such as described in (Chen et al. 2011), in this bake-off the distribution of incorrect characters will match the real world error distribution in the sub-task one. The first subtask aims at the evaluation of error detection. The input sentences might consist of no error to evaluate the false-alarm rate of a system (Wu et al. 2010). The second sub-task focuses on the evaluation of error correction. Each sentence includes at least one error. The ability to accomplish these two sub-tasks is the complete function of a spelling checker.

3.1 Spelling Error Detection

The training data and test data consist of 350 and 1000 sentences separately. Both of them are provided by the SIGHAN-7 organizer.

Table 1. Performance evaluation of the proposed method in subtask 1.

RUN	1	2	3
False-Alarm Rate	0.2371	0.2129	0.0929
Detection Accuracy	0.738	0.761	0.825
Error Location Accuracy	0.623	0.652	0.748
Detection Precision	0.5514	0.5850	0.7451
Detection Recall	0.68	0.70	0.6333
Detection F-score	0.609	0.6374	0.6847
Error Location Precision	0.2405	0.2813	0.4431
Error Location Recall	0.2967	0.3367	0.3767
Error Location F-score	0.2657	0.3065	0.4271

According to the results shown in Table 1, the suitability of the subtasks 1 is high enough. Compared to other approaches, we consider the mapping between the spelling error and correction more.

3.2 Spelling Error Correction

The training data is same as error detection. The test data consists of 1000 sentences those are not the same as the error detection subtask 1.

Table 2. Performance evaluation of the proposed method in subtask 2.

RUN	1	2	3
Location Accuracy	0.369	**0.663**	**0.663**
Correction Accuracy	0.307	**0.625**	**0.625**
Correction Precision	0.485	0.703	0.703

According to the results shown in Table 2, the suitability of the subtasks 2 is excellent. Due to the proposed approach considers both character confusing set and word contextual information, the performance is able to provide the right information to detect and correct the spelling error for users. Especially, The proposed approach outperforms the other approaches significantly in location accuracy and correction accuracy. These results show the N-gram ranked inverted index list able to obtain improvement for spelling error correction. The performance of run 3 outperforms that of run 2 due to some pruning for the word with more than two characters. According to the observations of the error pattern obtained from the training data, we know the spelling error usually appears with the word with less than three characters. By this, the performance is improved significantly.

4 Conclusions

A novel approach to detect and correct the spelling error in traditional Chinese text are proposed in this study. The algorithm is based on the idea of N-gram ranked inverted index list. For detecting the potential correction, the similar patters based on pronunciation and character shape are gathered in a dictionary. To capture the contextual information, the word based N-gram ranking is adopted to arrange the node order in the inverted index list. Finally, the optimal result is selected as the output. The experimental results verified that the proposed approach results in keeping more information either in character or word levels. The performance about the spelling error detection is acceptable and that about correction outperforms other approaches. The experimental results show the proposed method is practice.

Acknowledgments

The authors would like to acknowledge the National Science Council (NSC 100-2622-E-415-001-CC3) and Ministry of Education of Taiwan for financial support for this research.

References

Sun, X., Micol, D., Gao, J., Quirk, C., 2010. Learning Phrase-Based Spelling Error Models from Clickthrough Data. *Proceedings of ACL 2010*.

Ahmad, F., and Kondrak, G. 2005. Learning a spelling error model from search query logs. *In HLT-EMNLP*, pp 955-962.

Li, M., Zhu, M., Zhang, Y., and Zhou, M. 2006. Exploring distributional similarity based models for query spelling correction. *Proceedings of ACL 2006*, pp. 1025-1032.

Gao, J., Li, X., Micol, D., Quirk, C., and Sun, X., 2010. A Large Scale Ranker-Based System for Search Query Spelling Correction, The 23rd International Conference on Computational Linguistics 2010 (COLING 2010). Pp. 358–366.

Ahmad, F., and Kondrak, G., 2005. Learning a Spelling Error Model from Search Query Logs, *Proceedings of Human Language Technology Conference and Conference on Empirical Methods in Natural Language Processing (HLT/EMNLP)*, pp. 955–962.

Li, Y., Duan, H., Zhai, C.X. . 2011. CloudSpeller: Spelling Correction for Search Queries by Using a Unified Hidden Markov Model with Web-scale Resources. *Spelling Alteration for Web Search Workshop 2010*, pp.10-14.

Bao, Z., Kimelfeld, B., Li, Y., 2011. A Graph Approach to Spelling Correction in Domain-Centric Search, , *Proceedings of the 49th Annual Meeting of the Association for Computational Linguistics(ACL) 2011*, pp. 905–914.

Cucerzan, S., and Brill, E.. 2004. Spelling correction as an that exploits the collective knowledge of Web users. *Proceedging of Conference on Empirical Methods in Natural Language Processing EMNLP*, pp. 293–300.

Ingason, A.K., Johannsson, S.B., Rognvaldsson, E., Helgadóttir, S., Loftsson, H. 2009. Context-Sensitive Spelling Correction and Rich Morphology, *NODALIDA 2009 Conference Proceedings*, pp. 231–234.

Mitton, R. 2010. Fifty years of spellchecking. *Wring Systems Research*, 2:1–7.

Huang, Y.-H., Yen M.-C., Wu, G.-H., Wang, Y.-Y., Yeh, J.-F. 2010. Print Pickets Combined Language Models and Knowledge Resources. ROCLING 2010, pp.297-309.

Google. 2010. A Java API for Google spelling check service.http://code.google.com/p/google-api-spellingjava/.

Microsoft Microsoft web n-gram services. 2010. http://research.microsoft.com/web-ngram

Seobook. 2010. Keyword typo generator. http://tools.seobook.com/spelling/keywordstypos.

Christiane F. 1998. *WordNet: An Electronic Lexical Database* (Language, Speech, and Communication). The MIT Press.

Dong, Z.D., and Dong Q. 2006. *HowNet and the Computation of Meaning*. World Scientific Publishing Co. Pte. Ltd.

Liu, C.-L., Lai, M.-H., Tien, K.-W., Chuang, Y.-H., Wu, S.-H., and Lee, C.-Y. 2011. Visually and phonologically similar characters in incorrect Chinese words: Analyses, identification, and applications, *ACM Trans. Asian Lang. Inform. Process.* Vol. 10, No. 2, Article 10 (June 2011), 39 pages.

Chen, Y.-Z., Wu, S.-H., Yang, P.-C., Ku, T., and Chen, G.-D. 2011. Improve the detection of improperly used Chinese characters in students' essays with error model. *Int. J. Cont. Engineering Education and Life-Long Learning*, Vol. 21, No. 1, pp.103-116, 2011.

Wu, S.-H., Chen, Y.-Z., Yang, P.-C., Ku, T., and Liu, C.-L. 2010. Reducing the False Alarm Rate of Chinese Character Error Detection and Correction, *Proceedings of CIPS-SIGHAN Joint Conference on Chinese Language Processing (CLP 2010)*, pages 54 - 61, Beijing, 28-29 Aug., 2010.

Chen, W.-T., Lin, S.-C., Huang, S.-L., Chung, Y.-S., and Chen, K.-J. 2010, E-HowNet and Automatic Construction of a Lexical Ontology, *the 23rd International Conference on Computational Linguistics*, Beijng, China.

Bai, M.-H., Chen K.-J., and Chang, J. S. 2008, Improving Word Alignment by Adjusting Chinese Word Segmentation, *Proceedings of IJCNLP2008*.

Chinese Spelling Checker Based on Statistical Machine Translation

Hsun-wen Chiu **Jian-cheng Wu** **Jason S. Chang**
Department of Institute of Information Systems and Applications
National Tsing Hua University
{chiuhsunwen, wujc86, jason.jschang}@gmail.com

Abstract

Chinese spelling check is an important component for many NLP applications, including word processor and search engines. However, compared to checkers for alphabetical languages (e.g., English or French), Chinese spelling checkers are more difficult to develop, because there are no word boundaries in Chinese writing system, and errors may be caused by various Chinese input methods. In this paper, we proposed a novel method to Chinese spelling checking. Our approach involves error detection and correction based on the phrasal statistical machine translation framework. The results show that the proposed system achieves significantly better accuracy in error detecting and more satisfactory performance in error correcting.

1 Introduction

Chinese spelling check is a task involving automatically detecting and correcting typos, roughly corresponding to misspelled words in English. Liu et al. (2011) show that people tend to unintentionally generate typos that sound similar (e.g., "*措折 cuo zhe" and "挫折 cuo zhe"), or look similar (e.g., "*固難 gu nan" and "困難 kun nan"). On the other hand, some typos found on the Web (such as forums or blogs) are used deliberately for the purpose of speed typing or just for fun. Therefore, spelling check is an important component for many applications such as computer-aided writing and corpus cleanup.

The methods of spelling check can be broadly classified into two types: rule-based methods (Ren et al., 2001; Jiang et al., 2012) and statistical methods (Hung and Wu, 2009; Chen and Wu, 2010). Rule-based methods use knowledge resources such as a dictionary to identify a word as a typo if the word is not in the dictionary, and provide similar words in the dictionary as suggestions. However, simple rule-based methods have their limitations. Consider the sentence "心是很重要的。 xin shi hen zhong yao de" which is correct. However, the two single-character words "心 xin" and "是 shi" are likely to be regarded as an error by a rule-based model for the longer word "心事 xin shi" with identical pronunciation.

Data driven, statistical spelling check approaches appear to be more robust and performs better. Statistical methods tend to use a large monolingual corpus to create a language model to validate the correction hypotheses. Considering "心是 xin shi", the two characters "心 xin" and "是 shi" are a bigram which has high frequency in a monolingual corpus, so we may determine that "心是 xin shi" is not a typo after all.

In this paper, we propose a model, which combines rule-based with statistical approaches to detect errors and generate the most appropriate corrections in Chinese text. Once, an error is identified by the rule-based detection model, we use statistic machine translation (SMT) model (Koehn, 2010) to provide the most appropriate correction. Rule-based models tend to ignore context, so that we use SMT to deal with this problem. Our model treats spelling correction as a kind of translation, where typos are translated into correctly spelled words according to the translation probability and language model probability. Consider the same case "心是很重要的。 xin shi hen zhong yao de". The string "心是 xin shi" will not be incorrectly replaced with "心事 xin shi" because we would consider "心是 xin shi" is highly probable according to the language model.

The rest of the paper is organized as follows. We present the related work in the next section. Then we describe the proposed model for automatically detecting the spelling errors and correcting the found errors in Section 3. Section 4 and Section 5 present the experimental data and evaluation results. And we conclude in Section 6.

2 Related Work

Chinese spelling check is a task involving automatically detecting and correcting typos in a given Chinese sentence. Previous work typically takes the approach of combining a confusion set and a language model. Rule-based approach depends on dictionary knowledge and a confusion set, a collection set of a certain character consists of visually and phonologically similar characters. On the other hand, statistical-based methods usually use a language model, which is generated from a reference corpus. Statistical language model assigns a probability to a sentence of words by means of ngram probability to compute the likelihood of a corrected sentence.

Chang (1995) proposed a system that replaces each character in the sentence based on the confusion set and estimates the probability of all modified sentences according to a bigram language model built from a newspaper corpus, then comparing the probability before and after substitution. They used a confusion set consists of pairs of character with similar shape that are collected by comparing the original text and its OCR results. Similarly, Zhuang et al. (2004) proposed an effective approach using OCR to recognize possible confusion set. In addition, Zhuang et al. (2004) also used a multi-knowledge based statistical language model, the n-gram language model, and Latent Semantic Analysis. However, the experiments by Zhuang et al. (2004) seem to show that the simple n-gram model performs the best.

In recent years, Chinese spelling checkers have incorporated word segmentation. The method proposed by Huang et al. (2007) incorporates Sinica Word Segmentation System (Ma and Chen, 2003) to detect typos. With a character-based bigram language model and the rule-based methods of dictionary knowledge and confusion set, the method determines whether the word is a typo or not. There are many more systems that use word segmentation to detect errors. For example, in Hung and Wu (2009), the given sentence is segmented using a bigram language model. In addition, the method also uses confusion set and common error templates manually edited and provided by Ministry of Education in Taiwan. Chen and Wu (2010) modified the system proposed by Hung and Wu (2009), by combining statistic-based methods and a template matching module generated automatically to detect and correct typos based on language model.

In a work closer to our method, Wu et al. (2010) adopts the noise channel model, a framework used both in spell checkers and machine translation systems. The system combined statistic-based method and template matching with the help of a dictionary and a confusion set. They also used word segmentation to detect errors, but they did not use an existing word segmentation as Huang et al. (2007) did, because it might regard a typo as a new word. They used a backward longest first approach to segment sentences with an online dictionary sponsored by MOE, and a templates with a confusion set. The system also treat Chinese spelling check as a kind of translation, they combine the template module and translation module to get a higher precision or recall.

In our system, we also treat Chinese spelling checking problem as machine translation like Wu et al. (2010), with a different way of handling word segmentation to detect typos and translation model where typos are translated into correctly spelled words.

3 Method

In this section, we describe our solution to the problem of Chinese spelling check. In the error detection phase, the given Chinese sentence is segmented into words. (Section 3.1) The detection module then identifies and marks the words, which may be typos. (Section 3.2) In the error correction phase, we use a statistical machine translation (SMT) model to translate the sentences containing typos into correct ones (Section 3.3). In the rest of this section, we describe our solution to this problem in more details.

3.1 Modified Chinese Word Segmentation System

Unlike English text in which sentences are sequences of words delimited by spaces, Chinese texts are represented as strings of Chinese characters (called Hanzi) with word delimiters. Therefore, word segmentation is a pre-processing step required for many Chinese NLP applications. In this study, we also perform word segment to reduce the search space and the probability of false alarm. After segmentation, sequences of two or more singleton words are considered likely to contain an error. However, over-segmented might lead to falsely identified errors, which we will describe in Section 3.2. Considering the sen-

Replaced character	氣		份	
Translations	汽份	泣份	氣分	氣忿
	器份	契份	氣憤	氣糞
	企份	憩份	氣奮	氣氛

Table 1. Sample "translations" for "氣份 qi fen".

tence "除了要有超世之才，也要有堅定的意志 chu le yao you chao shi zhi cai, ye yao you jian ding de yi zhi", the sentence is segmented into "除了/要/有/超世/之/才/，/也/要/有/堅定/的/意志." The part "超世之才 chao shi zhi cai" of the sentence is over-segmented and runs the risk of being identified as containing a typo. To solve the problem of over-segmentation, we used additional lexicon items and reduce the chance of generating false alarms.

3.2 Error Detection

Motivated by the observation that a typo often causes over-segmentation in the form of a sequence of single-character words, so we target the sequences of single-character words as candidates for typos. To identify the points of typos, we take all n-grams consist of single-character words in the segmented sentence into consideration. In addition to a Chinese dictionary, we also include a list of web-based ngrams to reduce the false alarm due to the limited coverage of the dictionary.

When a sequence of singleton word is not found in the dictionary, or in the web-based character ngrams, we regard the ngram as containing a typo. For example, "森林 的 芳 多 精 sen lin de fang duo jing" is segmented into consecutive singleton words: bigrams such as "的 芳 de fang", and "芳 多 fang duo" and trigrams such as "的 芳 多 de fang duo" and "芳 多 精 fang duo jing" are all considered as candidates for typos since those ngrams are not found in the reference list.

3.3 Error Correction

Once we generate a list of candidates of typos, we attempt to correct typos, using a statistical machine translation model to translate typos into correct word. When given a candidate, we first generate all correction hypotheses by replacing each character of the candidate typo with similar characters, one character at a time.

Take the candidate "氣份 qi fen" as example, the model generates all translation hypotheses, according to a visually and phonologically confusion set. Table 1 shows some translation hypotheses. The translation hypotheses are then validated (or pruned from the viewpoint of SMT) using the dictionary.

Translations	Freq.	LM prob.	tp
氣憤	48	-4.96	-1.20
氣氛	473	-3.22	-1.11

Table 2. Translations for "氣份 qi fen".

The translation probability *tp* is a probability indicates how likely a typo is translated into a correct word. *tp* of each correction translation is calculated using the following formula:

$$tp = \log_{10}\left(\frac{freq(trans)}{freq(trans) - freq(candi)}\right) * \gamma$$

where *freq(trans)* and *freq(candi)* are the frequency of the translation and the candidate correspondingly, and γ is the weight of different error types: visual or phonological. *tp* is set to 0 if *freq(trans)* = 0.

Take "氣份 qi fen" from "不/一樣/的/氣/份 bu/yi yang/de/qi/fen" for instance, the translations with non-zero *tp* after filtering are shown in Table 2. Only two translations are possible for this candidate: "氣憤 qi fen" and "氣氛 qi fen".

We use a simple, publicly available decoder written in Python to correct potential spelling errors found in the detection module. The decoder reads in a Chinese sentence at a time and attempts to "translate" the sentence into a correctly spelled one. The decoder translates monotonically without reordering the Chinese words and phrases using two models — translation probability model and the language model. These two models read from a data directory containing two text files containing a translation model in GIZA++ (Och and Ney, 2003) format, and a language model in SRILM (Stolcke et al., 2011) format. These two models are stored in memory for quick access.

The decoder invokes the two modules to load the translation and language models and decodes the input sentences, storing the result in output. The decoder computes the probability of the output sentences according to the models. It works by summing over all possible ways that the model could have generated the corrected sentence from the input sentence. Although in general covering all possible corrections in the translation and language models is intractable, but a majority of error instances can be "translated" effectively by using the translation model and the language model.

4 Experimental Setting

To train our model, we used several corpora including Sinica Chinese Balanced Corpus, TWWaC (Taiwan Web as Corpus), a Chinese dictionary, and a confusion set. We describe the data sets in more detail below.

Sinica Corpus

"Academia Sinica Balanced Corpus of Modern Chinese", or Sinica Corpus for short, is the first balanced Chinese corpus with part-of-speech tags (Huang et al., 1996). Current size of the corpus is about 5 million words. Texts are segmented according to the word segmentation standard proposed by the ROC Computational Linguistic Society. We use the corpus to generate the frequency of bigram, trigram and 4-gram for training translation model and to train the n-gram language model.

TWWaC (Taiwan Web as Corpus)

We use TWWaC for obtaining more language information. TWWaC is a corpus gathered from the Web under the .tw domain, containing 1,817,260 Web pages, 30 billions Chinese characters. We use the corpus to generate the frequency of all character n-grams for n = 2, 3, 4 (with frequency higher than 10).

Words and Idioms in a Chinese Dictionary

From the dictionaries and related books published by Ministry of Education (MOE) of Taiwan, we obtained two lists, one is the list of 64,326 distinct Chinese words[1], and the other one is the list of 48,030 distinct Chinese idioms[2]. We combine the lists into a Chinese dictionary for validating words with lengths of 2 to 17 characters.

Confusion Set

After analyzing erroneous Chinese word, Liu et al. (2011) found that more than 70% of typos were related to the phonologically similar character, about 50% are morphologically similar and almost 30% are both phonologically and morphologically similar. We use the ratio as the weight for the translation probabilities. In this study, we used two confusion sets generated by Liu et al. (2011) and provided by SIGHAN 7 Bake-off 2013: Chinese Spelling Check Shared Task as a full confusion set based on loosely similar relation.

In order to improve the performance, we expanded the sets slightly and also removed some loosely similarly relations. For example, we removed all relations based on non-identical phonologically similarity. After that, we added the similar characters based on similar phonemes in Chinese phonetics, such as "ㄣ，ㄥ en, eng", "ㄤ，ㄢ ang, an", "ㄕ，ㄙ shi, si" and so on. We also modify the similar shape set to a more strongly similar set. The characters are checked automatically by comparing corresponding Cangjie code (倉頡碼). Two characters which differ from each other by at most one symbol in Cangjie code are considered as strongly similar and are retained. For example, the code of "徵 zheng" and "微 wei" are strongly similar in shape, since in their corresponding codes "竹人山土大" and "竹人山山大", differ only in one place.

5 Evaluation Results

In Bake-off 2013, the evaluation includes two sub-tasks: error detection and error correction. For the error detection, sub-task1, there are 1000 sentences with/without spelling errors. And sub-task2 for the error correction, there are also containing 1000 sentences but all with errors. The evaluation metrics, which computes false-alarm rate, accuracy, precision, recall, and F-Score is provided by SIGHAN 7 Bake-off 2013: Chinese Spelling Check Shared Task. In this paper, we describe Run3 system and results.

On sub-task1, evaluation results as follows:

Evaluation metrics	Score
False-Alarm Rate	0.0514
Detection Accuracy	0.861
Detection Precision	0.8455
Detection Recall	0.6567
Detection F-Score	0.7392
Error Location Accuracy	0.82
Error Location Precision	0.6695
Error Location Recall	0.52
Error Location F-Score	0.5854

Table 3. Evaluation metrics of Sub-task1.

We obtain higher detection accuracy, error location accuracy, and error location F-Score, which put our system in first place among 13 systems evaluated. On sub-task2, our system obtained

[1] Chinese Dictionary http://www.edu.tw/files/site_content/m0001/pin/yu7.htm?open

[2] Idioms http://dict.idioms.moe.edu.tw/cydic/index.htm

location accuracy, correction accuracy, and correction precision of 0.454, 0.443, and 0.6998, respectively.

6 Conclusions and Future Work

Many avenues exist for future research and improvement of our system. For example, new terms can be automatically discovered and added to the Chinese dictionary to improve both detection and correction performance. Part of speech tagging can be performed to provide more information for error detection. Named entities can be recognized in order to avoid false alarms. Supervised statistical classifier can be used to model translation probability more accurately. Additionally, an interesting direction to explore is using Web ngrams in addition to a Chinese dictionary for correcting typos. Yet another direction of research would be to consider errors related to a missing or redundant character.

In summary, we have introduced in this paper, we proposed a novel method for Chinese spelling check. Our approach involves error detection and correction based on the phrasal statistical machine translation framework. The error detection module detects errors by segmenting words and checking word and phrase frequency based on a compiled dictionary and Web corpora. The phonological or morphological spelling errors found are then corrected by running a decoder based on statistical machine translation model (SMT). The results show that the proposed system achieves significantly better accuracy in error detecting and the evaluation results show that the method outperforms other system in Chinese Spelling Check Shared Task.

References

Chao-Huang Chang. 1995. A new approach for automatic Chinese spelling correction. In *Proceedings of Natural Language Processing Pacific Rim Symposium*, pp. 278-283.

Yong-Zhi Chen and Shih-Hung Wu. 2010. *Improve the detection of improperly used Chinese characters with noisy channel model and detection template*. Master thesis, Chaoyang University of Technology.

Chu-Ren Huang, Keh-jiann Chen and Li-Li Chang. 1996. Segmentation standard for Chinese natural language processing. *Proceedings of the 1996 International Conference on Computational Linguistics (COLING 96)*, Vol. 2, pp. 1045-1048.

Chuen-Min Huang, Mei-Chen Wu and Chang Ching-Che. 2007. Error detection and correction based on Chinese phonemic alphabet in Chinese text. *Proceedings of the 4th International Conference on Modeling Decisions for Artificial Intelligence (MDAI IV)*, pp. 463-476.

Ta-Hung Hung and Shih-Hung Wu. 2009. *Automatic Chinese character error detecting system based on n-gram language model and pragmatics knowledge base*. Master thesis, Chaoyang University of Technology.

Ying Jiang, Tong Wang, Tao Lin, Fangjie Wang, Wenting Cheng, Xiaofei Liu, Chenghui Wang and Weijian Zhang. 2012. A rule based Chinese spelling and grammar detection system utility. *2012 International Conference on System Science and Engineering (ICSSE)*, pp. 437-440.

Philipp Koehn. 2010. Statistical Machine Translation. United Kingdom: Cambridge University Press.

Chao-Lin Liu, Min-Hua Lai, Kan-Wen Tien, Yi-Hsuan Chuang, Shih-Hung Wu and Chia-Ying Lee. 2011. Visually and phonologically similar characters in incorrect Chinese words: Analyses, identification, and applications. *ACM Trans. Asian Lang. Inform. Process.* 10, 2, Article 10, pp. 39.

Wei-Yun Ma and Keh-Jiann Chen. 2003. Introduction to CKIP Chinese word segmentation system for the first international Chinese Word Segmentation Bakeoff. *Proceedings of ACL, Second SIGHAN Workshop on Chinese Language Processing*, Vol. 17, pp. 168-171.

Franz Josef Och and Hermann Ney. 2003. A systematic comparison of various statistical alignment models. *Computational Linguistics*, Vol. 29, number 1, pp. 19-51.

Fuji Ren, Hongchi Shi and Qiang Zhou. 2001. A hybrid approach to automatic Chinese text checking and error correction. *2001 IEEE International Conference on Systems, Man, and Cybernetics*, Vol. 3, pp. 1693-1698.

Andreas Stolcke, Jing Zheng, Wen Wang and Victor Abrash. 2011. SRILM at Sixteen: Update and Outlook. In *Proceedings of IEEE Automatic Speech Recognition and Understanding Workshop*.

Shih-Hung Wu, Yong-Zhi Chen, Ping-che Yang, Tsun Ku and Chao-Lin Liu. 2010. Reducing the false alarm rate of Chinese character error detection and correction. *Proceedings of CIPS-SIGHAN Joint Conference on Chinese Language Processing (CLP 2010)*, pp. 54-61.

Li Zhuang, Ta Bao, Xiaoyan Zhu, Chunheng Wang and Satoshi Naoi. 2004. A Chinese OCR spelling check approach based on statistical language models. *2004 IEEE International Conference on Systems, Man and Cybernetics*, Vol. 5, pp. 4727-4732.

A Hybrid Chinese Spelling Correction Using Language Model and Statistical Machine Translation with Reranking

Xiaodong Liu, Fei Cheng, Yanyan Luo, Kevin Duh and Yuji Matsumoto
Graduate School of Information Science
Nara Institute of Science and Technology
8916-5 Takayama, Ikoma, Nara 630-0192, Japan
{xiaodong-l,fei-c,yanyan-l,kevinduh,matsu}@is.naist.jp

Abstract

We describe the Nara Institute of Science and Technology (NAIST) spelling check system in the shared task. Our system contains three components: a word segmentation based language model to generate correction candidates; a statistical machine translation model to provide correction candidates and a Support Vector Machine (SVM) classifier to rerank the candidates provided by the previous two components. The experimental results show that the k-best language model and the statistical machine translation model could generate almost all the correction candidates, while the precision is very low. However, using the SVM classifier to rerank the candidates, we could obtain higher precision with a little recall dropping. To address the low resource problem of the Chinese spelling check, we generate 2 million artificial training data by simply replacing the character in the provided training sentence with the character in the confusion set.

1 Introduction

Spelling check, which is an automatic mechanism to detect and correct human spelling errors in every written language, has been an active research area in the field of Natural Language Processing (NLP). However, spelling check in Chinese is very different from that in English or other alphabetical languages. First because there are no word delimiters between the Chinese words; moreover, the average length of a word is very short: usually one to four characters. Therefore, error detection is a hard problem since it must be done within a context, say a sentence or a long phrase with a certain meaning, and cannot be done within one word. For instance, in the words "自已"(self-control) and "自己"(oneself), the character "已" or "己" cannot be detected as an error without the context. Other challenge in the Chinese spelling check is that there is no commonly available data set for this task and the related resource is scarce.

The SIGHAN 2013 shared task is to provide a common evaluation data set to compare the error detection and correction rates between different systems. The evaluation includes two sub-tasks: 1) error detection and 2) error correction.

In this paper, we present a system that combines the correction candidates produced by the language model based method and the statistical machine translation approach, and then uses an SVM classifier to rerank the correction candidates. To address the low resource problem, firstly, we generate around 2 million artificial sentences following a simple rule, which replaces each character in the provided 700 sentences with the character in the confusion set to generate a new training corpurs; secondly, we use unlabeled data corpus, the Chinese Gigaword, to train a language model[1] to estimate the real Chinese texts.

The paper is organized as follows. We first briefly discuss the related work in Section 2 and overview of our system structure in Section 3. Subsections 3.1, 3.2 and 3.3 describe the components of our system respectively. In Section 4, we discuss the experiment setting and experimental results. Finally, we give the conclusions in the final section.

2 Related work

In Chinese spelling check, the confusion sets are collections of candidate error characters, and play a crucial role.

Chang (1995) manually edited confusion sets from 4 viewpoints, i.e., shape, pronunciation, meaning and input keystroke sequence. Then by

[1] We use the SRI Language Modeling Toolkit adopting the interpolated Kneser-Ney smoothing method.

substituting each character in the input sentence with the characters in the corresponding confusion set, they use a language model to generate a plausibility score to evaluate each possible substituted sentence. Because of the importance of confusion sets, some researchers attempted to automatically extend confusion sets by using different Chinese input methods. Intuitively, the characters with similar input key sequences are similar in shape. Zhang (2000) proposed a method to automatically generate confusion sets based on the Wubi method by replacing one key in the input key sequences of a certain character. Lin et al. (2002) used the Cangjie input method to extend confusion sets automatically.

Over the last few years, more and more models using NLP techniques were introduced into the Chinese spell check task. Huang et al. (2007) proposed a method which used a word segmentation tool to detect Chinese spelling errors. They used CKIP word segmentation toolkit to generate correction candidates (CKIP, 1999). By incorporating a dictionary and confusion sets, the system can detect whether a segmented word contains error or not. Hung et al. (2008) proposed a system which was based on manually edited error templates (short phrases with one error). For the cost of editing error templates manually, Cheng et al. (2008) proposed an automatic error template generation system. The basic assumption is that the frequency of a correct phrase is higher than the corresponding error template. Wu et al. (2010) proposed a system which implemented a translate model and a template module. Then the system merged the output of the two single models and reached a balanced performance on precision and recall.

3 System Architecture

Our system includes three components, as shown in Figure 1. Given a sentence with or without error characters, our procedure contains several steps: 1) we simultaneously generate the correction character candidates using the word segmentation based language model and the statistical machine translation model; and then 2) the SVM classifier reranks the candidates to output the most probable sentence. Each component in our system is described in Section 3.1, Section 3.2 and Section 3.3.

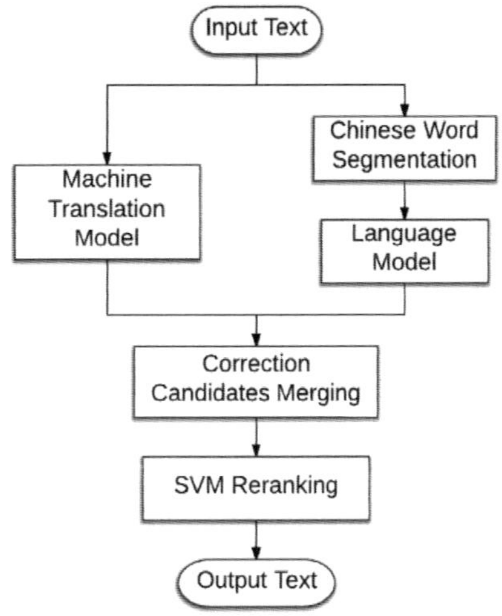

Figure 1: System structure.

3.1 Language Model Based Method

To generate the correction candidates, firstly we segment the sentence into words and then find all possible corrections based on the confusion set and a Chinese dictionary.

In this study, we use the character based Chinese word segmentation model[2] (Xue, 2003), which outperforms the word based word segmentation model in out-of-vocabulary recall. The model is trained on the Academia Sinica corpus, released under the Chinese word segmentation bake-off 2005[3] and the feature templates are the same in Sun (2011).

For example, given the following Chinese sentence (here, the Chinese character in red indicates an error character):

"我看過許多勇敢的人，不怕措折地奮鬥。".

Firstly, we segment the sentence into words separated by a slash as follows.

"我/看過/許多/勇敢/的/人/，/不怕/措折/的/奮鬥/。".

Secondly, we build a lattice, as shown in Figure 2, based on the following rules:

1. If a word only contains a single Chinese character, add all the candidates in the confusion set.

2. If a word contains more than one Chinese character and it is not in the dictionary, then

[2]The CRFsuite package is used in our experiment: http://www.chokkan.org/software/crfsuite/

[3]http://www.sighan.org/bakeoff2005/

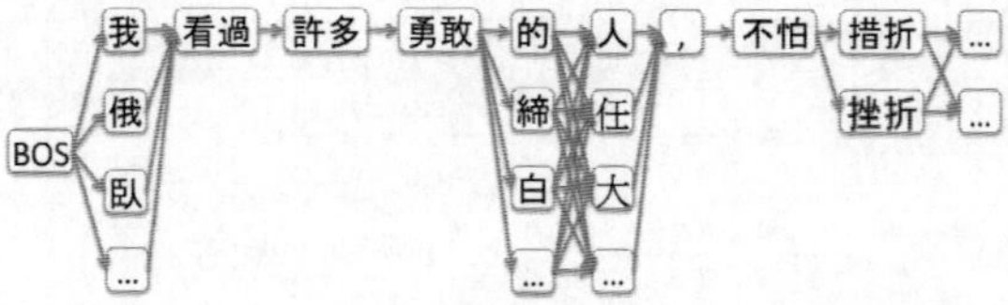

Figure 2: An example of generated candidates lattice.

replace all the characters in the word with candidates in the confusion set. If the generated word is in the dictionary, add it as a candidate.

3. If a word contains more than one Chinese character and it is in the dictionary, do nothing.

Finally, the forward algorithm (Rabiner, 1989) is used to find the k-best sentences using the n-gram language model.

3.2 Statistical Machine Translation Model

As an alternative, we also employ the statistical machine translation model as a new way to detect and correct character errors (Wu et al., 2010), which is widely used by the statistical machine translation community (Brown et al., 1993).

We treat each sentence with error as a source language. Our goal is to find the best correction sentence. Formally, given a sentence S which might contain error characters in it as a source sentence, the output is the sentence $\hat{C}$ in the target language with the highest probability of different replacement C. Symbolically, it is represent by:

$$\hat{C} = \arg\max_{c} p(C|S) \tag{1}$$

Using Bayes Rule, we can rewrite Formula 1 as:

$$\begin{aligned}\hat{C} &= \arg\max \frac{p(S|C)p(C)}{p(S)} \\ &\approx \arg\max p(S|C)p(C)\end{aligned} \tag{2}$$

Here, $p(S|C)^4$ is called "error model", which is the chance that a correct Chinese character could be written wrong, while $p(C)$ is the n-gram language model which evaluates the quality of the corrected Chinese sentence.

[4]We use GIZA++ to train the error model and Moses to decode.
https://code.google.com/p/giza-pp/
http://www.statmt.org/moses/

3.3 SVM Reranking

Support vector machines (SVMs) are supervised learning models used for classification and regression analysis (Burges et al., 1998). The goal of the Chinese spelling error detection task is to detect whether there are any errors in a given sentence, which we can treat as a binary classification problem: if the current character is an error character, the result is 0, otherwise, the result is 1. The probability output of the SVM classifier [5] can also be regarded as a confident score of how possible the current character is an error.

Given the original input text and the outputs of the other models, the system creates a candidate list for each character in the input text. Each character in the candidate list will be reranked based on the confidence score generated by the SVM classifier. The top character in the reranked candidate list will be treated as the correct character of our system. An example of SVM reranking is shown in Figure 3.

We denote a character token c_0 with a context sequence: $...c_{-2}c_{-1}c_0c_{+1}c_{+2}...$ and $c_{s:e}$ as a character sequence that starts at the position s and ends at position e. Our system creates the following features for each candidate.

- Character features: c_{-1}, c_0, c_{+1}, $c_{-1:0}$, $c_{0:+1}$.
- The pointwise mutual information (Gerlof, 2009) between two characters: $PMI(c_{-1}; c_0)$, $PMI(c_0; c_{+1})$.
- The identity of the character sequence if it exists in the dictionary and the n-gram word list. For instance: 2-character window $c_{-1:0}$, 3-character window $c_{-2:0}$, 4-character window $c_{-3:0}$, 5-character windows $c_{-4:0}$

However, the Chinese spelling check shared task provided a sample data with only 700 sentences. We split 80% as training data and 20% as test data and use 5-fold cross-validation to evaluate the SVM reranking results.

4 Experiments

4.1 Data Sets

We used two data sets in our experiments. The first data set is provided by the shared task, which

[5]LIBLINEAR with L2-regularized L2-loss support vector classification is used and optimized the cost parameter (C=3) on the sample data cross-validation result. http://www.csie.ntu.edu.tw/ cjlin/liblinear/.

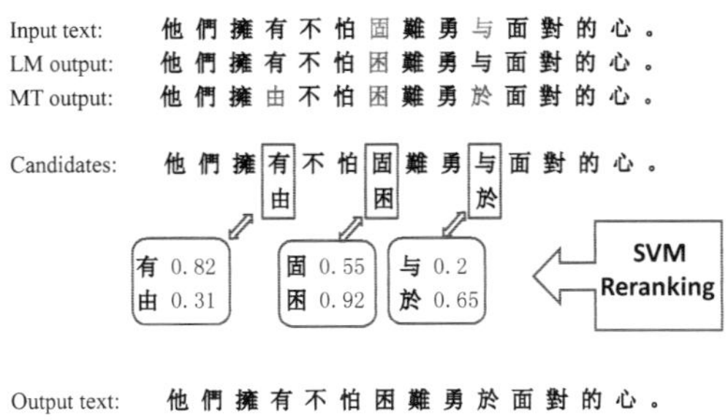

Figure 3: An example of SVM reranking.

includes similar shape confusion sets, similar pronunciation confusion sets, 350 sentences with error characters and 350 sentences without error characters. The second one includes the Chinese Gigaword Second Edition[6], the Chinese word segmentation bake-off 2005 corpus and a free traditional Chinese dictionary[7].

Since only 700 sample sentences are released, it is hard to estimate the error model using Formula 2. A better way is to extend the training corpus to estimate the translation probability. In our experiments, we replace each character in the provided sample sentence with the character in the confusion set to generate a new training instance. Guided by this procedure, around 2 million sentences are generated to train the "error model". However, it is too large for the SVM training. So we limited the candidate samples selecting 20-best sentences ranked by the language model.

4.2 Experiment Setting

For comparison, we combined the outputs of the translation model component and the language model component in three different ways:

1. **NAIST-Run1**: Union of the output candidates of the language model and the statistical machine translation model, and then reranked by SVM.

2. **NAIST-Run2**: Intersection of the output candidates of the language model and the statistical machine translation model, and then reranked by SVM.

3. **NAIST-Run3**: Only use the output of the language model and then reranked by SVM.

Here, we assume that union of the candidates might get a higher recall (NAIST-Run1), while the intersection of the candidates might get a higher precision (NAIST-Run2).

Submission	LocAcc	CorAcc	CorPrec
NAIST-Run1	0.508	0.467	0.5765
NAIST-Run2	0.261	0.254	0.653
NAIST-Run3	0.487	0.453	0.6155

Table 2: **Final results on sub-task 2.** LocAcc, CorAcc and CorPrec denote location accuracy, correction accuracy and correction precision respectively.

4.3 Experimental Results

In the final test, there are two data sets. Each task corpus contains 1000 sentences.

As shown in Table 1, NAIST-Run1 obtained the highest detection recall and NAIST-Run2 got the highest detection precision. However, NAIST-Run3 obtained the highest error location recall, the highest detection F-score and the error location F-score. We think the main reason is that the rate of sentences with error characters is much lower, around 5%, while NAIST-Run1 tends to find more correction candidates.

The final results of the error correction sub task are shown in Table 2. As we expect in Section 4.2, NAIST-Run2 obtained the correction precision, while NAIST-Run1 obtained both the highest location accuracy and the highest correction accuracy.

To evaluate the importance of the SVM reranking, we do another set of experiments on the 700 sample sentences with 5-fold cross-validation. We could obtain 34.7% of the error location precision and 69.1% of the error location recall using the language model based approach. After the reranking by the SVM, the error location precision increased to 70.2%, while the error location recall dropped to 67.0%. From this observation, the SVM reranking plays a crucial role for detection and correction of Chinese spelling errors.

5 Conclusion

We proposed a hybrid system which combines the language model and the statistical machine trans-

[6]Released by LDC. Here we only used the traditional Chinese news to train the language model. http://www.ldc.upenn.edu/Catalog/catalogEntry.jsp?catalogId=LDC2005T14

[7]CC-CEDICT, which is a free dictionary, is released by Creative Commons Attribution-Share Alike 3.0 License. http://www.mdbg.net/chindict/chindict.php?page=cedict

Submission	FAR	DAcc	DPr	DRe	DF-score	ELAcc	ELPr	ELRe	ELF-score
NAIST-Run1	0.2929	0.746	0.5504	0.8367	0.664	0.645	0.3289	0.5	0.3968
NAIST-Run2	0.0543	0.812	0.7979	0.5	0.6148	0.764	0.5426	0.34	0.418
NAIST-Run3	0.2243	0.777	0.5985	0.78	0.6773	0.698	0.3964	0.5167	0.4486

Table 1: **Final results on sub-task 1.** FAR denotes the false-alarm rate. DAcc, DPr, Dre and DF-score indicate detection accuracy, detection precision, detection recall and detection f-score respectively. ELAcc, ELPr, ELRe and ELF-score denote error location accuracy, error location precision, error location recall and error location f-score respectively.

lation model to generate almost all the correction candidates. To improve the precision of the Chinese spelling check, we employ SVM to rerank the correction candidates, where we could obtain a higher precision with a little recall dropping. We also proposed a simple approach to generate many artificial samples, which improved the recall of the statistical machine translation model. Our final test results reveal that our approach is competitive to other systems.

Acknowledgments

We would like to thank Keisuke Sakuchi, Komachi Mamoru and Lis Kanashiro for valuable discussions and comments.

References

Brown, Peter F and Pietra, Vincent J Della and Pietra, Stephen A Della and Mercer, Robert L. 2003. The mathematics of statistical machine translation: Parameter estimation. *Computational linguistics.*. 19-2, pp. 263–311.

Xue, Nianwen. 2003. Chinese word segmentation as character tagging *Computational Linguistics and Chinese Language Processing*. 8-1, pp. 29–48.

Sun, Weiwei. 2011. A Stacked Sub-Word Model for Joint Chinese Word Segmentation and Part-of-Speech Tagging. *Proceedings of the 49th Annual Meeting of the Association for Computational Linguistics: Human Language Technologies*. pp. 1385–1394, Portland, Oregon, USA.

Wu, Shih-Hung and Chen, Yong-Zhi and Yang, Ping-che and Ku, Tsun and Liu, Chao-Lin. 2010. Reducing the false alarm rate of Chinese character error detection and correction. *Proceedings of CIPS-SIGHAN Joint Conference on Chinese Language Processing*. pp. 54–61.

Burges, Christopher JC. 1998. A tutorial on support vector machines for pattern recognition *Data mining and knowledge discovery*. 2-2, pp. 121–167.

Chang, Chao-Huang. 1995. A new approach for automatic Chinese spelling correction. *Proceedings of Natural Language Processing Pacific Rim Symposium*. pp. 278–283.

Zhang, Lei and Huang, Changning and Zhou, Ming and Pan, Haihua. 2000. Automatic detecting/correcting errors in Chinese text by an approximate word-matching algorithm. *Proceedings of the 38th Annual Meeting on Association for Computational Linguistics*. pp. 248–254.

Huang, Chuen-Min and Wu, Mei-Chen and Chang, Ching-Che. 2007. Error detection and correction based on Chinese phonemic alphabet in Chinese text. *Modeling Decisions for Artificial Intelligence*. pp. 463–476.

Hung, Ta-Hung and Wu, Shih-Hung. 2008. Chinese Essay Error Detection and Suggestion System. *Taiwan E-Learning Forum*.

Hung, Ta-Hung and Wu, Shih-Hung. AutoTag. Academia Sinaca.

Chen, Yong-Zhi and Wu, Shih-Hung and Yang, Ping-Che and Ku, Tsun. 2008. Improve the detection of improperly used Chinese characters in students' essays with error model. *International Journal of Continuing Engineering Education and Life Long Learning*. 21-1, pp. 103–116.

Chen, Yong-Zhi and Wu, Shih-Hung and Yang, Ping-Che and Ku, Tsun. 2009. Chinese confusion word set for automatic generation of spelling error detecting template. *The 21th Conference on Computational Linguistics and Speech Processing, Taichung, Taiwan, September*. pp. 1–2

Lin, Yih-Jeng and Huang, Feng-Long and Yu, Ming-Shing. 2002. A Chinese spelling error correction system. *Proceedings of the Seventh Conference on Artificial Intelligence and Applications (TAAI)*.

Bouma, Gerlof. 2009. Normalized (pointwise) mutual information in collocation extraction. *Proceedings of the Biennial GSCL Conference*. pp. 31–40.

Rabiner, Lawrence. 1989. A tutorial on hidden Markov models and selected applications in speech recognition. *Proceedings of the IEEE*. 77-2, pp. 257–286.

Introduction to CKIP Chinese Spelling Check System for SIGHAN Bakeoff 2013 Evaluation

Yu-Ming Hsieh[1,2] **Ming-Hong Bai**[1,2] **Keh-Jiann Chen**[1]
[1] Institute of Information Science, Academia Sinica, Taiwan
[2] Department of Computer Science, National Tsing-Hua University, Taiwan
morris@iis.sinica.edu.tw, mhbai@sinica.edu.tw,
kchen@iis.sinica.edu.tw

Abstract

In order to accomplish the tasks of identifying incorrect characters and error correction, we developed two error detection systems with different dictionaries. First system, called CKIP-WS, adopted the CKIP word segmentation system which based on CKIP dictionary as its core detection procedure; another system, called G1-WS, used Google 1T uni-gram data to extract pairs of potential error word and correction candidates as dictionary. Both detection systems use the confusion character set provided by the bakeoff organizer to reduce the suggested correction candidates. A simple maximizing tri-gram frequency model based on Google 1T tri-gram was designed to validate and select the correct answers. The CKIP group of Academia Sinica participated in both Sub-Task1 (Error Detection) and Sub-Task2 (Error Correction) in 2013 SIGHAN bakeoff. The evaluation results show that the performances of our systems are pretty good on both tasks.

1 Introduction

Spelling check, an automatic mechanism to detect and correct document inputting errors, is a common task for every written languages. How to detect and correct error spellings in a document is an important and difficult task in particular for Chinese language. Since many Chinese characters have similar shape and similar pronunciation, improper use of characters in Chinese essays are hard to be detected (Liu et. al, 2011). Therefore, most Chinese character detection systems are built based on confusion sets and a language model. Some new systems also incorporate NLP technologies for Chinese character error detection in recent years (Huang et al., 2007; Wu et al., 2010). Huang et al. (2007) used a new word detection function in the CKIP word segmentation toolkit (Ma and Chen, 2003) to detect error candidates. With the help of a dictionary and confusion set, the system will be able to judge whether a monosyllabic word is probably error or not. The system we designed for this contest adopts CKIP word segmentation module for unknown word detection too, confusion sets for providing possible candidate characters, and a large-scale corpus for constructing language model for validation and correction of words.

In order to accomplish these two spelling check tasks, we designed two error detection systems with the capability of providing suggested correction candidates. Each system uses different dictionary for its knowledge source. The first system uses the CKIP dictionary, called CKIP-WS; another uses the correction pair dictionary extracted from Google 1T uni-gram data, called G1-WS. In CKIP-WS, we detect possible occurrences of errors through unknown word detection process (Chen and Bai, 1998). So that deeper morphological analysis is carried out only where morphemes of unknown word are detected (Chen and Ma, 2002). As a result, some false alarms caused by proper names and determinant-measure compounds can be avoided. For G1-WS, we build an error suggestion dictionary (or template) to match potential error spellings and suggest correction candidates. Finally we use an n-gram language model to select the corrected characters as our system output.

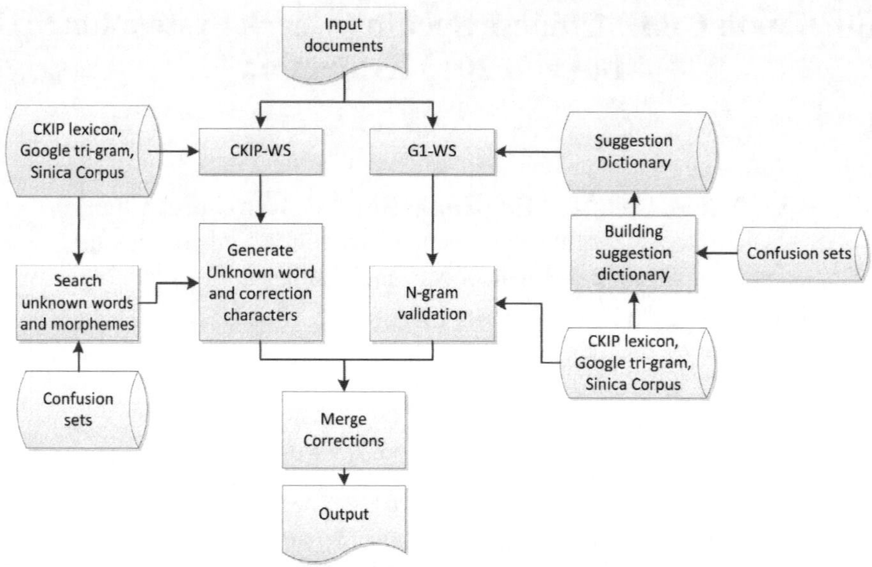

Figure 1. Flowchart of the system

The paper is organized as follows. Section 2 describes the architecture of our system. Section 3 states the bakeoff results evaluated by SIGHAN. In the section 4, we have some relevant discussions and provide analysis on the system performances. Section 5 is the conclusion.

2 System architecture

2.1 System flowchart

Figure 1 illustrates the block diagram of our Chinese Spelling Check system used in this contest. First, input documents are sent to two different error detection systems. The first one is CKIP-WS, which can detect error characters based on unknown word detection and n-gram verification. The second system is G1-WS, which treats error detection based on suggestion dictionary produced by using data of confusion sets, Sinica Corpus and Google Chinese 1T. Finally, the results of the two systems can be merged to get a final detection result. The details will be described in the following subsections.

2.2 Unknown word detection

The first step of our system is word segmentation to find possible error candidates. For example the input sentence "不怕措折地奮鬥" will be marked as "不() 怕() 措(?) 折(?) 地() 奮鬥()" by the unknown word detection process of the CKIP-WS, where (?) denotes the detected monosyllabic unknown word morpheme and () denotes common words. We focus on the morphemes marked with (?) only and provide possible replacement words by checking confusion sets and CKIP dictionary. After the process, the pattern "不 怕 {措,挫} 折 地 奮 鬥" is extracted. For another example, "也在一夕之門". After the detection process, the system marks the sentence as "也() 在() 一() 夕(?) 之() 門()". We use simple algorithm to produce "也 在 一 夕 之 {門, 間}" by left- or right- extension of the word by checking CKIP dictionary. To increase the recall rate, if there are still some monosyllabic words which are not stop words, those words will be also considered as possible error candidates. We will mark those problematic morphemes with (?) for further n-gram validation.

2.3 Building suggestion dictionary

In G1-WS, we first build a suggestion dictionary for potential error words. The data of the dictionary is extracted from Google 1T uni-gram. We use this uni-gram data, and the confusion set to search for similar word pairs and ranks the pair of words by their frequencies. The word of low frequency is considered as error candidate and the high frequency similar word is considered as correction suggestion. Note that the above process is based on the fact that Google 1T uni-gram contains many spelling-error words. Some extracted similar word pairs are shown follow:

Word	Suggestion
措折	挫折
讚同	贊同
讚助商	贊助商
...	

However, the extracted naive suggestion dictionary may have a lot of noises. So we use a simple method to confirm whether to adopt each similar word pair suggestions. First, we use word segmentation in Sinica Corpus by G1-WS. And then we count all words and suggestions. If the frequency ratio of freq(word)/freq(suggestion) > 0.1, we ignore this suggestion. The final G1-WS error detection and candidate suggestion process adopts the modified dictionary. After the first step CKIP-WS error detection, we use the new error detection system G1-WS with this suggestion dictionary to detect and provide additional correction suggestions.

2.4 Validation and correction by n-gram model

After two error detection steps an input document is marked with potential errors and suggest candidate characters. We were intended to develop a character n-gram language model to determine the best character sequence as the answers for detection and correction. However due to the limited developing time, we simply developed a maximizing tri-gram frequency approach instead. Based on the marked error spots, we set a window to count the frequency of these strings which contain potential errors. By simply maximizing tri-gram frequency based on Google 1T tri-gram data, we select the suggestion candidates with the highest string frequency as the answer.

For example, in "也 在 一 夕 之 {門,間}", in comparing with other string candidates as shown in Figure 2. We found the string of the highest frequency "在一夕之間" which is 37,709. So we detect the error spot and select '間' as the corrected character at the mean time.

```
L2L1C0: ("也在一夕之門", 0)
L1C0R1: ("在一夕之門，", 0)
C0R1R2: ("一夕之門，被", 0)
L1C0:   ("在一夕之門", 0)
C0R1:   ("一夕之門，", 0)
-----------------------------
L2L1C0: ("也在一夕之間", 0)
L1C0R1: ("在一夕之間，", 0)
C0R1R2: ("一夕之間，被", 0)
L1C0:   ("在一夕之間", 37709)
C0R1:   ("一夕之間，", 0)
```

Figure 2. Calculating the frequency of the target string in Google tri-gram corpus.

3 Evaluation Results

3.1 Data

The resources adopted in our system are described below:

- CKIP lexicon[1]: The CKIP lexicon is an electronic dictionary containing 88,000 entries for Mandarin Chinese. We use this word information for checking whether the target lexicon is a word or not.
- Google 1T n-gram lexicon[2]: It consists of Chinese word n-grams and their frequency counts generated from over 800 million tokens of text. The length of the n-grams ranges from unigrams (single words) to 5-grams. We use tri-gram data for our n-gram validation process and use uni-gram data for building the suggestion dictionary.
- Confusion sets: Confusion sets are a collection of each individual Chinese character (Liu et al., 2011). There were 5401 confusion sets for each of the 5401 high frequency characters. We use this data to generate possible correction characters.
- Sinica Corpus[3]: We employ the ten-million-word Sinica Corpus, a balanced modern Chinese Corpus with word segmentation and PoS tag. We use this corpus to check and filter our correction data.

3.2 Evaluation metrics

There are several evaluation indexes provided by SIGHAN, i.e. false-alarm rate (FAR), detection accuracy (DA), detection precision (DP), detection recall (DR), detection F-score (DF), error location accuracy (ELA), error location precision (ELP), error location recall (ELR), error location F-score (ELF), location accuracy (LA), correction accuracy (CA), and correction precision (CP).

3.3 Results of our CKIP-WS system

Table 1 shows the evaluation results of our CKIP-WS system in error detection and error correction tasks. In SIGHAN evaluation report, the CKIP-WS system is 'SinicaCKIP-Run1'. In

[1] http://www.aclclp.org.tw/use_ced.php

[2] http://www.ldc.upenn.edu/Catalog/catalogEntry.jsp?catalogId=LDC2010T06

[3] http://db1x.sinica.edu.tw/kiwi/mkiwi/

both tasks, our system achieves good performance.

Task1	**FAR**			
	0.13			
	DA	**DP**	**DR**	**DF**
	0.84	0.7174	0.77	0.7428
	ELA	**ELR**	**ELP**	**ELF**
	0.773	0.5093	0.5467	0.5273
Task2	**LA**	**CA**	**CP**	**CF**
	0.482	0.442	0.5854	0.5037

Table 1. Results of our CKIP-WS system

3.4 Results of our final system

In our final system, we merge CKIP-WS and G1-WS output into final correction data. The evaluations of our final system are shown in table 2. For sub-task 1, FAR score rises 0.03, from 0.13 to 0.1619, and DF and ELF improve 0.0214 and 0.025 respectively. For sub-task 2, the CF has improved 0.0578. From these results, we know that the two systems of CKIP-WS and G1-WS have a complementary relationship. With a better suggestion dictionary, the system performance will be better.

Task1	**FAR**			
	0.1619			
	DA	**DP**	**DR**	**DF**
	0.842	0.6919	0.8533	0.7642
	ELA	**ELR**	**ELP**	**ELF**
	0.771	0.8533	0.6167	0.5523
Task2	**LA**	**CA**	**CP**	**CF**
	0.559	0.516	0.6158	0.5615

Table 2. Results of our final system

From the final summary of SIGHAN Bake-off, our final system ranks the top among 33 submitted systems for detection F-score (DF) and rank 3rd for error location F-score (ELF) in sub-task 1. For sub-task 2, our system ranks second among 30 submitted systems.

4 Discussions

The evaluation results show that our system arrives the top three in both Sub-Task 1 and Sub-Task 2. However, our system performance is still low in both recall and precision. Following are discussions on the recall and precision problems for our systems. We have observes some reasons accounted for recall problems:

- Some correct characters are not in the confusion sets, for examples, "不怕[固→苦]難", "有特[銖→殊]的意義", "深深地敬[佩→佩]這", and etc.
- Dispute on the gold standard, for examples, "樹木 [經]不起 大雨的打擊", "有時候同學的 [嘻]笑怒罵", "不要 一時[胡]塗".
- The word pairs as (再,在),(得,的) cannot be distinguished in our system, such as, "是 個 [在] 平凡 不過 的", "覺 [的] 很 不 開心", "都 過 的 很 快樂", "從此變[的]不同", and etc.
- No information on the related words, such as "圈差" (correct suggestion "圈叉"), and "二 連 罷" (correct suggestion "二連霸").

As to the precision problem, we focus on the confusion set and n-gram language model:

- There are a lot of irrelevant characters in the confusion sets. There should be a way to filter out some of the irrelevant characters.
- A better n-gram language model needs to be developed.

The above discussions suggest that we should enrich our knowledge bases to increase the recall rate by including more suggestion candidates and on the other hand to design a more robust language model to increase the precision of the correction.

5 Conclusions

In this paper, we described the overview of our Chinese Spelling Check system for SIGHAN-7 bakeoff. We employ two word segmentation systems, and adopt some knowledge resources. With the help of these resources, we propose a method to select and filter these correction candidates. Finally, we merge these two systems' outputs for SIGHAN evaluation. The evaluation results show that our approaches are promising. In the future, we will be trying to merge the two word segmentation to a uniform system and develop a more robust language model.

References

Keh-Jiann Chen and Ming-Hong Bai. 1998. Unknown Word Detection for Chinese by a Corpus-based Learning Method. International Journal of Computational Linguistics and Chinese Language Processing, 3(1):27-44.

Keh-Jiann Chen and Wei-Yun Ma. 2002. Unknown word extraction for Chinese documents. In proceedings of the 19th international conference on Computational linguistics (COLING 2002), pages 1-7.

Chuen-Ming Huang, Mei-Che Wu, and Ching-Che Chang. 2007. Error Detection and Correction Based on Chinese Phonemic Alphabet in Chinese Text. In Proceedings of the Fourth Conference on Modeling Decisions for Artificial Intelligence (MDAIIV), pages 463-476.

Chao-Lin Liu, Min-Hua Lai, Kan-Wen Tien, Yi-Hsuan Chuang, Shih-Hung Wu, and Chia-Ying Lee. 2011. Visually and phonologically similar characters in incorrect Chinese words: Analyses, identification, and applications. ACM Transactions on Asian Language Information Processing, 10(2), 10:1-39. Association for Computing Machinery, USA, June 2011.

Wei-Yun Ma and Keh-Jiann Chen. 2003. Introduction to CKIP Chinese Word Segmentation System for the First International Chinese Word Segmentation Bakeoff. In Proceedings of ACL, Second SIGHAN Workshop on Chinese Language Processing, pages 168-171.

Shih-Hung Wu, Yong-Zhi Chen, Ping-Che Yang, Tsun Ku, and Chao-lin Liu. 2010. Reducing the False Alarm Rate of Chinese Character Error Detection and Correction. In Proceeding of CIPS-SIGHAN Joint Conference on Chinese Language Processing (CLP 2010), pages 54-61, Beijing, 28-29 Aug., 2010.

Automatic Chinese Confusion Words Extraction Using Conditional Random Fields and the Web

Chun-Hung Wang
Department of Computer Science
National Tsing Hua University
mars@cs.nthu.edu.tw

Jason S. Chang
Department of Computer Science
National Tsing Hua University
jason.jschang@gmail.com

Jian-Cheng Wu
Department of Computer Science
National Tsing Hua University
wujc86@gmail.com

Abstract

A ready set of commonly confused words plays an important role in spelling error detection and correction in texts. In this paper, we present a system named ACE (Automatic Confusion words Extraction), which takes a Chinese word as input (e.g., "不脛而走") and automatically outputs its easily confused words (e.g., "不徑而走", "不逕而走"). The purpose of ACE is similar to web-based *set expansion* – the problem of finding all instances (e.g. "Halloween", "Thanksgiving Day", "Independence Day", etc.) of a set given a small number of class names (e.g. "holidays"). Unlike *set expansion*, our system is used to produce commonly confused words of a given Chinese word. In brief, we use some hand-coded patterns to find a set of sentence fragments from search engine, and then assign an array of tags to each character in each sentence fragment. Finally, these tagged fragments are served as inputs to a pre-learned conditional random fields (CRFs) model. We present experiment results on 3,211 test cases, showing that our system can achieve 95.2% precision rate while maintaining 91.2% recall rate.

1 Introduction

Since many Chinese characters have similar forms and similar or identical pronunciation, improperly used characters in Chinese texts are quite common. Previous works collected these hard-to-distinguish characters to form confusion sets (Ren et al., 1994). Confusion sets are pretty helpful for online detecting and correcting improperly used Chinese characters in precision and speed. Zhang et al. (2000) build a confusion set based on a Chinese input method named Wubi. The basic assumption is that characters that have similar input sequences must have similar forms. Therefore, by replacing one code in the input sequence of a certain character, the system could generate characters with similar forms. Lin et al. (2002) used the Cangjie input method to generate confusion sets under the same assumption in Zhang et al. Another approach is to manually edit the confusion set. Hung manually compiled 6,701 common errors from different sources (Hung and Wu, 2008). These common errors were collected from essays of junior high school students and were used in Chinese character error detection and correction.

Since the cost of manual compilation is high, Chen et al. (2009) proposed an automatic method that can collect these common errors from a corpus. The idea is similar to template generation, which builds a question-answer system (Ravichandran and Hovy, 2001; Sung et al., 2008). The template generation method investigates a large corpus and mines possible question-answer pairs. In this paper, we present ACE system to automatically extract commonly confused words from the Web of a given word. Table 1 shows some examples of ACE's input and output.

input	兵荒馬亂	三令五申	伶牙俐齒
output	兵慌馬亂	三令五伸 三令五聲 三申五令	伶牙利齒 靈牙利齒

Table 1: Examples of ACE's input and output.

This paper is organized as follows. Section 2 illustrates the architecture of ACE. Section 3 explains the features we use for training model. Section 4 presents evaluation results. The last section summarizes this paper and describes our future work.

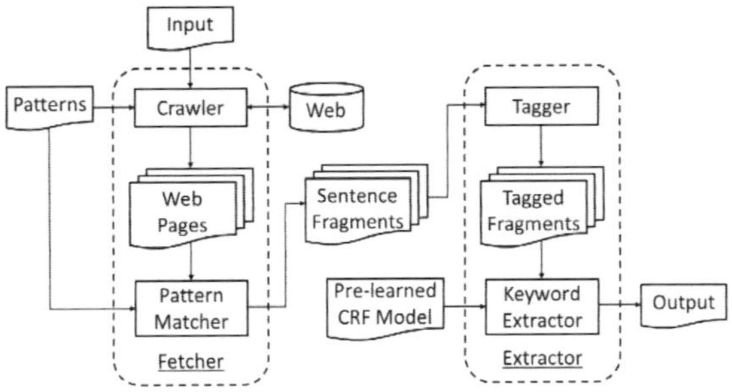

Figure 1: Flow chart of the ACE System.

2 System Architecture

ACE consists of two major components: the Fetcher and the Extractor. Given a Chinese word (assume it is correct), the Fetcher retrieves snippets from Google using hand-coded patterns, and then executes the pattern matching process to produce a set of sentence fragments. The Extractor is responsible for assigning an array of tags to each character in every sentence fragment depends on its features. These tagged fragments are served as inputs to a pre-learned CRFs model (see Section 3) for extracting commonly confused words of the input word. In this section, we will describe the Fetcher and the Extractor in more detail.

2.1 The Fetcher

The Fetcher first constructs a few query strings by using the combination of input word and a set of pre-defined patterns. Table 2 shows our query strings and their English translations.

Type I	**<w>** 誤作	**<w>** be misused as
	<w> 寫成	**<w>** be written as
	<w> 誤為	**<w>** be misused as
	<w> 不是	**<w>** not
Type II	應為 **<w>**	should be **<w>**
	應作 **<w>**	should be **<w>**
	改為 **<w>**	be revised as **<w>**

Table 2: Type I and Type II query strings and their English translations. In each query string, **<w>** is a placeholder for the input word.

There are two types of query strings: Type I are the ones that require the input word **w** to precede the pattern (e.g. "**w**寫成"), and Type II are the opposite ones (e.g. "應作**w**"). For every query, the Fetcher retrieves several Web pages of results from Google where each page contains up to 100 snippets due to Google's restriction. For each snippet, the Fetcher removes its HTML tags and extracts sentence fragments which contain the input word and possibly contain incorrect words with the help of regular expression. These sentence fragments are inputs of the Extractor we will describe later. For Type I query results, sentence fragment is orderly composed by 0 to 6 characters (including Chinese characters, alphanumeric symbols, punctuation marks, etc.), the input word, and 1 to n characters where n is the number of characters of the input word plus 14. For Type II query results, sentence fragment is orderly composed by 1 to n characters, the input word, and 0 to 6 characters. Table 3 shows some examples of extracted sentence fragments of the input word "不脛而走".

Type I
目。復原**不脛而走**" *誤作* "不徑而走" （'97
「**不脛而走**」*寫成*「不徑而走」- Y
Type II
"不徑而走" *應為* "**不脛而走**" big
月 5 日 - 不徑而走*應作***不脛而走**. 峻工

Table 3: Examples of sentence fragments of the input word "不脛而走". For clarification purposes, we make the input word bold and italicize the pattern.

2.2 The Extractor

The Extractor first assigns an array of tags to each character in every sentence fragment derived from the Fetcher by its features. We may assign up to four tags to each character according to system configurations. Table 4 shows an example of fully tagged fragment. Tag I denotes that this character is in the instance of the input word or not. Tag II and Tag III are pronunciation-related features, indicating pronunciation similarity between this character and any character of the input word. Tag IV is orthographic similarity between this character and any character of the input word. Meanings of tags and how to assign tags to characters will be detailed in Section 4.

After sentence fragments are tagged, these tagged fragments are served as inputs to a pre-learned CRFs model for labeling easily confused words of the input word. Finally, the Extractor combines these labeled characters into words, and then ranks these words based on frequency.

ACE outputs first few ranked words depend on system settings. Let a = $\langle a_1, a_2, \ldots, a_n \rangle$ be the set of ranked words and $f(a_i)$ denotes the frequency of a_i , $f(a_1) \geq f(a_2) \geq \cdots \geq f(a_n)$.

ACE outputs $a' = \langle a_1, \dots, a_j \rangle$ where $1 \le j \le i$ and $a_k \ge C * a_{k-1}$ for each $a_k \in a'$. The default value of C is 0.3 and can be configured in the system. Some example inputs and outputs are listed in Table 1, and Section 6 shows more examples.

characters	Tag I	Tag II	Tag III	Tag IV
“	N	O	O	O
不	N	Y	Y	Y
徑	N	N	N	N
而	N	Y	Y	Y
走	N	Y	Y	Y
”	N	O	O	O
應	N	O	O	O
為	N	O	O	O
“	N	O	O	O
不	Y	Y	Y	Y
脛	Y	Y	Y	Y
而	Y	Y	Y	Y
走	Y	Y	Y	Y
”	N	O	O	O

Table 4: An example of fully tagged fragment.

3 Features Set

One property that makes feature based statistical models like CRFs so attractive is that they reduce the problem to finding an appropriate feature set. This section outlines the four main types of features used in our evaluations.

3.1 Base Feature

One of simplest and most obvious features is the character itself of sentence fragment. Another intuitive feature is that the character is included in the input word (tagged as “Y”) or not (tagged as “N”). More accurately, let $\mathbf{o} = \langle o_1, o_2, \dots, o_n \rangle$ be a sequence of characters of sentence fragment. Let $\mathbf{w} = \langle w_1, w_2, \dots, w_m \rangle$ be a sequence of characters of the input word. $\mathbf{w} \subset \mathbf{o}$. For each $o_i \in \mathbf{o}$, we tag o_i as “Y” if $o_i \in \mathbf{w}$, otherwise tag o_i as “N”. In our experiments, we define the combination of those two features as base feature.

3.2 Sound Feature

Liu (2009) previously showed that pronunciation-related errors reach 79.88% among all types of incorrect writings in Chinese. This feature has three tag values: “Y”, “N”, and “O”. We continuously use notations of Section 4.1. Let $U_w = \langle u_{w_1}, u_{w_2}, \dots, u_{w_m} \rangle$ where u_{w_i} denotes the sound of w_i. Let u_{o_i} denotes the sound of o_i. For each $o_i \in \mathbf{o}$, we tag o_i as “Y” if $o_i \in \mathbf{w}$, else tag o_i as “N” if $u_{o_i} \in U_w$, otherwise tag o_i as “O”.

We build up a look-up table for quickly access a character’s sound. Table 5 is the list of characters grouped by sound. Note that characters in the same group may have different tones. We will consider the feature of same sound and same tone in Section 4.3.

sound	characters
suan	酸 痠 狻 匴 算 蒜 筭
wai	歪 咼 外
zai	哉 災 載 宰 仔 崽 縡 在 再 載

Table 5: Characters grouped by sound.

3.3 Phonetic Alphabet Feature

This feature differentiates two characters with same sound but different tone from each other. Let $H_w = \langle h_{w_1}, h_{w_2}, \dots, h_{w_m} \rangle$ where h_{w_i} denotes the phonetic symbol of w_i. Let h_{o_i} denotes the phonetic symbol of o_i. For each $o_i \in \mathbf{o}$, we tag o_i as “Y” if $o_i \in \mathbf{w}$, else tag o_i as “N” if $h_{o_i} \in H_w$, otherwise tag o_i as “O”. Table 6 is the list of characters grouped by phonetic alphabet.

phonetic alphabet	characters
suān	酸 痠 狻
suǎn	匴
suàn	算 蒜 筭
wāi	歪
wǎi	咼
wài	外

Table 6: Characters grouped by phonetic alphabet.

3.4 Orthography Feature

In addition to pronunciation-related features, the model could also benefit from orthographical similarity features. We have collected a list of 12,460 Chinese characters accompanied by a group of orthographically similar characters for each from Academic Sinica of Taiwan[1]. Two characters are considered to be orthographically similar according to their forms. In this list, each character may have more than one similar character. Let $\mathbf{r}_{w_i} = \langle r_{w_{i1}}, r_{w_{i2}}, \dots, r_{w_{ik}} \rangle$ be a set of orthographically similar characters of w_i. Let $\mathbf{R}_w = \langle \mathbf{r}_{w_1}, \mathbf{r}_{w_2}, \dots, \mathbf{r}_{w_m} \rangle$ be the collection of $\mathbf{r}_{w_i}$.

[1] http://cdp.sinica.edu.tw/cdphanzi/

For each $o_i \in \mathbf{o}$, we tag o_i as "Y" if $o_i \in \mathbf{w}$, else tag o_i as "N" if $o_i \in \mathbf{R}_w$, otherwise tag o_i as "O". Table 7 is the list of characters accompanied by their orthographically similar characters.

character	similar characters
亨	烹 哼 脝 京 享
佐	仜 左 佈 傞 倥 佑
別	捌 咧 唎 喇

Table 7: Characters and their orthographically similar characters.

4 Experiments

In this section, we describe the details of CRFs model training and evaluation. Secondly, we will compare performance of ACE system with two manually compiled confusion sets which can be anonymously accessed online.

4.1 Model Training and Testing

We obtained data set from a document named Terms Unified Usage[2] provided by National Science Council of Taiwan. This document contains 641 correct-and-incorrect word pairs. We randomly selected 577 of them for training and the rest for testing. For each word pair, we constructs query strings to retrieve sentence fragments by using the method described in Section 2.1, and then assigns tags to each character in every sentence fragment by using the method described in Section 2.2. In addition, we tagged target label (e.g. B-I, I-I, O) to each character for the purpose of training and evaluation.

There are 17,019 sentence fragments which containing 126,130 characters in training data, and 1,252 sentence fragments which containing 15,767 characters in testing data. Eight experiments were completed by different combinations of features. Detailed results are presented in table 7 (in next page). In Table 7, characters precision denotes number of correctly labeled characters divided by number of total characters in the testing data. Similarly, sentences precision denotes number of correctly labeled sentences (every character in sentence is correctly labeled) divided by number of total sentence. Since the output of ACE is a ranked list of extracted words, we set 0.3 to constant C (see Section 2.2) to compute precision ratio, recall ratio, and F_1 measure. More precisely, let:

- {A}=incorrect words indicated in Terms Unified Usage
- {B}=incorrect words extracted by ACE

Then, precision ratio $P = |\{A\} \cap \{B\}| / |\{B\}| * 100\%$, recall ratio $R = |\{A\} \cap \{B\}| / |\{A\}| * 100\%$, and F_1 measure = $2*P*R/(P+R)$.

From the result, the CRFs model using the combination of sound and orthography features or using all features performs best, achieving F_1 measure of 94.6%.

4.2 Comparisons to Manually Compiled Confusion Sets

We collected two manually compiled confusion sets for the purpose of comparisons. One is the *Common Error in Chinese Writings*[3] (CECW) provided by Ministry of Education (MOE) of Taiwan, which containing 1,491 correct-and-incorrect word pairs. Another is the *Commonly Misused Characters for Middle School Students*[4] (CMC), which containing 1,720 correct-and-incorrect word pairs. We feed these correct words to ACE system to evaluate the ability of automatic generation of confusion sets. We choose features combinations of "base + S + G" and set constant C to 0.3. Table 8 summarizes the evaluation results, showing that given a Chinese word, ACE system has about 93% chance to produce same result with manually compiled confusion sets.

	Precision	Recall	F_1 measure
CECW	95.2%	91.2%	93.2%
CMC	93.8%	92.0%	92.8%

Table 8: Evaluation results on two confusion sets.

input	output
滄海一粟	滄海一粟
半晌	半餉 半响
發憤圖強	發奮圖強 奮發圖強
掃描	掃瞄
彆扭	蹩扭 憋扭 變扭 辯扭

Table 9: Examples of ACE's input and output.

[2] http://www.nsc.gov.tw/sd/uniword.htm

[3] http://dict.revised.moe.edu.tw/htm/biansz/18a-1.htm

[4] http://kitty.2y.idv.tw/~mars/cset.xlsx

	Characters Precision	Sentences Precision	Extracted Words		
			Precision	Recall	F_1 measure
base only	94.1%	66.1%	89.7%	73.2%	80.6%
base + Sound (S)	97.6%	83.0%	89.7%	77.3%	83.0%
base + Phonetic (P)	97.9%	85.7%	93.1%	87.5%	90.2%
base + Orthography (G)	97.9%	86.6%	89.7%	85.6%	87.6%
base + S + P	97.7%	84.1%	89.7%	89.3%	89.5%
base + S + G	98.8%	92.4%	96.6%	92.7%	94.6%
base + P + G	98.9%	92.8%	96.6%	89.3%	92.8%
base + S + P + G	98.8%	92.9%	96.6%	92.7%	94.6%

Table 7: Test results by different combinations of features.

5 Conclusions and Future Work

In this paper, we present the ACE system which takes a Chinese word as input and automatically outputs its easily confused words. Table 9 shows some real examples of ACE's input and output. We have shown that a CRF-based model with pronunciation- and orthography-related features can achieve performance near that manually compiled confusion sets.

There are several future topics of research that we are currently considering. First, we plan to extend ACE system to support other languages, such as English and Japanese. Secondly, we will investigate another approach without the help of a pre-learned CRFs model. Third, we will look into automatic identification of possible words which can be easily misused as another one, so that we can generate confusion sets without any input. Lastly, we will apply our approach to another application, such as recognizing as many as entity pairs (e.g., <"Tokyo", "Japan">, <"Taipei", "Taiwan">, etc.) of a given semantic relation (e.g. "… is a city of …").

References

Andrew McCallum and Wei Li. 2003. Early results for named entity recognition with conditional random fields, feature induction and web-enhanced lexicons. *Proceedings of the Conference on Natural Language Learning*, 188–191.

Chao-Lin Liu, Kan-Wen Tien, Min-Hua Lai, Yi-Hsuan Chuang, and Shih-Hung Wu. 2009. Phonological and logographic influences on errors in written Chinese words. *Proceedings of the Seventh Workshop on Asian Language Resources, the Forty Seventh Annual Meeting of the Association for Computational Linguistics*, 84-91.

Cheng-Lung Sung, Cheng-Wei, Lee, Hsu0Chun Yen, and Wen-Lian Hsu. 2008. An Alignment-based Surface Pattern for a Question Answering System. *IEEE International Conference on Information Reuse and Integration*, 172-177.

Deepak Ravichandran and Eduard Hovy, E. 2001. Learning surface text patterns for a Question Answering system. In *Proceedings of the 40th Annual Meeting on Association for Computational Linguistics*, 41-47.

Fei Sha and Fernando Pereira. 2003. Shallow parsing with conditional random fields. In *Proceedings of the Human Language Technology and North American Association for Computational Linguistics Conference*, 134-141.

Fuji Ren, Hongchi Shi, and Qiang Zhou. 1994. A hybrid approach to automatic Chinese text checking and error correction. In *Proceedings of the ARPA Work shop on Human Language Technology*, 76-81.

John Lafferty, Andrew McCallum, and Fernando Pereira. 2001. Conditional random fields: Probabilistic models for segmenting and labeling sequence data. In *Proceedings of the International Conference on Machine Learning*.

Lei Zhang, Changning Huang, Ming Zhou, and Haihua Pan. 2000. Automatic detecting/correcting errors in Chinese text by an approximate word-matching algorithm. In *Proceedings of the 38th Annual Meeting on Association for Computational Linguistics*, 248-254.

Ta-Hung Hung and Shih-Hung Wu. 2008. Chinese essay error detection and suggestion system. *Taiwan E-Learning Forum*.

Yih-Jeng Lin, Feng-Long Huang, and Ming-Shing Yu. 2002. A Chinese spelling error correction System. In *Proceedings of the Seventh Conference on Artificial Intelligence and Applications* (TAAI).

Yong-Zhi Chen, Shih-Hung Wu, Chia-Ching Lu, and Tsun Ku. 2009. Automatic template feneration for Chinese essay spelling error detecting system. *The 13th Global Chinese Conference on Computer in Education*, 402-408.

Conditional Random Field-based Parser and Language Model for Traditional Chinese Spelling Checker

Yih-Ru Wang
National Chiao Tung University
HsinChu, Taiwan
yrwang@mail.nctu.edu.tw

Yuan-Fu Liao
National Taipei University of Technology, Taipei, Taiwan
yfliao@ntut.edu.tw

Yeh-Kuang Wu
Institute for Information Industry
Taipei, Taiwan
121590@gmail.com

Liang-Chun Chang
Institute for Information Industry
Taipei, Taiwan
lcchang@iii.org.tw

Abstract

This paper describes our Chinese spelling check system submitted to SIGHAN Bake-off 2013 evaluation. The main idea is to exchange potential error character with its confusable ones and rescore the modified sentence using a conditional random field (CRF)-based word segmentation/part of speech (POS) tagger and a tri-gram language model (LM) to detect and correct possible spelling errors. Experimental results on the Bakeoff 2013 tasks showed the proposed method achieved 0.50 location detection and 0.24 error location F-scores in subtask1 and 0.49 location and 0.40 correction accuracies and 0.40 correction precision in subtask2.

1 Introduction

Chinese spelling check is a difficult task for two reasons: (1) there are no word delimiters between words, (2) the length of each word is usually only one to three characters long. So it cannot be done within the word and must be solved within a context. Therefore, Chinese spell checking is usually divided into two steps: (1) segmentation of text into word sequence and (2) error checking of each word in sentence level.

Basically, word segmentation can be formulated as a sequential learning problem. In the past decade, many statistical methods, such as support vector machine (SVM) (Zhang, 2010), conditional random field (CRF) (Zhao, 2006), maximum entropy Markov models (MEMMs) (Berger, 1996), were proposed by NLP researchers to handle this sequential learning task. Among them, CRF-based approach has been shown to be effective with very low computational complexity.

On the other hand, error checking could be treated as an abnormal word sequence detection problem and is often based on language knowledge, and mainly includes rule-based methods and statistic-based methods. Rule-based methods use rule sets, which describe some exact dictionary knowledge such as word or character frequency, POS information and some other syntax or morphological features of a language, to detect dubious areas and generate candidate words list. This kind of methods achieves significant success in some special domains, but it is difficult to deal with open natural language. On the other hand, statistic-based methods often use a language model that is achieved by using some language knowledge and analyzing a huge of language phenomena on large corpus so more context information is utilized, and this kind of methods is suitable for general domains.

There are many advanced Chinese spelling check methods (Liu, 2011 and Chen, 2011). However, from the viewpoint of automatic speech recognition (ASR) research, the word segmentation and LM are the most important modules for ASR studies. Especially, it is known that a good LM can significantly improve ASR's recognition performance. And a sophisticated parser is required for building highly effective LM. So, in past few years, lots of works were conducted in our laboratory to build a CRF-based word segmentation/POS tagger and a tri-gram LM to improve the performance of ASR.

Although, we have already applied our parser and LM to ASR and achieved many successes (Chen, 2012), we would like to take the chance of Bakeoff 2013 evaluation to examine again how generalization and sophistication our parser and LM are. Therefore, the focus of this paper is on how to integrate our parser and LM originally built for ASR to deal with the Chinese spelling check task.

2 The Proposed Framework

The block diagram of the proposed method is shown in Fig. 1. Our main idea is to exchange potential error character with its confusable ones and rescore the modified sentence using our CRF-based parser and tri-gram LM to detect and correct possible spelling errors.

In this scheme, the input text is first checked if there are some high frequency error words in the rule-based frontend. The sentence is then segmented into a word sequence using our CRF-based parser and scored with tri-gram LM. Each character in short words (less than 3 characters) is considered as potential error character and is replaced with characters that have similar shape or pronunciation. The modified sentence is then re-segmented and rescored to see if the score of the changed sentence is higher. This process is repeated until the best sentence with maximum LM score is found.

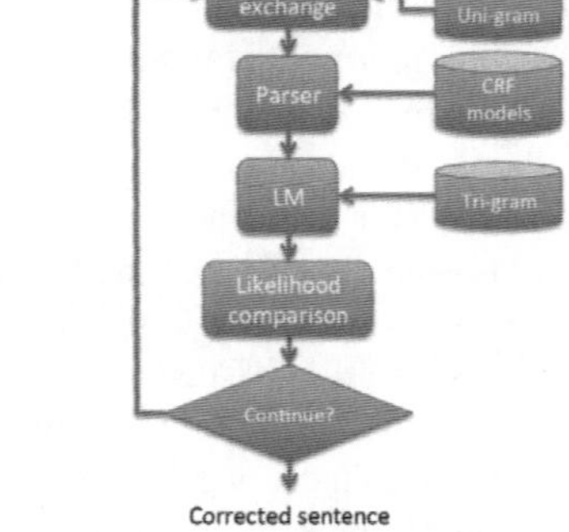

Fig. 1: The schematic diagram of the proposed Chinese spelling checker.

2.1 Rule-based Frontend

Basically, the rule-based spelling error correcting was easy and will not increase the complexity of our parser. In our parser, only the rules with high accuracy and low false alarm were added to the parser. It can also increase the accuracy of our parser.

There are about 600 high frequency error words in our database. Those words are basically collected from Internet. The rule to replace error words is in general as follows:

(1) Direct spelling errors correcting: Most of those cases are frequently error words, some interesting examples of the rules are:
- 倉惶 → 倉皇
- 翹課 → 蹺課
- 百摺裙 → 百褶裙
- 經不起 → 禁不起
- 明查秋毫 → 明察秋毫

It can be seen from those examples that some errors are due to misunderstanding of the meaning of words. Since these errors are often unconsciously replaced with other high-frequency characters, it is usually difficult to detect and corrected using LM.

(2) Errors correcting with constraints: In this case, the word *XX*, usually two characters, will be corrected to *YY*, with some constraints. We need to check if the *XX* is cross word boundary. If p_i is preceding character and P_i succeeding character of *XX*, and the p_i-*XX* can be segment into p_iX-*X* or *XX*-P_i can be segment into *X*-*X*P_i. In order to avoiding false alarm, the constraints were checked before the correcting.
For example: 一但 → 一旦, but the preceding character p_i is not 統, or the succeeding character P_i is not 書.

(3) Spelling errors correcting after parsing: Some frequently happened spelling errors were difficult to correction without the word segmentation information. The error words were added in the lexicon of parser in order to get the corrected word segmentation. And, the error words were correcting after parsing.

2.2 CRF-based Chinese PARSER

A block diagram of the proposed Chinese parser is shown in Fig. 2. There are three blocks including (1) text normalization, (2) word segmentation and (3) POS tagging. The last two modules are briefly described as follows.

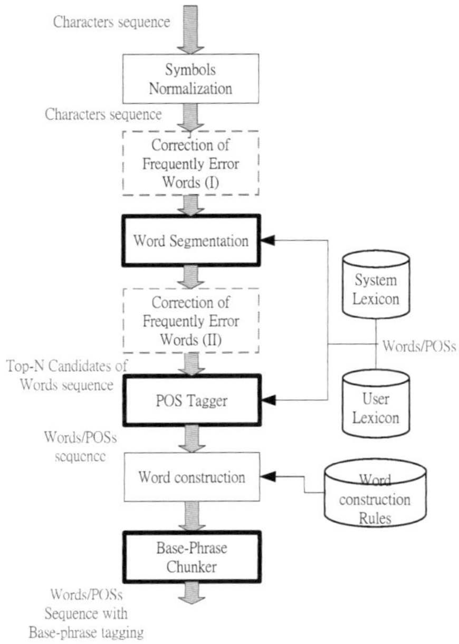

Fig. 2: The schematic diagram of the proposed Chinese parser.

2.2.1 Word Segmentation

Basically, it is based on CRF method and implemented following Zhao's work (Zhao, 2006). Six tags, denoted as B1, B2, B3, M, E and S, are used to represent the activated functions. The information used in feature template is listed in the following:

- C_n: Unicode of the current character (Unicode plain-0 only).
- B_n: radical of the current character ("bushu", 部首).
- SB_n: if B_n is equal to B_{n-1}.
- WL_n: length of the maximum-length word in lexicon that matches the string including the current character. Here, the 87,000-word lexicon released from Sinica (Sinica Chinese Electronic Dictionary[1]) is used as the basic internal lexicon. A user-defined lexicon is allowed to define more words, and in most cases they are named entities.
- WT_n: tags of the maximum-length word comprising the current character (indicating character position in word by B1, B2, B3, M, E, S).
- D/E_n: indicator showing whether the current character is a digit.
- PM_n: 0-1 tags to indicate whether the current character is a punctuation mark (PM).

Moreover, the CRF templates used in the word segmentation are shown in Table 1.

Information	Templates
Character n-gram	Cn-2, Cn-1, Cn, Cn+1, Cn+2, (Cn-2 Cn-1 Cn), (Cn Cn+1 Cn+2), (Cn-1 Cn Cn+1), (Cn-2 Cn-1 Cn Cn+1 Cn+2)
Digits/English	(D/En-1 D/En), (D/En D/En+1), (D/En-1 D/En D/En+1)
Bushu	(Bn BSn), (Bn-1 BSn-1), (Bn+1 BSn+1)
Tag of candidate word	WTn-1, WTn, WTn+1, (WTn-1 WTn), (WTn WTn+1), (WTn-1 WTn WTn+1)
Length of candidate word	WLn-1, WLn, WLn+1, (WLn-1 WLn), (WLn WLn+1), (WLn-1 WLn WLn+1)
Length/tag of candidate word	(WTn WLn), (WTn-1 WLn-1 WTn WLn), (WTn WLn WTn+1 WLn+1)
Repeated word	(LWn SW1n), (LWn SW2n)
PM	PMn-1, PMn, PMn+1

Table 1: List of CRF templates for word segmentation.

The word segmentation module is trained by using Sinica Balanced Corpus version 4.02. Before training the word segmentation CRF, data in the corpus are check to correct in-consist word-segmentation. More than 1% of data in the corpus are corrected manually.

The protocol of consistency check is described here. The unigram and bigram of Sinica Balanced corpus are first generated. Then all pairs of words, excepting the words with POS of "Nf" and "Neu", are checked to see whether they can be combined into a single word. There are about 10% of such word-pairs. For example:

(1) For the case that both a word-pair (e.g. 民意(Na) 代表(Na)) and the combination word (e.g. 民意代表(Na) appear in the corpus, we divide the combination word into two words.

(2) For a word-pair (e.g. /長途(A) 電話(Na)/) whose combination does not appear as a single word in the corpus but is a word entry (e.g. /長途電話(Na)/) in the Sinica lexicon, we keep the two words and remove the combination word from the lexicon.

(3) Most of the bound morphemes (i.e., prefixes and suffixes), named entities, compound words, idioms, and abbreviations in the corpus were checked for consistency.

(4) Some words, especially for function words, have different POSs and can be divided into smaller words, like "就是(T), 就是 (SHI), 就

[1] http://www.aclclp.org.tw/use_ced.php

[2] http://www.aclclp.org.tw/use_asbc.php

[2] http://www.aclclp.org.tw/use_asbc.php

是(Nc), 就(D) 是(SHI), 就是(D), 就是(Cbb)" and "真是(VG), 真是(D), 真(D) 是(SHI)]". Some of them need to be corrected according to the syntactic and/or sematic context in the sentence.

The corpus is divided into two parts: a training set containing 90% of the corpus (about 1 million words including PMs) and a test set containing 10% (about 120K words including PMs). The training set is used to train the word segmentation CRF. The F-measure of the word segmentation is 96.72% for the original database and 97.50% for the manually correct one. The difference between precision and recall rates is less than 0.1%. If all PMs are excluded, the F-measure reduces to 97.01%.

2.2.2 POS Tagger

Here is the features used in the CRF method:

- PM_n: Unicode of the first character of the current word when it is a PM, or "X" if it is not a PM. We note that some PMs, such as "?!" and "…", are formed by string of more than one character.
- WL_n: word length of the current word.
- $LPOS_n$: all possible POSs of the current word if it is in the internal or external lexicons, or "X" if it is not in those lexicons, e.g. the word "一"(one) can be "Cbb_Di_D_Neu".
- FC_n: first character of the current word if it is not in lexicon, or "X" if it is in lexicon.
- LC_n: last character if the word is not in lexicon, or "X" if it is in lexicon.

Table 2 shows the CRF templates used for POS tagging.

Information	Templates
Possible POS n-gram	$LPOS_{n-2}$, $LPOS_{n-1}$, $LPOS_n$, $LPOS_{n+1}$, $LPOS_{n+2}$, ($LPOS_{n-1}$ $LPOS_n$), ($LPOS_{nn}$ $LPOS_{n+1}$), ($LPOS_{n-1}$ $LPOS_{n+1}$)
PM	PM_{n-1}, PM_n, PM_{n+1}
Information of OOV word	(WL_n FC_n), (WL_n LC_n)

Table 2: List of CRF templates for POS tagging.

The POS tagger is trained by using the same training set used in the word segmentation. In the test, the POS tagger processes the top-N output sequences of the word segmentation. It combines the log-likelihood scores of word segmentation and POS tagging to find the best output word sequenc. The accuracy of the 47-type POS tagging is 94.22%. The performance is reasonable except "*Nv*".

2.3 Language Modeling

For constructing the LM, two corpora, the Sinica Balanced Corpus CIRB030 (Chinese Information Retrieval Benchmark, version 3.03), the Taiwan Panorama Magazine4 and the Wikipedia (zh-version, 2013/04/20), containing 440 million words totally, are parsed.

Some post-processing are done on the parsed text database, including

(1) text normalization,
(2) segment long number (the word with POS '*Neu*') into short number strings,
(3) change the hyphen between number and date (the word with POS '*Nd*') into "至" (to) to make the text readable,
(4) change some variation words (Here, variation word means a word have different written forms).

Finally, A lexicon with 100K words is used to build the LM. The coverage rate of the lexicon is about 97%.

3 Bakeoff 2013 Evaluation Results

3.1 Task

The task is divided into two sub-tasks including (1) error detection and (2) error correction. For the error detection sub-task, the system should return the locations of the incorrect characters. For the error correction sub-task, the system should return the locations of the incorrect characters, and must point out the correct characters. Moreover, one Sample Set (selected from students' essays) and two Similar Character Set (abbrev. Bakeoff 2013 CSC Datasets) are provided for this evaluation. There are two test data sets for the evaluation. Each set contains 1000 Chinese texts selected from students' essays.

3.2 Evaluation Results

Two configurations of our system (Run1 and Run2) were tested. Run1 applied only the rule-based frontend. Run2 utilized the whole system. The performances of the proposed spelling check method are shown in Table 3 and 4.

From Table 3, it can be found that Run1 has very low false alarm and recall rates, but higher accuracy in error detection. The reason is that it only modified few errors with high confidence.

[3] http://www.aclclp.org.tw/use_cir.php
[4] http://www.aclclp.org.tw/use_gh_c.php (in Chinese)

Run2 has much higher false alarm and recall rates, but lower accuracy, since it tried to change as much as possible errors and may introduce overkill. However, in general, Run2 has better F-score than Run1. Furthermore, Table 4 also shows that Run2 has higher location and correction accuracies (although it has lower correction precision than Run1). These results show the benefits of combining CRF-based parser and LM in the second stage of spelling check system.

Error	False-Alarm	Accuracy	Precision	Recall	F-score
Run1	0.0243	0.722	0.6964	0.13	0.2191
Run2	0.8329	0.411	0.3352	0.98	0.4995

(a)

Error Location	Accuracy	Precision	Recall	F-score
Run1	0.711	0.5	0.0933	0.1573
Run2	0.257	0.1596	0.4667	0.2379

(b)

Table 3: Evaluation results of the proposed system on Bakeoff 2013 sub-task 1: (a) detection error rates, (b) location error rates on 1000 test sentences.

	Location Accuracy	Correction Accuracy	Correction Precision
Run1	0.07	0.065	0.5118
Run2	0.485	0.404	0.404

Table 4: Evaluation results of the proposed system on Bakeoff 2013 sub-task 2. There are 1000 test sentences.

3.3 Error Analysis

Here are some examples that show the typical overkill behaviors of the proposed system ("O" original, "M" modified):

O: 人生 是 需要 巨浪 激出 美麗 的 浪花
M:人生 是 需要 巨浪 洗出 美麗 的 浪花
O: 很 難 感受到 快樂 的 人
M: 很 難看 受到 快樂 的 人

In brief, it was found that the most overkill errors are due to the out of vocabulary (OOV) problem. Especially, in the above three cases, the outputs of parser are in fact correct but unfortunately, the LM didn't recognize "激出" and "感受到" and our system gave them high penalties.

4 Conclusions

In this paper, a Chinese spelling check approach that integrating our CRF-based parser and LM originally built for ASR is proposed. Experimental results on the Bakeoff 2013 tasks confirmed the generalization and sophistication of our parser and LM. The work to improve our traditional Chinese parser and LM is still continued. Our latest Chinese parser is available online at http://parser.speech.cm.nctu.edu.tw.

Acknowledgments

This work was supported by the National Science Council, Taiwan, Republic of China, under the project with contract NSC 101-2221-E-009-149-MY2, 101-2221-E-027-129 and under the "III Innovative and Prospective Technologies Project" of the Institute for Information Industry which is subsidized by the Ministry of Economy Affairs of the Republic of China.

References

A. L. Berger, Stephen A. D. Della Pietra, and V. J. Della Pietra, 1996, A maximum entropy approach to natural language processing, Computational Linguistics, 22(1): 39-71.

Chao-Lin Liu, Min-Hua Lai, Kan-Wen Tien, Yi-Hsuan Chuang, Shih-Hung Wu, and Chia-Ying Lee 2011, Visually and phonologically similar characters in incorrect Chinese words: Analyses, identification, and applications, ACM Trans. Asian Lang. Inform. Process. 10, 2, Article 10.

Chongyang Zhang, Zhigang Chen, Guoping Hu, 2010, A Chinese Word Segmentation System Based on Structured Support Vector Machine Utilization of Unlabeled Text Corpus, Joint Conference on Chinese Language Processing

H. Zhao, C. N. Huang and M. Li, 2006, An Improved Chinese Word Segmentation System with Conditional Random Field, the Fifth SIGHAN Workshop on Chinese Language Processing, pp. 108-117.

S. H. Chen, J. H. Yang, C. Y. Chiang, M. C. Liu, and Y. R. Wang, 2012, A New Prosody-Assisted Mandarin ASR System, IEEE Trans. on Audio, Speech and Language Processing, Vol. 20, No, 6, pp. 1669-1684.

Y. Bengio, R. Ducharme, P. Vincent, and C. Jauvin, 2003, A neural probabilistic language model, Journal of Machine Learning Research, No. 3(2), pp. 1137–1155.

Yong-Zhi Chen, Shih-Hung Wu, Ping-che Yang, Tsun Ku, and Gwo-Dong Chen, 2011. Improve the detection of improperly used Chinese characters in students' essays with error model. Int. J. Cont. Engineering Education and Life-Long Learning, Vol. 21, No. 1, pp.103-116.

A Maximum Entropy Approach to Chinese Spelling Check

Dongxu Han, Baobao Chang
Institute of Computational Linguistics, Peking University
Key Laboratory of Computational Linguistics(Peking University), Ministry Education, China
Beijing, 100871, P.R.China
{handx,chbb}@pku.edu.cn

Abstract

Spelling check identifies incorrect writing words in documents. For the reason of input methods, Chinese spelling check is much different from English and it is still a challenging work. For the past decade years, most of the methods in detecting errors in documents are lexicon-based or probability-based, and much progress are made. In this paper, we propose a new method in Chinese spelling check by using maximum entropy (ME). Experiment shows that by importing a large raw corpus, maximum entropy can build a well-trained model to detect spelling errors in Chinese documents.

1 Introduction

Because of the popularity of computers, more and more documents are produced. For the carelessness of human or errors of OCR image recognition, many spelling errors occur in documents, which seriously interferes documents quality. Proofreading by human to correct the errors is laborious and expensive, so an automatic approach is badly in need. Automatic spelling check can identify incorrect writing words in documents, which plays an important role in documents writing and OCR post-processing.

Research on automatic spelling check of English documents began in the 1960s (Damerau F.J., 1964), many studies have been proposed and quite good results have been obtained. While spelling check of Chinese is still a challenging work due to some special processing difficulties arising from Chinese writing, which hardly occur in spelling check of English.

In English writing, each word is directly input by Latin letters, so the spelling errors are only the situation that one letter is mistaken written to another, such as writing "bcg" instead of "bag", or "son glasses" instead of "sun glasses". The former is a non-word spelling error, meaning the form of input word is definitely incorrect and latter is a real-word spelling error, meaning the form of input word can be found in the dictionary but incorrectly used.

In Chinese writing, unlike English, all legal characters (we call them hanzi) have been stored in a font lib and Chinese input system builds an effective map between Latin letters and hanzi fonts. For the reason of input methods, Chinese characters would not take the non-word errors such as missing or adding a part of character to form an illegal character in the dictionary. That is, all Chinese spelling errors are real-word errors. The treatment of real-word errors needs analyzing the context, which is much harder than the treatment of non-word errors. Chinese spelling check is still a challenging work.

In this paper, we propose a new but simple method in Chinese spelling check by using maximum entropy (ME) models. We train a maximum entropy model for each Chinese character based on a large raw corpus and use the model to detect the spelling errors in documents. Tentative experiment in the bakeoff shows the simple strategy works. However, further refinement and methodology combinations seem still needed to produce state-of-arts results.

The rest of the paper is organized as follows: In section 2, we give a brief introduction to the Chinese spelling check. In section 3 we introduce our approach to Chinese spelling check using maximum entropy model. Section 4 is description and discussion of our experiments. Section 5 is the conclusion.

2 Previous work

Research on Chinese automatic spelling check approaches appeared in 1990s (shih et al. 1992). Most of them are generally based on lexicon methods and statistic methods.

Lexicon-based methods use dictionaries, which contain as much as possible language information, such as word information, characters and words frequency information, encoding information, part-of speech tagging information and similar character information. Chinese characters are usually mistakenly written as some other characters, because their shapes or pronunciations are very similar or even the same in pronunciation. Such characters are called Chinese similar characters, and most of Chinese spelling errors are caused by them. In order to improve the performance of spelling check, these similar characters are summarized to similar character dictionaries, for example, the shape similar characters set and the pronunciation similar characters set provided by the bakeoff organization, are both similar character dictionaries (Liu, 2011).

Chang (1995) replaced each character in a sentence with another similar character by a large-enough similar character dictionary and calculated the replaced sentence score, to judge whether a character should be replaced with another. Zhang et al. (2000a) made use of characters and words frequency, similar character dictionary, and part of speech (POS) tagging information to detect dubious areas and generate candidate words. Zhang et al. (2000b, 2000c) used WuBi encoding information and Lin (2002) used Chong-Je encoding information to estimate dubious characters. These kinds of methods achieve success in some aspects, like Liu (2011) using Chong-Je encoding information could detect 93.37% error characters.

Statistic-based methods usually use a huge language corpus and the product of conditional probabilities to compute the appearance probability of a sentence (shih et al. 1992). Moreover, most of the statistic-based methods of Chinese spelling check jointly use lexicon-based methods together so as to achieve better performance. Like Ren (1994) used language model with word frequency dictionary, and Huang (2007) used language model with word dictionaries and similar character dictionary.

In the following, we will introduce our approach to Chinese spelling check in statistic-based methods totally without lexicon-based methods.

3 Chinese spelling check based on maximum entropy model

In this section, we first formalize spelling check as classifying each character into right or wrong categories based on the characters before and after it. We then briefly describe our feature setting in modeling the spelling check task using maximum entropy model.

3.1 Reformulating error characters detecting as a classification problem

Deciding whether a character is correctly or incorrectly written can be treated as a classification problem. To do this, we train each character a model that can classify the character into two categories named right or wrong, which means the character is correctly or incorrectly used.

In a Chinese sentence, no character can exist independently. They are all associated with the characters previous or next. In order to gain the whole data meaning, a complete context must be extracted, not just the target character. For example, when we train the character "國" (country), we select the n-gram "中華民國十三年" as the training data. In this way, we import a large raw corpus, segment the corpus into sentences by the pronunciations and remove these pronunciations, from the sentences we extract the n-grams whose middle character is the character to be trained (for example "國"). Then, the training data of character "國" could be like this:

中華民國十三年
$H_{-2}H_{-1}$美國總統布
到市區國會山莊
需要跨國 $H_1H_2H_3$
… … … … … …

In the training data, if there is not enough characters after the target character in an n-gram, we use padding characters "H_1", "H_2" and "H_3" as the characters after it (here is "國"). So are the characters "H_{-1}", "H_{-2}" and "H_{-3}".

To judge whether a target character is correctly or incorrectly written, in the training data of the target character, there should be enough positive instances and negative instances for classification training. Intuitively, the positive instances are all the n-grams in the corpus whose middle character is the target character, and the negative instances are all the n-grams in the corpus whose middle character should not be the target character but mistaken written as the target character. But usually there are no incorrectly used characters in corpus, so we don't have the negative instances like that way. Our method is that we replace all the n-grams in the corpus whose middle character is not the target character with the target character and choose these n-grams as the negative instances. In this way, the amounts of positive instances and negative instances are seriously imbalanced, the former too few and the latter too many. In order to reduce the amount of the negative instances, we import the similar character dictionaries provided by the bakeoff organization. We select the n-grams whose middle character is the similar character of the target character as the negative n-grams.

Then the positive instances are labeled right and the negative instances are labeled wrong. Also for example “國”:

Right	中華民國十三年
Right	$H_{-2}H_{-1}$美國總統布
Right	需要跨國 $H_1H_2H_3$
Wrong	小吃店國商店 H_1
Wrong	一個月國更長時
Wrong	巡守巾國不讓鬚

… … … … … … … … … …

We use maximum entropy to train the training data and achieve corresponding model of each character. We extract each character in the test data to be the n-gram in the same way and classify the n-grams into right or wrong categories by the character corresponding model, judging whether the character is correctly or incorrectly written, achieving the result of Chinese spelling check.

3.2 Feature templates

In our raw corpus, after segmented by pronunciations, the average length of characters in sentences is 7.443, so the n-gram we set here is seven-gram, namely we extract both 3 characters before and after the target character as a training seven-gram.

The target character is set C_0, the characters previous are set C_{-1}, C_{-2}, C_{-3} and the characters next are set C_1, C_2 and C_3. We have following maximum entropy feature templates:

(a) C_n (n=-3, -2, -1, 1, 2, 3)

(b) C_nC_{n+1} (n=-3, -2, 1, 2)

(c) $C_{-1}C_1$, $C_{-1}C_2$, $C_{-2}C_1$, $C_{-2}C_2$

(d) $C_{-2}C_{-1}C_1$, $C_{-1}C_1C_2$

(e) $C_{-2}C_{-1}C_1C_2$

From feature templates above, we can see that we train the character through the information of characters before and after it, so the C_0 actually cannot be used.

4 Experiments and discussions

We choose to use maximum entropy toolkit[1] as our model learner and we use traditional Chinese part of Chinese Gigaword corpus as our training data.

4.1 Training data

The traditional Chinese part of Gigaword corpus has about 800 million characters, covering over 9000 different characters. We select 5311 different characters mainly appear in the corpus, covering over 95% of the corpus.

Corresponded to the 5311 different characters, 5311 training data are made, each of which contains around 7.48 million seven-grams, and 5311 maximum entropy models are trained.

4.2 Error characters selection

Each character is associated with the characters previous or next, so if a target character with the character before or after it together appear in the test corpus, they are highly likely to appear in the training data. Then the target character would be highly classified into the right character category. Conversely, if a target character with the character before or after it together could not be found in the training data, the target character would be highly classified into the wrong category.

Affected by the incorrectly written character, even though the characters before and after it are correctly written, they all may be classified into wrong character category, for they are missed with the incorrectly written character in the training corpus. In the same way, if a certain character is classified into wrong character category while the characters before and after it are all classified into the right character category, it is highly likely mistakenly classified. We need to set thresholds to judge whether the characters are really incorrectly written or mistaken classified in the above two situations:

(a) To the situation that continuous two or more characters are classified into wrong character category, if all the calculated probabilities of the wrong character category of these characters are over the threshold X1, they will be treated as incorrectly written characters.

(b) To the situation that a single character is classified into wrong character category while the characters before and after it are all classified into the right character cate-

[1] Download from https://github.com/lzhang10/maxent/

gory, if the calculated probabilities of the wrong character category of the single character is over the threshold X2, it will be treated as incorrectly written characters.

In our experiment, we find that if the threshold X1 is set to 0.95 and the threshold X2 is set to 0.99, most of the characters incorrectly written can detected.

Though we set thresholds above, there are still too many mistaken classified characters. We need to set each character an accurate threshold, forming a cutoff table to filter out the mistaken classified characters.

We use the maximum entropy toolkit to classify the characters in the Dry-Run test set data, and achieve all the calculated probabilities of the wrong character category of incorrectly written characters. We calculate the mean probabilities of the wrong character category X, and set the smallest probability higher than X of each character as the threshold of the character. In our experiment, the X we calculated is 0.977.

As the number of the incorrectly written characters in the Dry-Run test set data is limited, we couldn't get all the probabilities of the characters. In order to avoid these characters mistaken classified as much as possible, a relatively high threshold is set. In our experiment, the threshold of it is set to 0.9999.

Corresponding to the 5311 characters in the experiment, we have 5311 characters thresholds. Using the cutoff table, we could achieve a better result on Chinese spelling check.

4.3 Experimental results

Spelling check performance is evaluated by F-score F=2RP/(R + P). The recall R is the ratio of the correctly identified spelling error sentences of the checker's output to all spelling error sentences in the gold-standard and the precision P refers to the ratio of the correctly identified spelling error sentences of the checker's output to all identified error sentences of the checker's output. Moreover, False-Alarm Rate and Detection Accuracy are also introduced to evaluate spelling check. The former is the ratio of the checker's output to all spelling error sentences with false positive error detection results to testing sentences without errors in the gold-standard, and the latter is the ratio of the checker's output to all spelling sentences with correctly detected results to all testing sentences.

Table 1: Performance of the final test

False-Alarm Rate	0.3986
Detection Accuracy	0.678
Detection Precision	0.4795
Detection Recall	0.8567
Detection F-score	0.6149
Error Location Accuracy	0.5
Error Location Precision	0.1474
Error Location Recall	0.2633

From the result, we achieve a relative better Detection Recall. As the maximum entropy can storage the knowledge of characters appearing together, most of the illegal continuous characters can be detected, and they are highly likely incorrectly written characters.

However, the Detection Precision is relative not high, as the maximum entropy mistaken classifies many single characters with high probabilities of the wrong character category such as "我", "的", "是", "不", "在" and so on. These characters are high frequency characters, almost appearing in every sentence. Even though the maximum entropy can classify over 99% of these characters correctly, the rest 1% mistaken classified would pull down the Detection Precision.

5 Conclusion

In this paper, we propose a maximum entropy method in Chinese spelling check. As the maximum entropy can storage the knowledge of characters appearing together, most of the illegal collocation can be detected. It also grows the problem that it could not handle the high frequency characters well, which affects the spelling check result a lot.

It is our first attempt on Chinese spelling check, and tentative experiment shows we achieve a not bad result. We don't use lexicon-based methods, easy to operate is the merit of our simple method.

However, we still have a long way from the state-of-arts results. Much work needs to be done, and further refinement and methodology combinations seem still needed. We need to find a better way to solve the problems of high frequency characters. In this work, we ignore the association of the n-grams formed by continuous characters. We need to explore a better way to train them. We also need to probe into other machine learning classifying tools, like Support Vector Machine (SVM).

6 Acknowledgment

This work is supported by National Natural Science Foundation of China under Grant No. 61273318.

Reference

Chao-Huang Chang. 1995. *A new approach for automatic Chinese spelling correction*, Proceedings of Natural Language Processing Pacific Rim Symposium: 278-283.

Chao-Lin Liu, Min-Hua Lai, Kan-Wen Tien, Yi-Hsuan Chuang, Shih-Hung Wu, and Chia-Ying Lee. 2011. *Visually and phonologically similar characters in incorrect Chinese words: Analyses, identification, and applications*, ACM Transactions on Asian Language Information Processing, 10(2), 10:1-39. Association for Computing Machinery, USA, June 2011.

Chuen-Min Huang, Mei-Chen Wu and Ching-Che Chang. 2007. *Error detection and correction based on Chinese phonemic alphabet in Chinese text*. Proceedings of the fourth conference on Modeling Decisions for Artificial Intelligence (MDAIIV). Springer Berlin Heidelberg: 463-476.

Damerau F.J., 1964. *A technique for computer detection and correction of spelling errors*. Communication of the ACM, 7(3):171-176.

Fuji Ren, Hongchi Shi and Qiang Zhou. 1994. *A hybrid approach to automatic chinese text checking and error correction*. Proceedings of the ARPA Workshop on Human Language Technology: 76-81.

Lei Zhang, Ming Zhou, Changning Huang, Lu Mingyu. 2000a. *Approach in automatic detection and correction of errors in Chinese text based on feature and learning* (In Chinese). Proceedings of the 3rd world congress on Intelligent Control and Automation, Hefei: 2744–2748.

Lei Zhang, Ming Zhou, Changning Huang, Haihua Pan. 2000b. *Automatic detecting/correcting Errors in Chinese text by an approximate word-matching algorithm*. Proceedings of the 38th Annual Meeting on Association for Computational Linguistics: 248-254.

Lei Zhang, Ming Zhou, Changning Huang, Maosong, Sun. 2000c. *Automatic Chinese text error correction approach based-on fast approximate Chinese word-matching algorithm*. In Intelligent Control and Automation, Proceedings of the 3rd World Congress on IEEE, 4: 2739-2743.

Shih, D.S. et al., 1992. *A statistical method for locating typo in Chinese sentences*. CCL Research Journal (8):19-26.

Yih-jeng Lin, Feng-long Huang, Ming-shing Yu. 2002. *A chinese spelling error correction system*. Proceedings of seventh conference on artificial intelligence and applications.

A Study of Language Modeling for Chinese Spelling Check

Kuan-Yu Chen[†*], **Hung-Shin Lee, Chung-Han Lee, Hsin-Min Wang**
[†]Academia Sinica, Taiwan
{kychen, hslee, chlee012, whm}@iis.sinica.edu.tw

Hsin-Hsi Chen
[*]National Taiwan University, Taiwan
hhchen@ntu.edu.tw

Abstract

Chinese spelling check (CSC) is still an open problem today. To the best of our knowledge, language modeling is widely used in CSC because of its simplicity and fair predictive power, but most systems only use the conventional *n*-gram models. Our work in this paper continues this general line of research by further exploring different ways to glean extra semantic clues and Web resources to enhance the CSC performance in an unsupervised fashion. Empirical results demonstrate the utility of our CSC system.

1 Introduction

Chinese is a tonal syllabic and character (symbol) language, in which each character is pronounced as a tonal syllable. A Chinese "word" usually comprises two or more characters. The difficulty of Chinese processing is that many Chinese characters have similar shapes or similar (or same) pronunciations. Some characters are even similar in both shape and pronunciation (Wu *et al.*, 2010; Liu *et al.*, 2011). However, the meanings of these characters (or words composed of the characters) may be widely divergent. Due to this reason, all the students in elementary school in Taiwan or the foreign Chinese learners need to practice to identify and correct "erroneous words" in a Chinese sentence, which is called the Incorrect Character Correction (ICC) test. In fact, the ICC test is not a simple task even for some adult native speakers in Taiwan.

Since most Chinese characters have other characters similar to them in either shape or pronunciation, an intuitive idea for CSC is to construct a confusion set for each character. Currently, many CSC systems use the confusion sets (Zhang *et al.*, 2000; Wu *et al.*, 2010; Liu *et al.*, 2011) to recursively substitute characters and find an optimal result to detect and correct erroneous words. Moreover, many researches have been focusing on automatically constructing the confusion sets from various knowledge sources, such as the Cangjie code (Liu *et al.*, 2011), psycholinguistic experimental results (Kuo *et al.*, 2004; Lee *et al.*, 2006; Tsai *et al.*, 2006), and templates generated from a large corpus (Chen *et al.*, 2009). Language modeling can be used to quantify the quality of a given word string, and most previous researches have adopted it as a method to predict which word might be a correct word to replace the possible erroneous word.

Although language modeling has been widely used in CSC, most researches only use the conventional *n*-gram models. To the best of our knowledge, the *n*-gram language models, aiming at capturing the local contextual information or the lexical regularity of a language, are inevitably faced with two fundamental problems. On one hand, it is brittle across domains, and the performance of the model is sensitive to changes in the genre or topic of the text on which it is trained. On the other hand, it fails to capture the information (either semantic or syntactic information) conveyed beyond the *n*-1 immediately preceding words. In view of these problems, this paper focuses on exploring the long-span semantic information for language modeling for CSC. Moreover, we make a step forward to incorporate a search engine to provide extra information from the Web resources to make a more robust system.

The rest of this paper is organized as follows. In Section 2, we briefly review the *n*-gram and topic language models. Section 3 details our proposed CSC system. A series of experiments are presented in Section 4. Finally, conclusions and future work are given in Section 5.

2 Language Modeling

2.1 *N*-gram Language Modeling

From the early 20th century, statistical language modeling has been successfully applied to various applications related to natural language processing (NLP), such as speech recognition (Chen and Goodman, 1999; Chen and Chen, 2011), information retrieval (Ponte and Croft, 1998; Lavrenko and Croft, 2001; Lavrenko, 2009), document summarization (Lin and Chen, 2010), and spelling correction (Chen *et al.*, 2009; Liu *et al.*, 2011; Wu *et al.*, 2010). The most widely-used and well-practiced language model, by far, is the *n*-gram language model (Jelinek, 1999), because of its simplicity and fair predictive power. Quantifying the quality of a word string in a natural language is the most commonly executed task. Take the tri-gram model for example, when given a word string $W_1^L = w_1, w_2, \ldots, w_L$, the probability of the word string is approximated by the product of a series of conditional probabilities as follows (Jelinek, 1999),

$$P(W_1^L) = P(w_1)\prod_{l=2}^{L} P(w_l \mid W_1^{l-1}) \approx P(w_1)P(w_2 \mid w_1)\prod_{l=3}^{L} P(w_l \mid w_{l-2}, w_{l-1}). \quad (1)$$

In the tri-gram model, we make the approximation (or assumption) that the probability of a word depends only on the two immediately preceding words.

The easiest way to estimate the conditional probability in Eq. (1) is to use the maximum likelihood (ML) estimation as follows,

$$P(w_l \mid w_{l-2}, w_{l-1}) = \frac{c(w_{l-2}, w_{l-1}, w_l)}{c(w_{l-2}, w_{l-1})}, \quad (2)$$

where $c(w_{l-2}, w_{l-1}, w_l)$ and $c(w_{l-2}, w_{l-1})$ denote the number of times the word strings " w_{l-2}, w_{l-1}, w_l " and " w_{l-2}, w_{l-1} " occur in a given training corpus, respectively. Without loss of generality, the tri-gram model can be extended to higher order models, such as the four-gram model and the five-gram model, but the high-order *n*-gram models usually suffer from the data sparseness problem, which leads to some zero conditional probabilities. Various language model smoothing techniques have been proposed to deal with the zero probability problem. For example, Good-Turing (Chen and Goodman, 1999), Kneser-Ney (Chen and Goodman, 1999), and Pitman-Yor (Huang and Renals, 2007) are well-known state-of-the-art smoothing approaches. The general formulation of these approaches is (Chen and Goodman, 1999):

$$P(w_l \mid w_{l-n+1}, \ldots, w_{l-1}) = \begin{cases} f(c(w_{l-n+1}, \ldots, w_l)) & , \text{ if } c(w_{l-n+1}, \ldots, w_l) \neq 0 \\ \beta(w_{l-n+1}, \ldots, w_{l-1}) f(c(w_{l-n+1}, \ldots, w_l)), & \text{if } c(w_{l-n+1}, \ldots, w_l) = 0 \end{cases} \quad (3)$$

where $f(\cdot)$ denotes a discounting probability function and $\beta(\cdot)$ denotes a back-off weighting factor that makes the distribution sum to 1.

2.2 Topic Modeling

The *n*-gram language model, aiming at capturing only the local contextual information or the lexical regularity of a language, is inevitably faced with the problem of missing the information (either semantic or syntactic information) conveyed by the words before the *n*-1 immediately preceding words. To mitigate the weakness of the *n*-gram model, various topic models have been proposed and widely used in many NLP tasks. We can roughly organize these topic models into two categories (Chen *et al.*, 2010): document topic models and word topic models.

2.2.1 Document Topic Modeling (DTM)

DTM introduces a set of latent topic variables to describe the "word-document" co-occurrence characteristics. The dependence between a word and its preceding words (regarded as a document) is not computed directly based on the frequency counts as in the conventional *n*-gram model, but instead based on the frequency of the word in the latent topics as well as the likelihood that the preceding words together generate the respective topics. Probabilistic latent semantic analysis (PLSA) (Hofmann, 1999) and latent Dirichlet allocation (LDA) (Blei *et al.*, 2003; Griffiths and Steyvers, 2004) are two representatives of this category. Take PLSA for example, we can interpret the preceding words, $W_1^{L-1} = w_1, w_2, \ldots, w_{L-1}$, as a document topic model used for predicting the occurrence probability of w_L:

$$P_{\text{PLSA}}(w_L \mid W_1^{L-1}) = \Sigma_{k=1}^{K} P(w_L \mid T_k) P(T_k \mid W_1^{L-1}), \quad (4)$$

where T_k is the *k*-th latent topic; $P(w_L \mid T_k)$ and $P(T_k \mid W_1^{L-1})$ are respectively the probability that the word w_L occurs in T_k and the probability of T_k conditioned on the preceding word string W_1^{L-1}. The latent topic distribution $P(w_L \mid T_k)$ can be estimated beforehand by maximizing the total log-likelihood of the training corpus. However, the preceding word string varies with context, and thus the corresponding topic mixture weight $P(T_k \mid W_1^{L-1})$ has to be estimated on the fly using inference algorithms like the expectation-maximization (EM) algorithm.

On the other hand, LDA, having a formula analogous to PLSA, is regarded as an extension to PLSA and has enjoyed much success for various NLP tasks. LDA differs from PLSA mainly in the inference of model parameters (Chen *et al.*, 2010). PLSA assumes that the model parameters are fixed and unknown while LDA places additional a priori constraints on the model parameters by thinking of them as random variables that follow some Dirichlet distributions. Since LDA has a more complex form for model optimization, which is hardly to be solved by exact inference, several approximate inference algorithms, such as the variational approximation algorithm, the expectation propagation method (Blei *et al.*, 2003), and the Gibbs sampling algorithm (Griffiths and Steyvers, 2004), have been proposed for estimating the parameters of LDA.

2.2.2 Word Topic Modeling (WTM)

Instead of treating the preceding word string as a document topic model, we can regard each word w_l of the language as a word topic model (WTM) (Chen, 2009; Chen *et al.*, 2010). To crystalize this idea, all words are assumed to share the same set of latent topic distributions but have different weights over the topics. The WTM model of each word w_l in W_1^{L-1} for predicting the occurrence of a particular word w_L can be expressed by:

$$P_{\text{WTM}}(w_L \mid \mathrm{M}_{w_l}) = \Sigma_{k=1}^{K} P(w_L \mid T_k) P(T_k \mid \mathrm{M}_{w_l}). \quad (5)$$

Each WTM model M_{w_l} can be trained in a data-driven manner by concatenating those words occurring within the vicinity of each occurrence of w_l in a training corpus, which are postulated to be relevant to w_l. To this end, a sliding window with a size of *S* words is placed on each occurrence of w_l, and a pseudo-document associated with such vicinity information of w_l is aggregated consequently. The WTM model of each word can be estimated by maximizing the total log-likelihood of words occurring in their associated "vicinity documents" using the EM algorithm. Notice that the words in such a document are assumed to be independent of each other (the so-called "*bag-of-words*" assumption). When we calculate the conditional probability $P(w_L | W_1^{L-1})$, we can linearly combine the associated WTM models of the words occurring in W_1^{L-1} to form a composite WTM model for predicting w_L:

$$P_{\text{WTM}}(w_L | W_1^{L-1}) = \sum_{l=1}^{L-1} \alpha_l \cdot P_{\text{WTM}}(w_L | M_{w_l}), \quad (6)$$

where the values of the nonnegative weighting coefficients α_l are empirically set to decay exponentially with *L-l* and sum to one (Chen, 2009).

Word vicinity model (WVM) (Chen *et al.*, 2010) bears a certain similarity to WTM in its motivation of modeling the "word-word" co-occurrences, but has a more concise parameterization. WVM explores the word vicinity information by directly modeling the joint probability of any word pair in the language, rather than modeling the conditional probability of one word given the other word as in WTM. In this regard, the joint probability of any word pair that describes the associated word vicinity information can be expressed by the following equation, using a set of latent topics:

$$P_{\text{WVM}}(w_i, w_j) = \sum_{k=1}^{K} P(w_i | T_k) P(T_k) P(w_j | T_k), \quad (7)$$

where $P(T_k)$ is the prior probability of a given topic T_k. Notice that the relationship between words, originally expressed in a high-dimensional probability space, are now projected into a low-dimensional probability space characterized by the shared set of topic distributions. Along a similar vein, WVM is trained by maximizing the probabilities of all word pairs, respectively, co-occurring within a sliding window of *S* words in the training corpus, using the EM algorithm. To calculate the conditional probability $P(w_L | W_1^{L-1})$, we first obtain the conditional probability $P(w_L | w_l)$ from the joint probability $P(w_L, w_l)$ by,

$$P_{\text{WVM}}(w_L | w_l) = \frac{\sum_{k=1}^{K} P(w_L | T_k) P(T_k) P(w_l | T_k)}{\sum_{k=1}^{K} P(w_l | T_k) P(T_k)}. \quad (8)$$

Then, a composite WVM model $P_{\text{WVM}}(w_L | W_1^{L-1})$ is obtained by linearly combining $P_{\text{WVM}}(w_L | w_l)$, as in WTM.

2.3 Other Language Models

In addition to topic models, many other language modeling techniques have been proposed to complement the *n*-gram model in different ways, such as recurrent neural network language modeling (RNNLM) (Tomáš *et al.*, 2010), discriminative language modeling (DLM) (Roark *et al.*, 2007; Lai *et al.*, 2011; Chen *et al.*, 2012), and relevance modeling (RM) (Lavrenko and Croft, 2001; Chen and Chen, 2011; Chen and Chen, 2013). RNNLM tries to project W_1^{L-1} and w_L into a continuous space, and estimate the conditional probability in a recursive way by incorporating the full information about W_1^{L-1}. DLM takes an objective function corresponding to minimizing the word error rate for speech recognition or maximizing the ROUGE score for summarization as a holy grail and updates the language model parameters to achieve the goal. RM assumes that each word sequence W_1^L is associated with a relevance class *R*, and all the words in W_1^L are samples drawn from *R*. It usually employs a local feedback-like procedure to obtain a set of pseudo-relevant documents to approximate *R* in the practical implementation.

3 The Proposed CSC System

3.1 System Overview

Figure 1 shows the flowchart of our CSC system. The system is mainly composed by three components: text segmenters, confusion sets, and language models. It performs CSC in the following steps:

1. Given a test word string, the CSC system treats the string as a query and posts it to a search engine to obtain a set of query suggestions.
2. Both the original word string and query suggestions will be segmented by using the maximum matching algorithm.
3. After segmentation, we assume that only the single-character words can be erroneous, so the system will iteratively substitute these words with possible characters by referring to the confusion sets.
4. Finally, the system will calculate the probability for each possible word string (by using the *n*-gram model, topic models, or both), and the most likely word string will be chosen as the final output.

3.2 Word Segmentation

Although the CKIP Chinese word segmentation system (Ma, 2003) is a famous and widely-used tool for the NLP community in Taiwan, we are aware that it has implemented an automatically merging algorithm, which might merge some error characters to a new word. To avoid the unexpected result, we have implemented our own forward and backward word segmentation tools based on the maximum matching algorithm. Given a word string, the CSC system will perform both forward and backward word segmentation, and then both forward

Table 1. Results of our CSC system.

	Sub-task1				Sub-task 2		
	Detection Accuracy	Detection F-score	Error Location F-score	False-Alarm Rate	Location Accuracy	Correction Accuracy	Correction Precision
Tri-gram	0.654	0.607	0.368	0.447	0.507	0.467	0.467
Tri-gram + Search Engine	0.835	0.739	0.458	0.141	0.489	0.445	0.445
Tri-gram + Search Engine + PLSA	0.836	0.741	0.467	0.141	0.494	0.450	0.450

and backward language models are applied to calculate the probabilities of the string.

3.3 Confusion Sets

The confusion sets are constructed from a pre-defined confusion corpus (Wu *et al.*, 2010; Liu *et al.*, 2011) and augmented by referring to the basic units of Chinese characters. We calculate the Levenshtein distance between any pair of Chinese characters based on their Cangjie codes. If the distance is smaller than a pre-defined threshold, the character pair is added to the confusion sets.

3.4 Language Modeling

Although language modeling has been widely used in the CSC task, most researches only use the conventional *n*-gram models. In this work, we evaluate the tri-gram language model as well as various topic models in our CSC system. The *n*-gram model and topic model are combined by a simple linear interpolation. Our lexicon consists of 97 thousand words. The tri-gram language model was estimated from a background text corpus consisting of over 170 million Chinese characters collected from Central News Agency (CNA) in 2001 and 2002 (the Chinese Gigaword Corpus released by LDC) and Sinica Corpus using the SRI Language Modeling Toolkit (Stolcke, 2000) with the Good-Turing smoothing technique. The topic models were also trained by using the same text corpus with 32 latent topics. Due to the space limitation, only the results with the PLSA topic model will be reported in the paper. Our preliminary experiments show that all the topic models discussed in Section 2 achieve similar performance.

3.5 Search Engine

In addition to topic models, we have also incorporated Web information in our CSC system by using a search engine. Given a test word string, our system treats the string as a query and posts it to a search engine to obtain a set of query suggestions. These query suggestions will also be treated as candidates. We use Baidu (http://www.baidu.com/) as the search engine.

4 Experimental Results

The experiments include two sub-tasks: error detection and error correction. All the experimental materials are

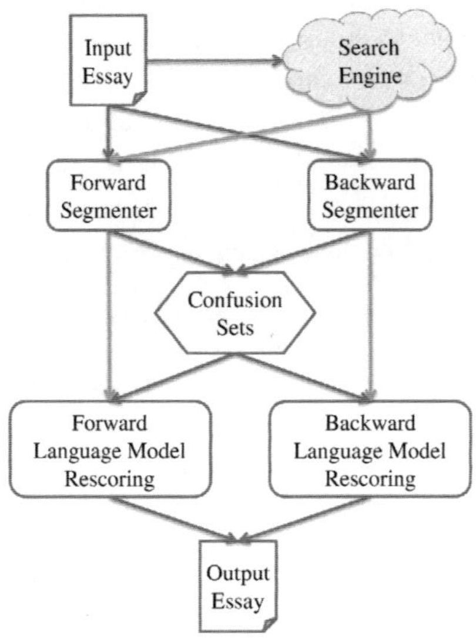

Figure 1. The flowchart of the CSC system.

collected from students' written essays. The first sub-task focuses on the evaluation of error detection. The input word string might consist of no error to evaluate the false-alarm rate of a system. The evaluation metrics include the detection accuracy, detection F-score, error location F-score, and false-alarm rate. As can be seen from the left part of Table 1, the tri-gram language model (denoted as "Tri-gram") can achieve a certain level of performance. Incorporating the suggestions from a search engine (denoted as "Tri-gram+Search Engine") in the CSC system yields significant improvements over Tri-gram in all evaluation metrics. Further incorporating topic modeling (denoted as "Tri-gram+Search Engine+PLSA") can slightly improve the detection F-score and error location F-score. The results demonstrate that the Web information is an indispensable reference for error detection, and the topic models can further improve the precision and recall rate without increasing the false alarm rate.

The second sub-task focuses on the evaluation of error correction. Each sentence includes at least one error. The evaluation metrics are the location accuracy, correction accuracy, and correction precision. The experimental results are listed in the right part of Table 1. To our surprise, Web information and the PLSA topic model cannot complement the conventional tri-gram model to achieve better performance. The reasons could be two-fold. First, we do not have a sufficient set of development documents to select a reasonable interpolation weight between the tri-gram model and the topic model. Second, the confusion sets should be further modified by some unsupervised or supervised methods to separate the wheat from the chaff.

5 Conclusions & Future Work

This paper has proposed a systematic way to render the semantic clues and Web resources to improve the performance of Chinese spelling check. The experimental results have demonstrated that our proposed system can improve error detection in terms of detection accuracy, detection F-score, error location F-score, and false-alarm rate. Our future research directions include: 1) investigating more elaborate language models for CSC, 2) seeking the use of discriminative training algorithms for training language models to directly optimize the detection and correction performance, and 3) applying and exploring unsupervised or supervised methods to construct the confusion sets.

References

Andreas Stolcke. 2000. SRI Language Modeling Toolkit (http://www.speech.sri.com/projects/srilm/).

Berlin Chen. 2009. Word Topic Models for Spoken Document Retrieval and Transcription. *ACM Transactions on Asian Language Information Processing,* Vol. 8, No. 1, pp. 2:1-2:27.

Berlin Chen, and Kuan-Yu Chen. 2013. Leveraging Relevance Cues for Language Modeling in Speech Recognition. *Information Processing & Management,* Vol. 49, No. 4, pp. 807-816.

Brian Roark, Murat Saraclar, and Michael Collins. 2007. Discriminative *N*-gram Language Modeling. *Computer Speech and Language,* Vol. 21, No. 2, pp. 373-392.

Chao-Lin Liu, Min-Hua Lai, Kan-Wen Tien, Yi-Hsuan Chuang, Shih-Hung Wu, and Chia-Ying Lee. 2011. Visually and Phonologically Similar Characters in Incorrect Chinese Words: Analyses, Identification, and Applications. *ACM Transactions on Asian Language Information Processing,* Vol. 10, No. 2, pp. 1-39.

Chia-Ying Lee, Jie-Li Tsai, Hsu-Wen Huang, Daisy L. Hung, and Ovid J.L. Tzeng. 2006. The Temporal Signatures of Semantic and Phonological Activations for Chinese Sublexical Processing: An Event-Related Potential Study. *Brain Research,* Vol. 1121, No. 1, pp. 150-159.

David M. Blei, Andrew Y. Ng, and Michael I. Jordan. 2003. Latent Dirichlet Allocation. *Journal of Machine Learning Research,* Vol. 3, pp. 993-1022.

Frederick Jelinek. 1999. *Statistical Methods for Speech Recognition.* The MIT Press.

Jay M. Ponte and W. Bruce Croft. 1998. A Language Modeling Approach to Information Retrieval. In Proceedings of SIGIR.

Jie-Li Tsai, Chia-Ying Lee, Ying-Chun Lin, Ovid J. L. Tzeng, and Daisy L. Hung. 2006. Neighborhood Size Effects of Chinese Words in Lexical Decision and Reading. *Language & Linguistics,* Vol. 7, No. 3, pp. 659-675.

Kuan-Yu Chen, Hsin-Min Wang, and Berlin Chen. 2012. Spoken Document Retrieval Leveraging Unsupervised and Supervised Topic Modeling Techniques. *IEICE Transactions on Information and Systems,* Vol. E95-D, No. 5, pp. 1195-1205.

Kuan-Yu Chen, and Berlin Chen. 2011. Relevance Language Modeling for Speech Recognition. In Proceedings of ICASSP.

Kuan-Yu Chen, Hsuan-Sheng Chiu, and Berlin Chen. 2010. Latent Topic Modeling of Word Vicinity Information for Speech Recognition. In Proceedings of ICASSP.

Min-Hsuan Lai, Bang-Xuan Huang, Kuan-Yu Chen, and Berlin Chen. 2011. Empirical Comparisons of Various Discriminative Language Models for Speech Recognition. In Proceedings of ROCLING.

Lei Zhang, Ming Zhou, Changning Huang, and Mingyu Lu. 2000. Approach in Automatic Detection and Correction of Errors in Chinese Text based on Feature and Learning. In Proceedings of WCICA.

Mikolov Tomáš, Karafiát Martin, Burget Lukáš, Černocký Jan and Khudanpur Sanjeev. 2010. Recurrent Neural Network based Language Model. In Proceedings of INTERSPEECH.

Shih-Hsiang Lin and Berlin Chen. 2010. A Risk Minimization Framework for Extractive Speech Summarization. In Proceedings of ACL.

Shih-Hung Wu, Yong-Zhi Chen, Ping-che Yang, Tsun Ku, and Chao-Lin Liu. 2010. Reducing the False Alarm Rate of Chinese Character Error Detection and Correction. In Proceedings of SIGHAN.

Song-Fang Huang and Steve Renals. 2007. Hierarchical Pitman-Yor Language Models for ASR in Meetings. In Proceedings of ASRU.

Stanley F. Chen and Joshua Goodman. 1999. An Empirical Study of Smoothing Techniques for Language Modeling. *Computer Speech and Language,* Vol. 13, No. 4, pp. 359-393.

Thomas L. Griffiths and Mark Steyvers. 2004. Finding Scientific Topics. In Proceedings of PNAS.

Thomas Hofmann. 1999. Probabilistic Latent Semantic Analysis. In Proceedings of UAI.

Victor Lavrenko and W. Bruce Croft. 2001. Relevance-based Language Models. In Proceedings of SIGIR.

Wei-Yun Ma and Keh-Jiann Chen. 2003. Introduction to CKIP Chinese Word Segmentation System for the First International Chinese Word Segmentation Bakeoff. In Proceedings of SIGHAN.

W.-J. Kuo, T.-C. Yeh, J.-R. Lee, L.-F. Chen, P.-L. Lee, S.-S. Chen, L.-T. Ho, D.-L. Hung, O.J.-L. Tzeng, and J.-C. Hsieh. 2004. Orthographic and Phonological Processing of Chinese Characters: An fMRI Study. In Proceedings of NeuroImage.

Yong-Zhi Chen, Shih-Hung Wu, Chia-Ching Lu, and Tsun Ku. 2009. Chinese Confusion Word Set for Automatic Generation of Spelling Error Detecting Template. In Proceedings of ROCLING.

Description of HLJU Chinese Spelling Checker for SIGHAN Bakeoff 2013

Yu He
School of Computer Science and Technology
Heilongjiang University
Harbin 150080, China
heyucs@yahoo.com

Guohong Fu
School of Computer Science and Technology
Heilongjiang University
Harbin 150080, China
ghfu@hotmail.com

Abstract

In this paper, we describe in brief our system for Chinese Spelling Check Backoff sponsored by ACL-SIGHAN. It consists of three main components, namely potential incorrect character detection with a multiple-level analysis, correction candidate generation with similar character sets and correction scoring with n-grams. We participated in all the two sub-tasks at the Bakeoff. We also make a summary of this work and give some analysis on the results.

1 Introduction

As one typical task in written language processing, spelling check is aiming at detecting incorrect characters within a sentence and correcting them. While a number of successful spelling checker have been available for English and many other other alphabetical languages, it is still a challenge to develop a practical spelling checker for Chinese due to its language-specific issues, in particular the writing system of Chinese without explicit delimiters for word boundaries. Furthermore, no data set are commonly available for spelling check in Chinese. As such, ACL-SIGHAN sponsor a Backoff on Chinese spelling check, which consists of two subtasks, namely spelling error detection and spelling error correction.

Based on the task specification the data sets for SIGHAN Backoff 2013, we develop a spelling checker for Chinese. It consists of three main components, namely potential incorrect character detection with a multiple-level analysis, correction candidate generation with similar character sets and correction scoring with n-grams. We have participated in all the two sub-tasks at the Bakeoff. We also make a summary of this work and give some analysis on the results.

The rest of this paper is organize as follows. First, we describe in brief our system for Chinese spelling check in Section 2. Then in Section 3, we present the settings or configuration of our system for different subtasks, and report the relevant results at this Bakeoff. Finally, we give our conclusions on this work in Section 4.

2 Proposed Method

2.1 System Architecture

Figure 1 shows the architecture of our system. It works in three main steps. Given a plain Chinese sentence with/without spelling errors, our system first segments it to words. Then, a multi-level analysis module is used to detect potential incorrect characters within the input and thus a 5401×5401 similarity matrix generated from the similar character set (viz. the Bakeoff 2013 CSC Datasets) (Liu et al., 2011) is further employed to generate set of corrections for the input. Finally, n-grams are used to score and decode a sentence as the best correction for the input. For convenience, we refer to this sentence as output sentence. If the output sentence is same as the original input sentence, then the input sentence does not contain any spelling errors; Or else, it has incorrect characters, and the output sentence would be its correction.

In the figure above, CLA is the abbreviation for character level analysis, WLA means word level analysis and CLA_2 represents context level analysis.

2.2 Potential Incorrect Character Detection

2.2.1 Types of incorrect words in Chinese

In general, Chinese words with incorrect characters (refered to as incorrect Chinese words thereafter) have three main ways of segmentations.

(1) The segmentation of an incorrect Chinese word would be a sequence of single-character

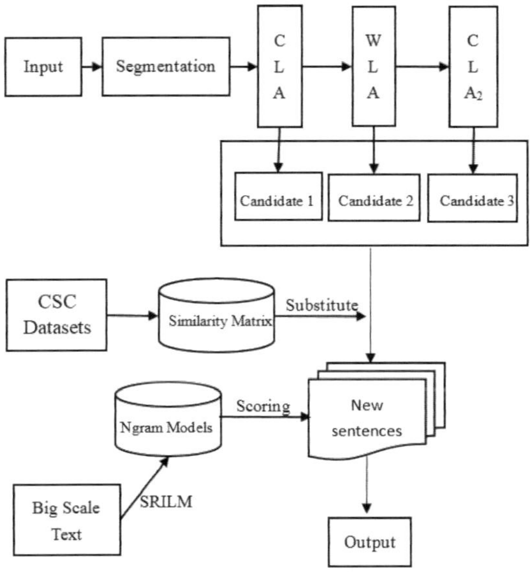

Figure 1: The architecture of our system

words. For example, 煩腦 is a common incorrect form of the word 煩惱 fan-nao 'trouble', and it will be segmented into two separate single-character words, namely, 煩 and 腦, during word segmentation;

(2) The segmentation of an incorrect word is still a word. For example, 措折 is a typical incorrect form of the word 挫折 cuo-zhe 'setback', and is usually segmented into one word 措折(Vt) after word segmentation. Here, we refer such

(3) An incorrect word and its adjacent characters in the context will form another word after segmentation. For example, the fragment 一番新的进攻 yi-fan-xin-de-jin-gong 'some new offensive' may be wrongly written as 一翻新的进攻. Here, the incorrect word 翻 fan 'turn over' and its left character 新 xin 'new' in the fragment will form a verb 翻新 fan-xin 'retread' during word segmentation.

In terms of the above different ways of segmentation, we can classify incorrect words in Chinese into three types, namely as character-level errors (CLEs), word-level errors (WLEs) and context-level errors (CLEs), respectively.

2.2.2 Detecting incorrect characters with a multi-level analysis

In order to reduce the space and noise in decoding for spelling error correction, we employ a three-level analysis strategy to identify the above mentioned three types of incorrect words and thus detect all potential incorrect characters within the input sentence.

Character－level analysis is for detection CLES within a given input sentence. After the statistical analyzing of the large formal tokenized text, we use the following formula to calculate each character w's probability to be a single-character word:

$$P_{sw}(w) = \frac{Count(w \text{ is a single word})}{Count(w)}$$

For each single-character word within a segmented sentence, if the value of P_{sw} is less than a given threshold, then we will regards it as a candidate incorrect character.

Word-level analysis is for identifying WLEs. In this case, we just need to take all the out-of-vocabulary words (OOVs) as the candidates for the word layer processing. The candidate contains two cases, one is the wrong word, and the other is OOVs.

Context-level analysis is for CLEs. Here, we use n-grams to detect such types of errors. Considering the previous example 一翻新的, we can observe that P(的|一,翻新) $= 0$, P(的|翻新) $= 0.385$, P(翻新|一) $= 0$ through n-gram models, indicating that the word does not exist. This may be due to the word 一 yi 'one'. However, the incorrect character is 翻 rather than 一. So we can conclude that its neighbor is not reliable when CLEs occur. Thus we take "一" and all words around it within a window range of 1 as the incorrect character candidates.

2.3 Correction Candidate Generation with Similarity Matrix

Organizers have provided us with a group of similar character sets (CSC)(Liu et al., 2011), which includes similar shape and similar pronunciation, and latter are divided into "same sound and same tone (SS)", "same sound and different tone (SD)", "similar sound and same tone (MS)" and "similar sound and different tone (MD)" and so on. As follows:

Similar Shape: 可, 何呵坷奇河柯苛阿倚寄崎...
Similar Pronunciation: 右, 幼鼬誘宥柚祐有侑...

Through the statistical analyzing of the sample data, we found that the similar pronunciation errors accounting for more than 80%, nevertheless, only 10% of similar shape errors, and the other errors accounted for about 10%. Therefore, we believe that similar pronunciation words should have greater weight. We take the words (5401 words) of the data set as the matrix's rows and columns, the elements of the matrix are the similar weights between two words. The degree of similarity is divided into five levels, namely, the same sound and same tune (SS) is 1, similar morphology is 2, the same sound and different tune (SD) is 3, similar sound and same tone (MS) is 4 and similar sound and same tone (MS) is 5. So we can get a diagonal matrix (the value of diagonal elements all is 0), called the similarity matrix.

2.4 Correction Scoring with n-grams

We take all the candidate words and the words around them within the window range of 1 in a sentence S to be replaced by the similar words successively. Using the following formula to calculate the new sentence $S^{'}$ probability score.

$$
\begin{aligned}
score(S^{'}) = \prod \alpha \times P_{trigram}(w|w_{i-1}w_{i-2}) \\
+ (1-\alpha) \times \beta \times P_{bigram}(w|w_{i-1} \\
+ (1-\alpha) \times (1-\beta) \times P_{unigram}(w)
\end{aligned}
$$

The value of α in the models determine the weight of $P_{trigram}$, the greater of α, the more greater proportion of $P_{trigram}$; The value of β determine the weight of P_{bigram} .

3 Experimental Results

Our system participated in both subTask at the Chinese Spelling Check Bakeoff. This section reports the results and discussions on its evaluation.

3.1 Experimental Settings

As mentioned above, SIGHAN Bakeoff 2013 consists of two sub-tasks: namely error detection (viz. Subtask 1) and error correction (viz. Subtask2). For the error detection task, the system should return the locations of the incorrect characters for a given Chinese sentence that may have or do not have spelling errors, while in Subtask2, the system should return the locations of the incorrect characters within the input and correct them. Obviously, Subtask2 is a follow-up problem of error detection for sentences with errors.

In SIGHAN Bakeoff 2013, ninth measures for subTask1 and three measures for subTask2 are employed to score the performance of a spelling correction system. They are False-Alarm Rate(FAR), Detection Accuracy(DA), Detection Precision(DP), Detection Recall(DR), Detection F-score(DF), Error Location Accuracy(ELA), Error Location Recall(ELR), Error Location F-score(ELF), Location Accuracy(LA), Correction Accuracy(CA) and Correction Precision(CP).

In our system, we employ the SRILM Toolkit(Stolcke and others, 2002) to build n-gram models for spelling correction selection from the Academia Sinica Segmentation Corpus(3.0) (Chen et al., 1996). Furthermore, we use the similar character sets (CSC datasets)(Liu et al., 2011) to build the similarity matrix for correct sentence candidate generation. In addition, we also uses Academia Sinica Segmentation System (CKIP)(Ma and Chen, 2003) to perform word segmentation.

4 Experimental results and discussion

We use three different sets of parameters presented three sets of results, namely HLJU_Run1, HLJU_Run2 and HLJU_Run3. See the table 1 below for details:

	Model α	Model β	Similarity
Run1	0.8	0.8	$5 \leq$
Run2	0.8	0.8	$2 \leq$
Run3	0.6	0.8	$5 \leq$

Table 1: Parameter Selection.

α and β have been introduced in section 2.4. The Similarity less than or equal a value x , it represents only consider the similarity less than x characters in similarity matrix. For example, the Similarity of Run2 is less than 2, so we consider only two cases, the "same sound and same tone (SS)" and "similar shape".

Table 2 shows the result of sub-Task1 and Table 3 shows the result of sub-Task2. The "Best" indicates the high score achieved in Chinese Spelling Check task. The "Average" represents the average level. The numbers in boldindicate the highest values of each metric.

From the above table, we can see that results are not satisfactory, and many metrics from the best score is still a certain gap. The value of FAR is too high, and the precision is low. It means our method causes a lot of false positive errors and shows our system is not strictly for candidate list. And the parameter setting remains to be determined. In ad-

	FAR	DA	DP	DR	DF	ELA	ELP	ELR	ELF
Run1	0.6857	0.514	0.3798	0.98	0.5474	0.301	0.1047	0.27	0.1509
Run2	**0.6529**	**0.529**	**0.3849**	0.9533	**0.5484**	**0.339**	**0.1292**	**0.32**	**0.1841**
Run3	0.6929	0.51	0.3782	**0.9833**	0.5463	0.296	0.1038	0.27	0.15
Average	0.3222	0.698	0.5847	0.7454	0.6064	0.591	0.3472	0.3887	0.3418
Best	0.0229	0.861	0.9091	1	0.7642	0.82	0.7102	0.6167	0.5854

Table 2: Evaluation Results of Sub-Task1.

	LA	CA	CP
Run1	0.265	0.225	0.2432
Run2	**0.323**	**0.277**	**0.3081**
Run3	0.264	0.222	0.2403
Average	0.415	0.3788	0.5026
Best	0.663	0.625	0.705

Table 3: Evaluation Results of Sub-Task2.

dition, I think there are some other reasons for this results:

1) There are some errors in the training and CSC data set, and we do not deal with it;

2) Our methods are still based on ngram models for correcting spelling errors, and we failed to the breakthrough.

However, the performance of Run2 is much better than other schemes. We can conclude that low character similarity has no any help for the correction task.

5 Conclusion

In this paper, we have presented a spelling checker for Chinese. It consists of three main modules, namely potential incorrect character detection with a multiple-level analysis, correct sentence candidate generation with similar character sets and correction scoring with n-grams. We have participated in all the two sub-tasks at the ACL-SIGHAN Chinese Spelling Check Bakeoff. Since our system is still under development, the results are not satisfactory. For future work, we hope to explore more complicated techniques to achieve precise error detection and correction decoding.

Acknowledgments

This study was supported by National Natural Science Foundation of China under Grant No.60973081 and No.61170148, the Returned Scholar Foundation of Educational Department of Heilongjiang Province under Grant No.1154hz26, and Harbin Innovative Foundation for Returnees under Grant No.2009RFLXG007, respectively.

References

Keh-Jiann Chen, Chu-Ren Huang, Li-Ping Chang, and Hui-Li Hsu. 1996. Sinica corpus: Design methodology for balanced corpora. *Language*, 167:176. `http://rocling.iis.sinica.edu.tw/CKIP/publication.htm`.

C-L Liu, M-H Lai, K-W Tien, Y-H Chuang, S-H Wu, and C-Y Lee. 2011. Visually and phonologically similar characters in incorrect chinese words: Analyses, identification, and applications. *ACM Transactions on Asian Language Information Processing (TALIP)*, 10(2):10.

Wei-Yun Ma and Keh-Jiann Chen. 2003. Introduction to ckip chinese word segmentation system for the first international chinese word segmentation bakeoff. In *Proceedings of the second SIGHAN workshop on Chinese language processing-Volume 17*, pages 168–171. Association for Computational Linguistics.

Andreas Stolcke et al. 2002. Srilm-an extensible language modeling toolkit. In *INTERSPEECH*.

Graph Model for Chinese Spell Checking*

Zhongye Jia, Peilu Wang and Hai Zhao†
MOE-Microsoft Key Laboratory for Intelligent Computing and Intelligent Systems,
Center for Brain-Like Computing and Machine Intelligence
Department of Computer Science and Engineering, Shanghai Jiao Tong University
800 Dongchuan Road, Shanghai 200240, China
jia.zhongye,plwang1990@gmail.com,zhaohai@cs.sjtu.edu.cn

Abstract

This paper describes our system in the Bake-Off 2013 task of SIGHAN 7. We illustrate that Chinese spell checking and correction can be efficiently tackled with by utilizing word segmenter. A graph model is used to represent the sentence and a single source shortest path (SSSP) algorithm is performed on the graph to correct spell errors. Our system achieves 4 first ranks out of 10 metrics on the standard test set.

1 Introduction and Task Description

Spell checking is a common task in every written language, which is an automatic mechanism to detect and correct human errors. However, spell checking in Chinese is very different from that in English or other alphabetical languages. In Bake-Off 2013, the evaluation includes two sub-tasks: detection and correction for Chinese spell errors. The errors are collected from students' written essays.

The object of spell checking is word, but "word" is not a natural concept for Chinese since there are no word delimiters between words. Most Chinese natural language processing tasks require an additional word segmentation phase beforehand. When a word is misspelled, the word segmentation could not be processed properly. Another problem with Chinese is that the difference between "characters" and "words" is not very clear. Most Chinese characters itself can also be words which are called "single-character words" in Chinese. Thus Chinese is a language that may never encounter "out-of-vocabulary (OOV)" problem. Spell errors in alphabetical languages, such as English, are always typically divided into two categories:

- The misspelled word is a non-word, for example "come" is misspelled into "cmoe";
- The misspelled word is still a legal word, for example "come" is misspelled into "cone".

Spell errors in Chinese are quite different. In Chinese, if the misspelled word is a non-word, the word segmenter will not recognize it as a word, but split it into two or more words with fewer characters. For example, if "你好世界 (hello world)" is misspelled into "你好世节", the word segmenter will segment it into "你好/世/节" instead of "你好/世节". For non-word spell error, the misspelled word will be mis-segmented.

Thus spell checking for Chinese cannot directly use those edit distance based methods which are commonly used for alphabetical languages. Spell checking for Chinese have to deal with word segmentation problem first, since misspelled sentence cannot be segmented properly by a normal word segmenter. And it is necessary to use information beyond word level to detect and correct those mis-segmented words.

In this paper, we describe the system submitted from the team of Shanghai Jiao Tong University (SJTU). We are inspired by the idea of shortest path word segmentation algorithm. A directed acyclic graph (DAG) is built from the input sentence similar to the shortest path word segmentation algorithm. The spell error detection and correction problem is transformed to the SSSP problem on the DAG. We also tried filters based on sen-

*This work was partially supported by the National Natural Science Foundation of China (Grant No.60903119, Grant No.61170114, and Grant No.61272248), and the National Basic Research Program of China (Grant No.2009CB320901 and Grant No.2013CB329401).

†Corresponding author

tence perplexity (PPL) and character mutual information (MI).

2 System Architecture

We utilize a modified shortest path word segmenter as the core part of spell checker. The original shortest path word segmentation algorithm is revised for spell checking. Instead of the segmented sentence, the output sentence of the modified word segmenter is both segmented and spell-checked.

2.1 The Shortest Path Word Segmentation Algorithm

Shortest path word segmentation algorithm (Casey and Lecolinet, 1996) is based on the following assumption: a reasonable segmentation should maximize the lengths of all segments or minimize the total number of segments. For a sentence S of m characters $\{c_1, c_2, \dots, c_m\}$, the best segmented sentence S^* of n^* words $\{w_1^*, w_2^*, \dots, w_{n^*}^*\}$ should be:

$$S^* = \underset{\{w_1, w_2, \dots, w_n\}}{\arg\min} \; n. \tag{1}$$

This optimization problem can be easily transformed to a SSSP problem on a DAG.

First a graph $G = (V, E)$ must be built to represent the sentence to be segmented. The vertices of G are possible candidate words of adjacent characters. The words are fetched from a dictionary $\mathbb{D}$. Two special vertices $w_{-,0}$ = “<S>” and $w_{n+1,-}$ = “</S>” are added to represent the start and end of the sentence:

$$V = \{w_{i,j} | w_{i,j} = c_i \dots c_j \in \mathbb{D}\} \cup \{w_{-,0}, w_{n+1,-}\}.$$

The edges are from a word to the next word:

$$E = \{< w_{i,j} \to w_{j+1,k}, \omega > | w_{i,j}, w_{j+1,k} \in V\},$$

where ω is the weight of edge which is set to 1, $\omega = \omega_0 \equiv 1$.

For example, the Chinese sentence “床前明月光” can be represented by the graph shown in Figure 1. It can be easily proved that the graph G is a DAG, and finding the best segmentation according to Equation 1 is finding the shortest path from “<S>” to “</S>”, which is an SSSP problem on DAG.

The SSSP problem on DAG have an simple algorithm (Eppstein, 1998) with time complexity of $O(|V| + |E|)$, The algorithm is shown in Algorithm 1.

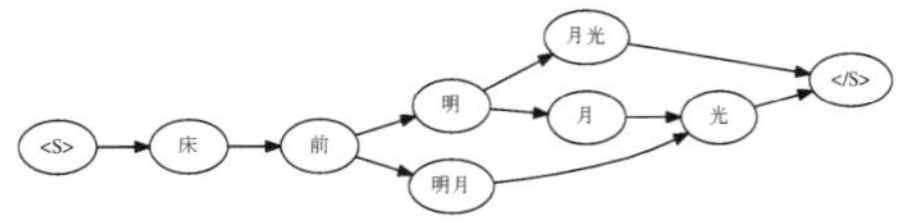

Figure 1: A sample of graph for segmentation

Algorithm 1 SSSP algorithm for word segmentation

Require: sentence of characters S
Require: dictionary $\mathbb{D}$
Ensure: segmented sentence s^*

Build DAG $G = (V, E)$ from S with $\mathbb{D}$
Topologically sort G into L
Init $D[v] \leftarrow -\infty, \forall v \in V$
Init $B[v] \leftarrow \Phi, \forall v \in V$
$D[\text{<S>}] \leftarrow 0$
for $u \in L$ **do**
  for v, ω s.t. $< u \to v, \omega > \in E$ **do**
    if $D[v] > D[u] + \omega$ **then**
      $D[v] \leftarrow D[u] + \omega$
      $B[v] \leftarrow u$
    end if
  end for
end for
$S^* = \Phi$
$v \leftarrow \text{</S>}$
while $v \neq \Phi$ **do**
  Insert v into the front of S^*
  $v \leftarrow B[V]$
end while

The segmented sentence of the above example “床前明月光” is “床/前/明月/光” or “床/前/明/月光” by using the SSSP algorithm.

2.2 Using SSSP Algorithm fo Spell Checking

The basic idea of using SSSP algorithm for spell checking comes from the observation that a misspelled word is often splitted into two or more words by the shortest path word segmenter. If we can substitute the misspelled character with the correct one and provide it as a candidate word, then the shortest path word segmenter will choose the correct one, since it has less words.

Then there is no need to change the SSSP algorithm. Only the graph of sentence is built in a different way. The vertices consists not only candidate words composed of original adjacent characters, but also characters substituted by those similar to the original ones. An additional map of similar characters $\mathbb{C}$ is needed. The revised vertices V are:

$$\begin{aligned} V = & \{w_{i,j} | w_{i,j} = c_i \dots c_j \in \mathbb{D}\} \\ & \cup \{w_{i,j}^k | w_{i,j}^k = c_i \dots c_k' \dots c_j \in \mathbb{D}, \\ & \qquad \tau \le j - i \le T, \\ & \qquad c_k' \in \mathbb{C}[c_k], k = i, i+1, \dots, j\} \\ & \cup \{w_{-,0}, w_{n+1,-}\}. \end{aligned}$$

The substitution is only performed on those words with lenth between some thresholds τ and T. The weight of edges are respectively changed:

$$\omega = f(\omega_0, \omega_s),$$

where ω_s measures the similarity between the two characters and $f(\cdot,\cdot)$ is a function to be selected.

With the modified DAG G, the SSSP algorithm can perform both segmentation task and spell checking task. Suppose the sentence "床前明月光" is misspelled as "床前名月光", the modified graph is shown in Figure 2. The output of the

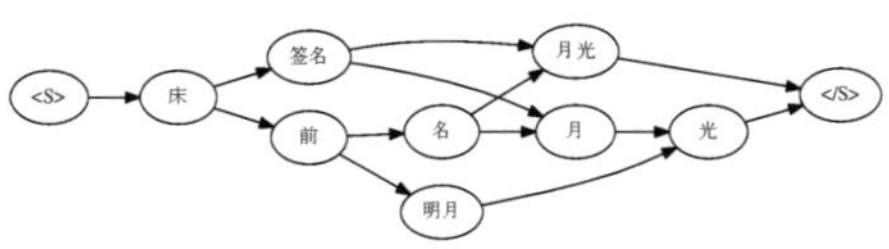

Figure 2: A sample of graph for spell checking

spell checker is "床/签名/月光", note this is not the expected result.

2.3 Using Language Model with SSSP Algorithm

The problem with simple SSSP spell chekcer is that it only tries to merge short words into longer ones without considering whether that is reasonable. To reduce the false-alarm rate (Wu et al., 2010), we add some statistical criteria to the SSSP spell checker.

A natural statistical criteria is the conditional probability between words, P, which can be given by a language model (LM). The conditional probability are combined into the weights of edges by some function $g(\cdot,\cdot,\cdot)$:

$$\omega = g(\omega_0, \omega_s, \frac{1}{P}),$$

Note that the higher conditional probability means the sentence is more reasonable, so for the SSSP algorithm, the inverse of conditional probability $\frac{1}{P}$ is used.

2.4 LM and MI Filter

In the sample set of Bake-Off 2013, we observed that there is at most one error in each sentence (Chen et al., 2011). But the spell checker may detect multiple errors. To choose the best correction, we run a filter and the one with lowest PPL or highest MI gain is selected.

For LM filter, sentence PPL is used as the metric. The correction with lowest PPL is considered as best.

MI indicates how possible two characters are collocated together. Character based MI is used, for two adjacent characters c_1 and c_2, the MI is:

$$\text{MI}(c_1, c_2) = \log \frac{P(c_1)P(c_2)}{P(c_1c_2)}$$

The correction with highest MI gain Δ_{MI} is considered as best:

$$\begin{aligned} \Delta_{\text{MI}} = \max(& \text{MI}(c_{i-1}, c_i') - \text{MI}(c_{i-1}, c_i), \\ & \text{MI}(c_i', c_{i+1}) - \text{MI}(c_i, c_{i+1})). \end{aligned}$$

3 Experiments

3.1 Data Sets and Resources

The Bake-Off 2013 sample data, SAMPLE, consists 350 sentences without errors and 350 sentences with one error per sentence. The official test data, TEST, consists of 1,000 unlabeled sentences for subtask 1 and another 1,000 sentences for subtask 2. All the sentences are collected from students' written essays. All the data are in traditional Chinese.

The dictionary used in SSSP algorithm is *SogouW*[1] dictionary from *Sogou inc.*, which is in simplified Chinese. The *OpenCC*[2] converter is used to convert it into traditional Chinese. For similar character map the data set provided by (Liu et al., 2011) is used. The LM is built on the Academia Sinica corpus (Emerson, 2005) with IRSTLM toolkit (Federico et al., 2008). Prefix tree data structure is used to speed up the dictionary look-up. The implementation of Perl module `Tree::Trie`[3] is used with some modification.

3.2 Edge Weight Function selection

A series of experiments are performed to choose a good edge weight function $g(\cdot,\cdot,\cdot)$. A simplified metric is used to evaluate different functions:

[1] `http://www.sogou.com/labs/dl/w.html`

[2] `http://code.google.com/p/opencc/`

[3] `http://search.cpan.org/~avif/Tree-Trie-1.5/`

- Correction precision:

$$\mathcal{P} = \frac{\text{\# of correctly corrected characters}}{\text{\# of all corrected characters}};$$

- Correction recall:

$$\mathcal{R} = \frac{\text{\# of correctly corrected characters}}{\text{\# of wrong characters of gold data}};$$

- F1 macro:

$$\mathcal{F} = \frac{2\mathcal{P}\mathcal{R}}{\mathcal{P}+\mathcal{R}}.$$

The LM is set to 2-gram according to the observations of (Yang et al., 2012). Improved Kneser-Ney (Chen and Goodman, 1999) algorithm is used for LM smoothing.

Multiplication of similarity and log conditional probability is firstly used as weight function:

$$\omega^M = -\alpha(\omega_0 + \omega_s)\log P$$

where $\omega_0 \equiv 1$, and ω_s for different kinds of characters are shown in Table 1. The settings of ω_s is inspired by (Yang et al., 2012), in which pinyin[4] edit distance is used as weight. Word length threshold is set to $\tau = 2$ and $T = 5$. Experiments show that the choice of α does not have notable influence on the result which remains at $\mathcal{P} = 0.49$, $\mathcal{R} = 0.61$, $\mathcal{F} = 0.55$ on SAMPLE.

Type	ω_s
same pronunciation same tone	0
same pronunciation different tone	0
similar pronunciation same tone	1
similar pronunciation different tone	1
similar shape	1

Table 1: ω_s used in ω^M

Linear combination of similarity and log conditional probability is then tried:

$$\omega^L = \omega_s - \beta \log P$$

where $\omega_0 \equiv 0$ which is omitted in the equation, and ω_s for different kinds of characters are shown in Table 2.

We experimented with different β and observed that with lager β, the spell checker tends to get more reasonable corrections so $\mathcal{P}$ goes higher, but $\mathcal{R}$ goes lower. The $\mathcal{P}$, $\mathcal{R}$ and $\mathcal{F}$ on SAMPLE of different β are shown in Figure 3.

LM and MI filters slightly improves the result of the spell checker. The results of applying two filters are shown in Figure 4.

[4]Pinyin is the official phonetic system for transcribing the sound of Chinese characters into Latin script.

Type	ω_s
same pronunciation same tone	1
same pronunciation different tone	1
similar pronunciation same tone	2
similar pronunciation different tone	2
similar shape	2

Table 2: ω_s used in ω^L

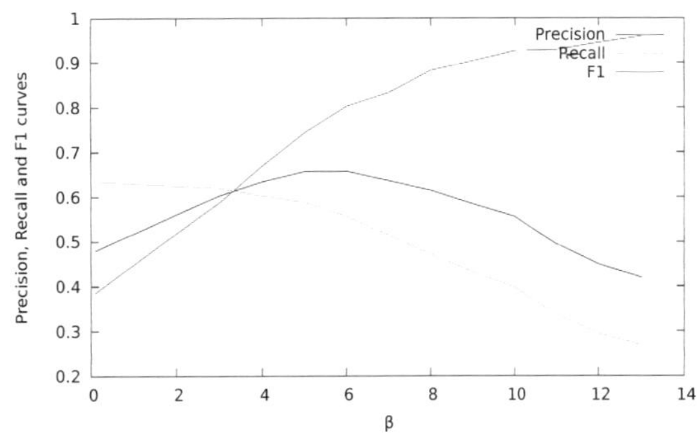

Figure 3: $\mathcal{P}$, $\mathcal{R}$ and $\mathcal{F}$ achieved by different β

3.3 Results

In the final test we submitted 3 runs, using edge weight function ω^L, of which β is set to 0, 6, and 10. Since there is no remarkable improvement by applying filters and the final test data has no claim that there's only one error per sentence, no filters are applied in the final test. The results on TEST are listed in Table 3 and Table 4, in which those metrics that we got first rank are marked as bold.

Metric	Run1	Run2	Run3
False-Alarm Rate	0.44	0.0957	**0.0229**
Detection Accuracy	0.662	0.856	0.844
Detection Precision	0.4671	0.769	**0.9091**
Detection Recall	0.9	0.7433	0.5333
Error Location Accuracy	0.522	0.805	0.809
Error Location Precision	0.2249	0.5931	**0.7102**
Error Location Recall	0.4333	0.5733	0.4167

Table 3: Final test results of subtask 1

Metric	Run1	Run2	Run3
Location Accuracy	0.372	0.475	0.37
Correction Accuracy	0.338	0.442	0.356
Correction Precision	0.3828	0.636	**0.705**

Table 4: Final test results of subtask 2

4 Conclusion and Future Work

In this paper we presented the system from team of Shanghai Jiao Tong University that participated in the Bake-Off 2013 task. A graph model is utilized to represent the spell checking problem and SSSP algorithm is applied to solve it. By adjusting edge weight function, a trade-off can be made between precision and recall.

A problem with the current result is that the test data set is a manually collected one with very high error rate. In subtask 1, nearly 50% sentences contains spell errors and in subtask 2, every sentence contains at least one spell error. This error rate is far higher than that in normal text. We may consider using data from normal text in future work.

References

Richard G Casey and Eric Lecolinet. 1996. A survey of methods and strategies in character segmentation. *Pattern Analysis and Machine Intelligence, IEEE Transactions on*, 18(7):690–706.

Stanley F Chen and Joshua Goodman. 1999. An empirical study of smoothing techniques for language modeling. *Computer Speech & Language*, 13(4):359–393.

Yong-Zhi Chen, Shih-Hung Wu, Ping-Che Yang, and Tsun Ku. 2011. Improve the detection of improperly used chinese characters in students' essays with error model. *International Journal of Continuing Engineering Education and Life Long Learning*, 21(1):103–116.

Thomas Emerson. 2005. The second international chinese word segmentation bakeoff. In *Proceedings of the Fourth SIGHAN Workshop on Chinese Language Processing*, pages 123–133.

David Eppstein. 1998. Finding the k shortest paths. *SIAM Journal on computing*, 28(2):652–673.

Marcello Federico, Nicola Bertoldi, and Mauro Cettolo. 2008. Irstlm: an open source toolkit for handling large scale language models. In *Interspeech*, pages 1618–1621.

C.-L. Liu, M.-H. Lai, K.-W. Tien, Y.-H. Chuang, S.-H. Wu, and C.-Y. Lee. 2011. Visually and phonologically similar characters in incorrect chinese words: Analyses, identification, and applications. 10(2):10:1–10:39, June.

Shih-Hung Wu, Yong-Zhi Chen, Ping-Che Yang, Tsun Ku, and Chao-Lin Liu. 2010. Reducing the false alarm rate of chinese character error detection and correction. In *CIPS-SIGHAN Joint Conference on Chinese Language Processing*.

Shaohua Yang, Hai Zhao, Xiaolin Wang, and Baoliang Lu. 2012. Spell checking for chinese. In *International Conference on Language Resources and Evaluation*, pages 730–736, Istanbul, Turkey, May.

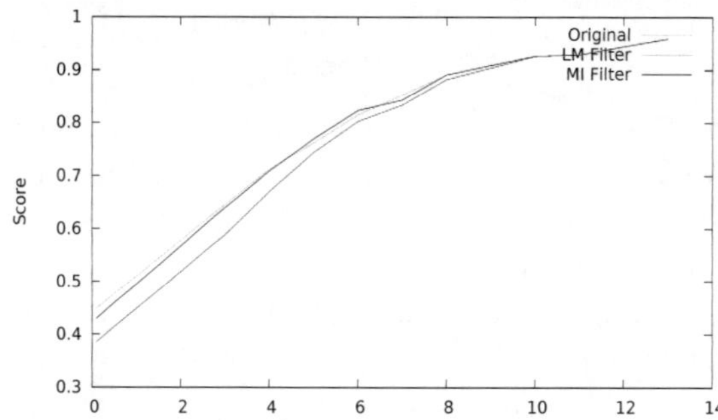

(a) Precision

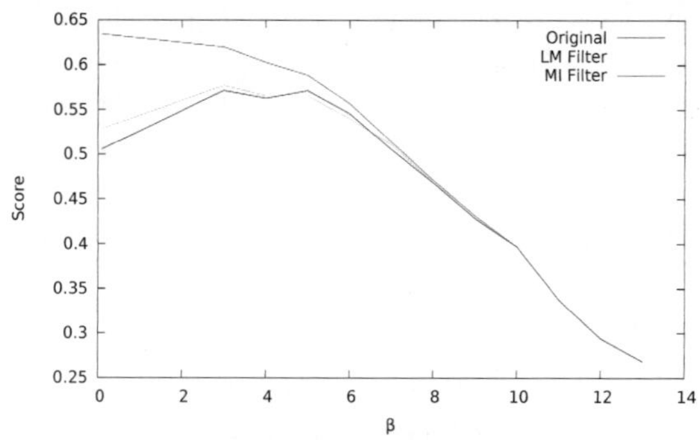

(b) Recall

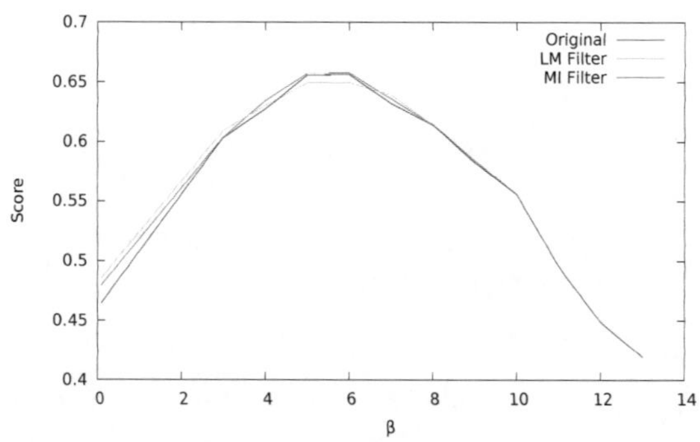

(c) F1

Figure 4: Precision, recall and F1 scores with filters

Sinica-IASL Chinese Spelling Check System at SIGHAN-7

Ting-Hao Yang*
Institute of Information Systems and Applications
National Tsing-Hua University
tinghaoyang@iis.sinica.edu.tw

Yu-Lun Hsieh*
Institute of Information Science
Academia Sinica
morphe@iis.sinica.edu.tw

Yu-Hsuan Chen
Institute of Information Science
Academia Sinica
smallright@iis.sinica.edu.tw

Michael Tsang
Electrical Engineering and Computer Sciences
University of California, Berkeley
themichaeltsang@gmail.com

Cheng-Wei Shih
Institute of Information Science
Academia Sinica
dapi@iis.sinica.edu.tw

Wen-Lian Hsu
Institute of Information Science
Academia Sinica
hsu@iis.sinica.edu.tw

Abstract

We developed a Chinese spelling check system for error detection and error correction subtasks in the 2013 SIGHAN-7 Chinese Spelling Check Bake-off. By using the resources of Chinese phonology and orthographic components, our system contains four parts: high confidence pattern matcher, the detection module, the correction module, and the merger. We submitted 2 official runs for both subtasks. The evaluation result show that our system achieved 0.6016 in error detection F-score of subtask 1, and 0.448 in correction accuracy of subtask 2.

1 Introduction

Chinese spelling check is a task which detects and corrects errors in text. These errors may result from writing, optical character recognition (OCR), typing, and so on. Chinese spelling check has been considered useful in many area such as language learning or error-tolerated language processing, and there are many researches around this topic (Y.-Z. Chen, Wu, Yang, Ku, & Chen, 2011; Liu et al., 2011; Wu, Chen, Yang, Ku, & Liu, 2010).

The SIGHAN Bake-off 2013 Chinese Spelling Check contains two subtasks. The first subtask requires each team to detect whether a sentence contains errors. If the answer is yes, the error location(s) should be provided. For each sentence in subtask2, there is at least one error. Participants have to locate and correct those errors in the sentence.

The organization of this paper is as follows. Section 2 describes the architecture and different modules in our spelling check system. Section 3 shows our evaluation results and some discussion. Lastly, Section 4 concludes this work and shares some insights we gained participating this Bake-off.

2 Method

Our system can be divided into four parts. They are high confidence pattern matcher, detection module, correction module and merger. High confidence pattern matcher finds patterns that are very unlikely to contain any error, and exclude them from the rest of the process. Detection module is used to detect the error locations in a sentence. Correction module generates suggestions for erroneous words. Merger receives these suggestions and chooses the most possible result. Figure 1 shows the structure of our system.

* Authors with equal contributions.

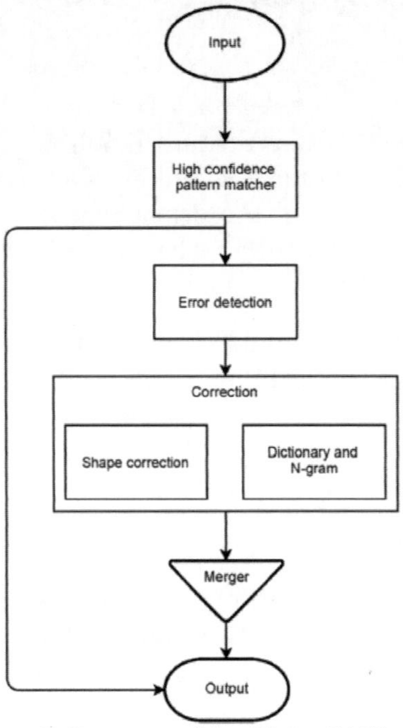

Figure 1. Structure of the Sinica-IASL Spelling Check System

2.1 High Confidence Pattern Matchers

Reliable Phonological Sequence Matcher

There are many homophones in Chinese. In order to detect errors caused by such a phonological similarity, we prepared an in-house dictionary with words which are longer than 2 characters, converted these words to phonetic symbols (注音) to form a syllable-word mapping table. Then we apply every syllable sequences in a syllable-annotated corpus based on CIRB (K.-H. Chen) to compute the matching percentage of each syllable-word pair in the mapping table. Syllable-word pairs with high percentage are considered as high confidence syllable-to-word patterns, means that these syllable sequences most likely map to the corresponding words in the corpus.

In the reliable phonological sequence matching of our system, we first convert the input sentence to phonetic symbols. If the phonetic symbols match one of the high confidence syllable-word pairs, the module checks the difference between the mapping word and the original input sequence. The overlapped characters are marked as correct. The remaining characters in the original input sentence are marked as error candidates and the correcting suggestions will be deliver to the correction module. For example, we found the syllable sequence of an input sentence "銼折" match a high confidence phonetic-word pair "ㄘㄨㄛˋ ㄓㄜˊ" — "挫折" (setback). Then the overlapped character "折" is marked as correct. On the other hand, the character "銼" will be regarded as an error candidate and the correcting suggestion of "挫" will be preserved.

Reliable Long Words

This module handles errors that happened in long Chinese in-vocabulary words based on the idea of maximum matching. We collected Chinese words, idioms, and sayings which are longer than four words, such as "一毛不拔" (stingy). Any part of the input text that exactly matches the patterns in this list are considered reliable, thus are marked as error-free.

Frequent Errors

We collected frequent errata and misused words from a dataset of junior high school students' composition. For example, "一但" is a frequent error from the correct one "一旦" (once). Whenever this module finds a part of the text contained in this frequent error list, a suggestion will be generated based on this list.

2.2 Detection Module

Detection module locates possible errors by integrating information from high confidence pattern matchers in Section 2.1 and word segmentation result described below, and passes these error locations to the correction module.

Word Segmentation

We used CKIP Chinese word segmentation tool (Ma & Chen, 2003) to get segmented sentences. Our presumption is that words containing erroneous characters are more likely to be split into different segments. For example, "佈告欄" (bulletin board) would be tagged as one segment by the tool, while the erroneous case "怖告欄" would be split into singlets such as "怖", "告" and "欄". This module would then check for consecutive singles and try to merge them into one segment. Then those segments were verified by a two-step checking. The first one is using a dictionary (Ministry of Education, 1994) to ensure there is no out-of-vocabulary being generated. The second one is using the frequency of n-grams from Google web 1T. The frequency of the generated segment has to surpass the pre-set threshold. Only those suggestions that pass at least one of the checks are kept.

2.3 Correction Module

Possible error positions from detection modules are received by the following correction modules to generate candidates for corrections. Both similar pronunciation and shape correcting process will be activated, and the results will be sent to the merger for the final decision.

Homophone Dictionary and N-gram Correction

We check the received error locations and generate possible corrections by using homophones and Google web 1T n-gram frequency. For example, there is an error "書貴" and the detection modules say that "貴" is an error. This module will generate possible candidates by finding all homophones of "貴". The frequency of each candidate in Google web 1T n-gram is used as the confidence. In this case, the frequency of "書櫃" (bookcase) is higher than the frequency of the original text, and all other homophones. Thus, a correction for "書貴" is given by this module as "書櫃".

Errors with Similar Shape

Shape correction module utilized data from Xiaoxuetang Chinese character database (National-Taiwan-University & Academia-Sinica, 2013), which consists of decomposed components of almost every Chinese character, to find corrections with similar shapes. We retrieved the components of each character that were marked as a possible error by the detection module, and calculate the Damerau-Levenshtein edit distance (Damerau, 1964; Levenshtein, 1966) between this character and all other characters. We slightly altered this edit distance formula to favor those with identical parts regardless of the order. For example, a character with parts (A, B) are considered more similar to (B, A) than to (A, D). From our observation of the training data, this method can better rank the most similar characters. We then select those characters that have an edit distance score less than 1, and filter out the ones that do not form a word with its neighboring 1 to 3 characters using a dictionary (Ministry of Education, 1994).

Across-the-board Search and Correction

This process will only be activated when no answer was provided by any previous modules. It checks all locations which are not covered by high confidence pattern matcher, and generates suggestions that have similar shapes to the characters in these locations using the shape correction module. We do not consider phonetic errors in this step because we assume phonetic errors can be detected by previous modules.

	Run 1	Run 2	Best	Average
False-Alarm Rate	0.3	**0.1857**	0.0229	0.4471
Detection Accuracy	0.713	**0.754**	0.861	0.654
Detection Precision	0.5161	**0.5873**	0.9091	0.4603
Detection Recall	0.7467	0.6167	1	0.89
Detection F-Score	0.6103	0.6016	0.7642	0.6068
Error Location Accuracy	0.605	**0.686**	0.82	0.549
Error Location Precision	0.2673	**0.3714**	0.7102	0.2793
Error Location Recall	0.3867	0.39	0.6167	0.54
Error Location F-Score	0.3161	**0.3805**	0.5854	0.3682

Table 1. Evaluation Results of Subtask 1

	Run 1	Run 2	Best	Average
Location Accuracy	0.468	**0.49**	0.663	0.418
Correction Accuracy	0.429	**0.448**	0.625	0.409
Correction Precision	0.4286	0.4476	0.705	0.6956

Table 2. Evaluation Results of Subtask 2.

2.4 Merger

The merger receives all suggestions from the aforementioned correction modules, and decides whether a suggestion is accepted or not. In our system, we used a probabilistic language model trained by LDC news corpus as the kernel of this merger. This module generates possible combinations of suggestions and calculates scores. The combination of suggestions with the best score is selected as our answer.

3 Experimental Results

We submitted two runs to compare the effect of high confidence patterns. Run 1 used patterns which have a confidence level of 50% or higher, and run 2 used those having over 80%. Table 1 and 2 are our experimental results for subtask 1 and 2, respectively. Bold typed numbers indicate that our performance is above the average.

We can see that, generally speaking, our performance of both subtasks is above average among participants. The effect of the confidence level of our high confidence patterns can be observed when we compare the results of our 2 runs. Using a higher confidence threshold (run 2) would yield a higher accuracy, while a lower threshold (run 1) would sometimes yield a higher recall.

4 Conclusion

This paper introduced our Sinica-IASL Chinese spelling checking system, implemented for the 2013 SIGHAN-7 Bake-off. By using phonological and orthographical data of Chinese characters, dictionaries and frequent error data, we were able to achieve reasonable performances. During the process of our work, we noticed that about 80% of the texts are covered by all words in our dictionary. The minimum coverage of a sentence is 50%. It implies that we can handle at least 50% of the text by only using a dictionary. If we use frequent n-grams, the coverage is over 90%. A method for finding useful n-grams is a way to boost our performance. The experimental results showed that there is plenty of room for improvement in our system's ability to detect errors. Further works also include using a web corpus to find frequent errors, possible error locations and corrections. In conclusion, our system can benefit from more resources in order to become a more competitive Chinese spelling checker.

Acknowledgement

We would like to thank the reviewers of the SIGHAN 2013 Program Committee for their helpful suggestions and comments on this paper, and Dr. Chiang-Chi Liao for his assistance on this work. This research was supported by the National Science Council of Taiwan under Grants NSC101-3113-P-032-001.

References

Kuang-Hua Chen. Chinese Information Retrieval Benchmark. http://lips.lis.ntu.edu.tw/cirb/index.htm

Yong-Zhi Chen, Shih-Hung Wu, Ping-Che Yang, Tsun Ku, and Gwo-Dong Chen. (2011). *Improve the detection of improperly used Chinese characters in students' essays with error model.* Paper presented at the Engineering Education and Life-Long Learning.

Fred J. Damerau. (1964). *A technique for computer detection and correction of spelling errors.* Paper presented at the Communications of the ACM 7.3.

Vladimir I. Levenshtein. (1966). Binary codes capable of correcting deletions, insertions and reversals. *Soviet physics doklady., 10.*

Chao-Lin Liu, Min-Hua Lai, Kan-Wen Tien, Yi-Hsuan Chuang, Shih-Hung Wu, and Chia-Ying Lee. (2011). Visually and phonologically similar characters in incorrect Chinese words: Analyses, identification, and applications. *ACM Transactions on Asian Language Information Processing, 10*, 1-39.

Wei-Yun Ma and Keh-Jiann Chen. (2003). *Introduction to CKIP Chinese word segmentation system for the first international Chinese Word Segmentation Bakeoff.* Paper presented at the The Second SIGHAN Workshop on Chinese Language Processing.

R.O.C. Ministry of Education. (1994). *教育部重編國語辭典修訂本 Revised Chinese Dictionary.*

National-Taiwan-University and Academia-Sinica (Producer). (2013). 小學堂文字學資料庫 Xiaoxuetang Philology Database. Retrieved from http://xiaoxue.iis.sinica.edu.tw/

Shih-Hung Wu, Yong-Zhi Chen, Ping-Che Yang, Tsun Ku, and Chao-Lin Liu. (2010). *Reducing the False Alarm Rate of Chinese Character Error Detection and Correction.* Paper presented at the CIPS-SIGHAN Joint Conference on Chinese Language Processing, Beijing.

Automatic Detection and Correction for Chinese Misspelled Words Using Phonological and Orthographic Similarities

Tao-Hsing Chang
Department of Computer Science and Information Engineering, National Kaohsiung University of Applied Sciences
changth@kuas.edu.tw

Hsueh-Chih Chen
Department of Educational Psychology and Counseling
National Taiwan Normal University
chcjyh@ntnu.edu.tw

Yuen-Hsien Tseng
Information Technology Center
National Taiwan Normal University
samtseng@ntnu.edu.tw

Jian-Liang Zheng
Department of Computer Science and Information Engineering, National Kaohsiung University of Applied Sciences
chaosgodyi@gmail.com

Abstract

How to detect and correct misspelled words in documents is a very important issue for Mandarin and Japanese. This paper uses phonological similarity and orthographic similarity co-occurrence to train linear regression model. Using ACL-SIGHAN 2013 Bake-off Dataset, experimental results indicate that the detection F-score, error location F-score of our proposed method for Subtask 1 is 0.70 and 0.43 respectively, and the correction accuracy of the proposed method for Subtask 1 is 0.39.

1 Introduction

How to automatically detect and correct misspelled words in documents is a very important issue. It is not an easy task for programs to spot misspelled words automatically. In English sentences, words are separated by space, thereby leading to the result that it is not difficult to distinguish if there are characters with non-existing orthography and unknown words. However, Chinese sentences are constructed by successive single-character, and a word could consist of one character or more. As a result, it is difficult to identify whether a character is a part of a misspelled word or not.

Based on our observation, misspelled words mainly occur as the following cases: phonological similarity and orthographic similarity. For example, word '已經' is mistakenly written as '以經' due to the fact that characters '已' and '以' are pronounced as 'yi'. In addition, word '代表' is mistakenly written as '伐表' because the orthographic of characters '代' and '伐' are quite confusing. As a result, it may work to identify the possible misspelled words within sentences by phonological similarity and orthographic similarity between two characters.

The purpose of the study is to propose a method to detecting and correcting misspelled words in sentences. The proposed method does not rely on the collection of similar words, but based on the following assumption. Supposing there was no misspelled word in sentences, ideal word segmentation method could divide sentence into serial correct words. However, if there was a misspelled word, the segmentation could separate words containing misspelled character by serial characters. For instance, sentence '我們都喜歡學伇' will be segmented into '我們 都 喜歡 學 伇' due to the fact that '學伇' cannot be found in the dictionary, thus segmenting '學' and '伇' respectively.

By the observation mention above, a sentence may include several character sequences consisting of two or more than two characters, denoted as sentential fragments. Each character in fragments may be the wrong part of a misspelling word while other characters are the correct part of the word. Hence, for each character treated as correct part of a misspelled word, the proposed method picks up the words containing the character. The words will be denoted as "candidate words". On the other hand, all characters in the fragment may be single-character words. The sentential fragment referring to candidate words is called "original string" in this paper. By calculating the probability of candidate words and original strings, the proposed method can determine whether the original strings contain misspelled words or not and correct the words. Next section will address the details.

2 Related Works

Chang (1995) proposed detecting technique of Mandarin misspelled word. Although it was able to find out misspelled words, there were some defects needed to be improved. For example, too much False Alert, long detection time, not able to refer to entire paragraph. Ren et al. (2001) utilized rule-based with linguistic model to detect mistakes. Although it was not very efficient, it was a new concept at the time. Lin et al. (2002) focused on misspelled words occurred in Cangjie input method and put forward a detecting system. Huang et al. (2008) designed a correcting system for wrong phonological words which built up similar phonological word collection for every single word. The correcting system also used bi-gram linguistic model to position the misspelled word, and replaced it with the most likely fit word.

Afterwards, there were many proposes under different circumstances. For example, Chen (2010) following previous studies, he amended detecting templates in order to automatically generate positive and negative knowledge corpus by Using Template and Translate modules to correct sentences. And final correction was conducted by part-of-speech Language Model to improve the accuracy probability of misspelled word correction.

3 Methods

Chang et al. (2012)'s approach is refined as the algorithm for automatically correcting misspelled words in this paper. They observed that there is a specific phenomenon when misspelled words occur. They envisaged that there was no misspelled words in sentences, ideal tokenization system would divide sentence into correct vocabulary combinations. However, if there is a misspelled word, the system would segment the majority of vocabulary contained misspelled words by means of single-character formation.

According to this property, existing misspelled words was assumed to appear in a string formed by successive single-character words in this paper. As a result, for a string including two or more than two single-characters, the words which contain some characters in a string from the dictionary can be listed. In this study, these words are called candidate word while the string is called original string.

Linear regression prediction model was used to determine whether an original string should be replaced with a candidate word or not. Three parameters between candidate word and original string are used in linear regression model as an input. The values of three parameters are respectively called similarity, the probability of character co-occurrence, and the probability of POS co-occurrence. The values are utilized as the input in linear regression formula, and then the probability of misspelled words in original string can be obtained. If several candidate words are predicted as the correct words of original string by prediction model at the same time, the word with highest score is treated as correct word.

The similarity between candidate word and original string is the average between phonological similarity and orthographic similarity. The Mandarin phonetic code was employed to compute phonological similarity. High similarity means that the two characters are easily represented as misspelled words for each other. On the other hand, radical structures are utilized to determine spatial structure of two fonts. Two characters with higher graphic resemblance easily represents as misspelled words. In the following sections, the detail of similarity will be addressed.

3.1 Candidate Words

For each sentence, it is segmented into words and the part-of-speeches of words are tagged by WeCAn system (Chang et al., 2012). Based on the assumption mentioned earlier in this paper, words which contain misspelled words can result in consecutive single-character string. Hence, the model will identify all words contained in consecutive single-character string from dictionary. As seen from Figure 1, a sentence '人生又何償不是如此' is segmented into '人生_又_何_償_不是_如此'. '償' is a misspelled words of '嘗' in this sentence, '何' and '償' are thus segmented respectively. Followed by, for the string with successive single-character '又何償', the system will select the candidate word from each character in the string. For the '何' in string, the proposed method identifies '何' as the second word and its length less than or equal to 3 in the dictionary, such as '任何', '如何' and so on. Additionally, the word '何' identified as the first word and its length less than or equal to 2 is also the candidate word, such as '何必', '何嘗'and so on.

All candidate words will be compared to correspondent original string with their phonological similarity and orthographic similarity. In Figure 1, the phonological similarity and orthographic similarity between the character '任' in candidate word '任何' and character '又' in original string will be computed. The similarities determine whether '任何' is needed to be further analyzed.

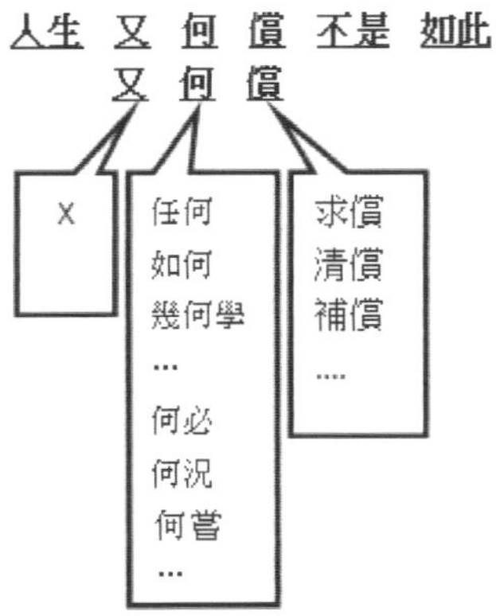

Figure 1. An Example of Candidate Words and an Original String.

3.2 Phonological Similarity

Mandarin phonetic symbols are used to evaluate phonological similarity. There are 37 symbols in Mandarin phonetic symbols dividing into initial (ㄅ/b/,ㄆ/p/,ㄇ/m/), medial (ㄧ /yi/, ㄨ /wu/, ㄩ /yu/), final (ㄚ /a/, ㄛ /o/, ㄜ /e/) and five tones. Chang et al.(2010) mentioned that some Chinese phonetic alphabets have identical articulation method and speech position, whereas articulation confusability is the causes of misspelled words. For example, symbols 'ㄅ' and 'ㄆ' have similar speech position ; symbols 'ㄕ' and 'ㄙ' have identical articulation; symbols 'ㄣ' and 'ㄥ' in final category belongs to a confusable articulation set.

This paper compares two characters with their Mandarin phonetic symbols of its initial, medial, final and tone respectively to measure phonetic similarity. The rules for comparison are as follows:

1. If there are identical initial, a similarity score will achieve one point. The score will achieve 0.5 point for initials of two characters which are 'ㄅ' and 'ㄆ', 'ㄉ' and 'ㄊ', 'ㄋ' and 'ㄌ', 'ㄍ' and 'ㄎ', 'ㄓ' and 'ㄗ', 'ㄔ' and 'ㄘ', or 'ㄕ' and 'ㄙ'.
2. If there are identical finals, the score will increase one point. The score will increase 0.5 point for finals of two characters which are 'ㄣ' and 'ㄥ'.
3. If there are identical medial in two characters, the score will increase one point.
4. If the tones are consistent in two characters, the score will increase one point.
5. Phonetic similarity between two characters can be obtained by dividing the similarity score by 4.

Phonological similarity between candidate word and original string is the average of phonological similarity of all characters in the candidate word. For instance, given candidate word '應該' corresponding to original string '因該', phonetic symbol of characters '因' and '應' is 'ㄧㄣ' and 'ㄧㄥ' respectively. Hence, the phonological similarity is (1+1+0.5+1)/4 = 0.875. The similarity between the same two characters '該' is one. Therefore, phonological similarity between candidate word '應該' and original string '因該'is (1+0.875)/2=0.9375.

3.3 Orthographic Similarity

Measurement of orthographic similarity in this paper is based on the method proposed by Chang et al. (2012). The measurement first disassembles two characters into a set of basic components and compare the differences between the two using Chinese Orthography Database proposed by Chen et al. (2011). There are 446 basic constituents in the database, and each unit of a character is linked by their spatial relations. There are 11 types of spatial relations, such as vertical combination and horizontal combination.

Through the database, a Chinese character can be converted into a series of branch-like structure consisting of parts and combination relations. The structure is called the constituent structure. Figure 2 shows the constituent structure of the Chinese character '查' in which '-' represents horizontal combination, and '木', '日', '一' are constituents.

In the constituent structure of a character, nodes represent combination relations while leaves represent constituents. Every relation and constituent in the whole structure has a level representing the position as well as a weight representing the strokes for that constituent. The weight for each relation denotes the total number of strokes for all relevant constituents. Chang et al.(2012) used the level and weight of constituent structure of two characters to calculate the degree of orthographic similarity.

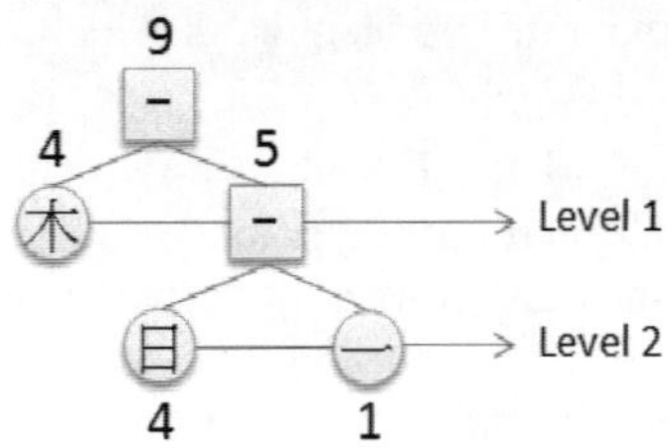

Figure. 2. Constituent Strucutre in the Chinese Character '查'.

This paper modifies measuring formula for similarity in previous study Chang et al. (2012). In previous formula, only the similarity between two identical constituents is scored. It is suggested that two similar constituents should increase the score. Therefore, this paper uses the stroke information in the database for constituents to calculate the similarity between two constituents. For example, stroke information of constituents '已' and '己' in the database is as follows:

'已' :[{口 2},{一}~(1:9@9),{乚}~(2:0@2)]
'己': [{口 2},{一}~(1:9@9),{乚}~(2:0@0)]

It is noted that most constituents for Chinese characters '已'and '己' are very similar which would receive a score close to 1 in similarity measure.

3.4 Probability of Co-occurrence

In large corpuses, some specific characters may have high frequency to be adjacent to another character, and this is called co-occurrence. The probability of co-occurrence between two characters is called probability of character co-occurrence (PCC). If a sentence has misspelled words, the PCC among characters in the sentence should be lower than the sentence which has no misspelled words. Hence, if the PCC of character in the candidate word is great higher than that in original string, misspelled words may occur in the sentence. In addition, there exists co-occurrence in part-of-speeches. The probability of co-occurrence between two characters is called probability of character co-occurrence (PPC).

Bi-gram method is utilized in both this paper and the previous study to calculate the PCC of characters in candidate words as well as that in original string. Ratio of PCC (RPCC) can be obtained by dividing the PCC of characters in candidate word by that in original string. The ratio of the probability of part-of-speech co-occurrence (RPPC) can be obtained by the same methods. The higher the two values, the possible the misspelled words occur in original string. As a result, both ratios will be two inputs for prediction model.

3.5 Prediction Model

This paper adopts linear regression formula to be the prediction model. For a candidate word and correspondent original string, the values of three inputs can be obtained by using approaches in subsection 3.2 to 3.4. Candidate words and correspondent original string in training data are utilized in this paper to compute each regression coefficient in formula 1.

$$y = \beta_1 X_1 + \beta_2 X_2 + \beta_3 X_3 \qquad (1)$$

For any set of candidate words and correspondent original string, three parameters are substituted into formula 1 to obtain *y*. The *y* value represents the probability of the original string within misspelled words. Based on the values of *y* obtained from training data, a threshold can be set. If *y* is higher above the threshold, there are misspelled words in original string. If *y* is lower than threshold value, there are no misspelled words in original string.

4 Experiments

This paper use the data provided by ACL-SIGHAN 2013 Bake-off to conduct performance evaluation. The data is divided into two sets called 'dry run' and 'final test' while the evaluation includes two tasks sub-task 1 and sub-task 2. Each set consist of two subsets which is employed to evaluate the performance of methods for two tasks respectively. In dry run, sub-task 1 and sub-task 2 each use 50 example sentences for testing. In final test, sub-task 1 and sub-task 2 each use 1000 example sentences for testing. The purposes of sub-task 1 and sub-task 2 are to respectively evaluate the performance of error detection and error correction of methods.

Table 1 presents the evaluation result of Sub-task 1 in our proposed method, denoted as KUAS-NTNU, and results of sub-task 2 are shown in Table 2. Since SIGHAN has not reported the F-score for sub-task 1 in dry run, Table 1 does not show the detection F-score and error location F-score of dry run.

	Dry Run	Final Test
False-alarm Rate	0.23	0.23
Detection Accuracy	0.80	0.79
Detection Precision	0.50	0.61
Detection Recall	0.90	0.82
Detection F-score	-	0.70
Error Location Accuracy	0.76	0.69
Error Location Precision	0.39	0.38
Error Location Recall	0.70	0.51
Error Location F-score	-	0.43

Table 1. The Performance of KUAS-NTNU System for Subtask 1.

	Dry Run	Final Test
Location Accuracy	0.30	0.44
Correction Accuracy	0.28	0.39
Correction Precision	0.36	0.51

Table 2. The Performance of KUAS-NTNU System for Subtask 2.

5 Discussion

Methods suggested by previous studies often rely on data collected from confusable character sets. Although corresponding characters in the set are high in similarity and can be easily confused, they could not be assessed correctly if they are not from the confusable sets. Our proposed methods calculate phonological similarity and orthographical similarity between misspelled words and original string, which are not restricted by confusable sets. The proposed method can still obtain a reliable estimation by other parameters with characters in low similarity.

Some issues and works could be explored and developed in the further. First, this study only examines characters with misspelled words. The detection and correction of single-character misspelled words only rely on simple rule-based approaches. It results in many single-character misspelled words cannot be extracted. Second, collections of unknown words in sentences are often considered having misspelled words which might cause a decrease in system accurate rate but an increase in false-alarm rate. Differences analysis for unknown words and misspelled words are issues that must be dealt with in future research.

Acknowledgments

This research was partially supported by National Science Council (NSC), Taiwan, under the grant NSC 100-2511-S-003-053-MY2 and NSC 102-2511-S-151-002, and the "Aim for the Top University Project" of National Taiwan Normal University (NTNU), sponsored by the Ministry of Education, Taiwan. We are also grateful to the support of International Research-Intensive Center of Excellence Program of NTNU and NSC, Taiwan, R.O.C., under the grant 101WFA0300229.

References

Chang C.-H. 1995. *A New Approach for Automatic Chinese Spelling Correction.* Proceedings of Natural Language Processing Pacific Rim Symposium'95, 278-283.

Chang C.-H., Lin S.-Y., Li S.-Y., Tsai M.-F., Liao H.-M., Sun C.-W., and Huang N.-E. 2010. *Annotating Phonetic Component of Chinese Characters Using Constrained Optimization and Pronunciation Distribution.* International Journal of Computational Linguistics and Chinese Language Processing, 15(2):145-160.

Chang T.-H., Su S.-Y., and Chen H.-C. 2012. *Automatic Correction for Graphemic Chinese Misspelled Words.* Proceedings of ROCLING 2012, 125-139.

Chang T.-H., Sung Y.-T., & Lee Y.-T. 2012. *A Chinese word segmentation and POS tagging system for readability research.* Proceedings of 42nd SCiP.

Chen H.-C., Chang L.-Y., Chiou Y.-S., Sung Y.-T., and Chang K.-E. 2011. *Chinese Orthography Database and Its Application in Teaching Chinese Characters.* Bulletin of Educational Psychology, 43:66-86.

Chen, Y.-Z. 2010. *Improve the Detection of Improperly Used Chinese Characters with Noisy Channel Model and Detection Template.* Chaoyang University of Technology, Taiwan, R.O.C.

Huang C.-M, Wu M.-C., and Chang C.-C. 2008. *Error Detection and Correction Based on Chinese Phonemic Alphabet in Chinese Text.* World scientific publishing company, International Journal of Uncertainty, Fuzziness and Knowledge-Based Systems, 16(1):89-105.

Lin Y.-J., Huang F.-L., and Yu M.-S. 2002. *A Chinese Spelling Error Correction System.* Proceedings of the 7th Conference on Artificial Intelligence and Applications.

Ren F., Shi H., and Zhou Q. 2001. *A hybrid approach to automatic Chinese text checking and error correction.* Proceedings of IEEE SMC, 1693-1698.

NTOU Chinese Spelling Check System in SIGHAN Bake-off 2013

Chuan-Jie Lin and Wei-Cheng Chu
Department of Computer Science and Engineering
National Taiwan Ocean University
No 2, Pei-Ning Road, Keelung 202, Taiwan R.O.C.
{cjlin, wcchu.cse}@ntou.edu.tw

Abstract

This paper describes details of NTOU Chinese spelling check system participating in SIGHAN-7 Bakeoff. The modules in our system include word segmentation, N-gram model probability estimation, similar character replacement, and filtering rules. Three dry runs and three formal runs were submitted, and the best one was created by bigram probability comparison without applying preference and filtering rules.

1 Introduction

Automatic spell checking is a basic and important technique in building NLP systems. It has been studied since 1960s as Blair (1960) and Damerau (1964) made the first attempt to solve the spelling error problem in English. Spelling errors in English can be grouped into two classes: non-word spelling errors and real-word spelling errors.

A non-word spelling error occurs when the written string cannot be found in a dictionary, such as in *fly *fron Paris*. The typical approach is finding a list of candidates from a large dictionary by edit distance or phonetic similarity (Mitten, 1996; Deorowicz and Ciura, 2005; Carlson and Fette, 2007; Chen *et al.*, 2007; Mitten 2008; Whitelaw *et al.*, 2009).

A real-word spelling error occurs when one word is mistakenly used for another word, such as in *fly *form Paris*. Typical approaches include using confusion set (Golding and Roth, 1999; Carlson *et al.*, 2001), contextual information (Verberne, 2002; Islam and Inkpen, 2009), and others (Pirinen and Linden, 2010; Amorim and Zampieri, 2013).

Spelling error problem in Chinese is quite different. Because there is no word delimiter in a Chinese sentence and almost every Chinese character can be considered as a one-syllable word, most of the errors are real-word errors. On the other hand, there can be a *non-character error* where a hand-written character is not legal (thus not collected in a dictionary). Such an error cannot happen in a digital document because all characters in Chinese character sets such as BIG5 or Unicode are legal.

There have been many attempts to solve the spelling error problem in Chinese (Chang, 1994; Zhang *et al.*, 2000; Cucerzan and Brill, 2004; Li *et al.*, 2006; Liu *et al.*, 2008). Among them, lists of visually and phonologically similar characters play an important role in Chinese spelling check (Liu *et al.*, 2011).

This bake-off is the first Chinese spell checking evaluation project. It includes two subtasks: error detection and error correction. The task is organized based on some research works (Wu *et al.*, 2010; Chen *et al.*, 2011; Liu *et al.*, 2011).

2 Architecture

Figure 1 shows the architecture of our Chinese spelling checking system.

A sentence under consideration is first word-segmented. All one-syllable words are replaced by similar characters and the newly created sentences are word segmented again. If a new sentence results in a better word segmentation, spelling error is reported. Details are described in the following subsections. All the examples are selected from the development set.

2.1 Similar character replacement

We only handle the case that a misused character becomes a one-syllable word. In other words, only one-syllable words will be checked whether it is correct or misused. The case of misusing a

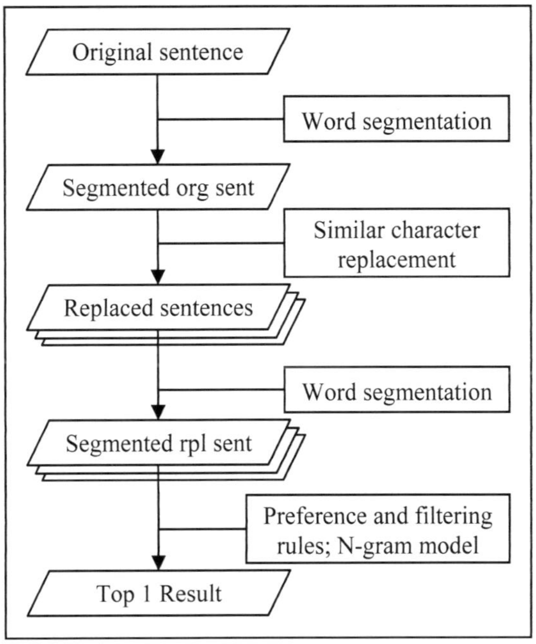

Figure 1. Architecture of NTOU Chinese Spelling Check System

two-syllable word instead of another two-syllable word (or longer words in either side) remains as our future work.

For each one-syllable word, its corresponding character in the original un-segmented sentence is replaced by its similar characters. The organizers of this evaluation project provided two kinds of similar character lists, one for phonologically similar characters and one for visually similar characters. We adopted all these lists except the one consisting of characters written in the same number of strokes with the same radical.

Taking Doc#00076 in the development set as an example. The original sentence is

...不能輕意半途而廢...

and it is segmented as

...不能 輕 意 半途而廢...

"輕" and "意" are one-syllable words so they are candidates of spelling errors. According to the similar character lists provided by the organizers, the phonologically similar characters of 輕 include 青情傾鯖氫... and its visually similar characters include 逕經涇經徑... Replacing 輕 with similar characters will produce the following new sentences.

...不能青意半途而廢...
...不能情意半途而廢...
......
...不能逕意半途而廢...
...不能經意半途而廢...
......

The newly created sentences are again word segmented and passed to the next steps.

2.2 Preference and filtering rules

Before determining a spelling error, some rules are applied to prefer or discard a similar-character replacement. These rules are defined as follows.

Rule 1: Long word preference

If a replacement results in a word whose length are 3 or more characters, this replacement is ranked first; if there are more than one such replacements, break ties by their N-gram probabilities. Take Doc#00028 as an example:

豐富 的 學識 更 如 海綿 受到 壓迫 而 盪 然 無 存

"蕩" is phonologically similar to "盪". The newly created sentence is segmented as

豐富 的 學識 更 如 海綿 受到壓迫 而 蕩然無存

where "蕩然無存" is a word with 4-character long. We will prefer such a replacement.

Rule 2: No error at the beginning

If a replacement takes place at the beginning of a sub-sentence, discard it. We assume that a writer seldom makes mistakes at the beginning of a sub-sentence. A sub-sentence is defined as a passage ended by a comma, period, exclamation, question mark, colon, or semicolon.

Take Doc#00001 as an example:

不 怕 措 折 地 奮鬥

Although "不" is a one-syllable word, it occurs at the beginning of a sub-sentence therefore no replacement is performed on this word.

Rule 3: No error in personal names

If a replacement results in a personal name, discard it. Our word segmentation system performs named entity recognition at the same time. If the replacing similar character can be considered as a Chinese family name, the consequent characters might be merged into a personal name. As most of the spelling errors do not occur in personal names, we simply ignore these replacements. Take Doc#00002 as an example:

突然 一 陣 巨 晃

"甄" is phonologically similar to "陣" and is one of the Chinese family names. The newly created sentence is segmented as

突然 一 甄巨晃(PERSON)

where "甄巨晃" is recognized as a personal name. We will discard such a replacement.

Rule 4: Stopword filtering

If the replaced (original) character is a personal anaphora (你 'you' 我 'I' 他 'he/she') or numbers from 1 to 10 (一二三四五六七八九十), discard the replacement. We assume that a writer seldom misspell such words. Take Doc#00002 as an example:

突然 一 陣 巨 晃

Although "一" is a one-syllable word, it is in our stoplist therefore no replacement is performed on this word.

2.3 N-gram probabilities

The newly created sentences are again word segmented. If a new sentence results in a better word segmentation, it is very likely that the replaced character is misused and its similar character is the correct one. But if no replacement is better than the original sentence, it is reported as "no misspelling".

The possibility of a sequence of words can be measured in its generation probability measured by a language model. We used smoothed unigram and bigram models in our experiments.

2.4 Error detection

The detail of our error detection algorithm is delivered here. Given a sentence,

1. Perform word segmentation on the original sentence
2. For each one-syllable word not violating the filtering rules (leading words or stop words), for each of its similar characters:
   (1) Its corresponding character in the original un-segmented sentence is replaced by the similar character
   (2) Perform word segmentation on the new sentence
   (3) If the new word sequence matches a preference rule (long words), rank this replacement to the top.
   (4) If the new word sequence matches a filtering rule (personal names), discard this replacement.
   (5) Otherwise, measure the N-gram probability (ungiram and bigram in this paper) of the new word sequence. Assign the rank of this replacement according to its N-gram probability.
3. If the top one segmentation is of the original sentence, report "no error" (either in error detection or correction subtasks).
4. If the top one segmentation is of a new sentence:
   - For error detection subtask, report "with error"
   - For error correction subtask, report the location of the replaced character and its similar character as the correction

Some examples of successful and wrong corrections by unigram and bigram probabilities are given in Table 1 to Table 4. All the values in "prob" columns are the logarithms of the probabilities.

Table 1 shows an example of correctly detecting an error by unigram probabilities. In Doc#00076, although replacing "輕" by "情" or "經" can form longer words, their unigram probabilities are less than the segmentation produced by replacing "意" by "易".

However, Table 2 gives an example of incorrectly detecting an error by unigram probabilities. In Doc#00002, the segmentation produced by replacing "晃" by "星" has a higher unigram probability than the correct replacement of "貴" by "櫃".

Table 3 shows an example of correctly detecting an error by bigram probabilities. In Doc#00001, although replacing "怕" by "必" or "地" by "抵" can form longer words, their bigram probabilities are less than the segmentation produced by replacing "措" by "挫".

However, Table 4 gives an example of incorrectly detecting an error by bigram probabilities. In Doc#00046, the segmentation produced by replacing "每" by "個" has a higher bigram probability than the correct replacement of "蹟" by "跡".

3 Performance

There are two sub-tasks in this bake-off: error detection and error correction.

Original sub-sentence in Doc#00076			Unigram prob	Bigram prob
不能 輕 意 半途而廢			-237.12	-360.48
Org	Rpl	Segmentation	Unigram prob	Bigram prob
輕	青	不能 青 意 半途而廢	-238.49	-362.78
輕	情	不能 情意 半途而廢	-230.79	-360.48
:	:	……		
輕	逕	不能 逕 意 半途而廢	-239.45	-360.48
輕	經	不能 經意 半途而廢	-234.12	-360.48
:	:	……		
意	易	不能 輕易 半途而廢	☺ -229.78	-357.08

Table 1. Success example of finding errors by unigram probability

Original sub-sentence in Doc#00002			Unigram prob	Bigram prob
突然 一 陣 巨 晃 ， 我們 家書 貴 倒 了			-262.14	-385.31
Org	Rpl	Segmentation	Unigram prob	Bigram prob
晃	星	突然 一 陣 巨星 ， 我們 家書 貴 倒 了	☹-256.13	-385.31
貴	櫃	突然 一 陣 巨 晃 ， 我們 家 書櫃 倒 了	-257.76	-385.31

Table 2. Failure example of finding errors by unigram probability

Original sub-sentence in Doc#00001			Unigram prob	Bigram prob
不 怕 措 折 地 奮鬥			-201.12	-308.93
Org	Rpl	Segmentation	Unigram prob	Bigram prob
怕	必	不必 措 折 地 奮鬥	-192.34	-308.93
措	挫	不 怕 挫折 地 奮鬥	-193.31	☺ -305.53
地	抵	不 怕 措 折抵 奮鬥	-198.82	-308.93

Table 3. Success example of finding errors by bigram probability

Original sub-sentence in Doc#00046			Unigram prob	Bigram prob
…都 有 它 的 蹤 蹟 ， 可以 算是 每 個人 長大 的 東西			-280.11	-405.72
Org	Rpl	Segmentation	Unigram prob	Bigram prob
蹟	跡	…公 車站 等 都 有 它 的 蹤跡	-273.85	-399.71
每	個	可以 算是 個 個人 長大 的 東西	-268.56	☹ -399.06

Table 4. Failure example of finding errors by bigram probability

Error detection is evaluated by the following metrics:

False-Alarm Rate = # of sentences with false positive error detection results / # of testing sentences without errors

Detection Accuracy = # of sentences with correctly detected results / # of all testing sentences

Detection Precision = # of sentences with correctly error detected results / # of sentences the system return as with errors

Detection Recall = # of sentences with correctly error detected results / # of testing sentences with errors

Detection F-Score= (2 * Detection Precision * Detection Recall) / (Detection Precision + Detection Recall)

Error Location Accuracy = # of sentences with correct location detection / # of all testing sentences

Error Location Precision = # of sentences with correct error locations / # of sentences the system returns as with errors

Error Location Recall = # of sentences with correct error locations / # of testing sentences with errors

Error Location F-Score= (2 * Error Location Precision * Error Location Recall) / (Error Location Precision + Error Location Recall)

Error correction is evaluated by the following metrics:

Location Accuracy = # of sentences correctly detected the error location / # of all testing sentences

Correction Accuracy = # of sentences correctly corrected the error / # of all testing sentences

Correction Precision = # of sentences correctly corrected the error / # of sentences the system returns corrections

We submitted 3 dry runs and 3 formal runs based on different system settings. The settings and evaluation results are described as follows.

3.1 Dry run evaluation

We submitted 3 dry runs in this Bake-off. The first run used only visually similar characters. The second run used only phonologically similar characters. And the third run used both kinds of similar characters. All three runs used bigram probability to detect errors.

Table 5 and 6 illustrate the evaluation results of dry runs in Subtask 1 and Subtask 2. (Evaluation results of Dryrun3_NTOU in Subtask 2 will be provided in the camera-ready version.) As we can see, using only phonologically similar characters achieve better F-scores than other strategies.

3.2 Formal run evaluation

We submitted 3 formal runs in this Bake-off. The first run used unigram probability while the other runs used bigram probability to detect errors. Besides, preference and filtering rules were applied only on the first run and the third run. All three runs used all similar characters to do the replacement.

Table 7 and 8 illustrate the evaluation results of formal runs in Subtask 1 and Subtask 2. As we can see, using bigram probability without preference and filtering rules achieve the best performance.

4 Conclusion

We submitted 3 dry runs and 3 formal runs based on different system settings. The evaluation results show that using bigram probability without preference and filtering rules achieve the best performance. Besides, phonologically similar characters are more useful than visually similar characters.

In the future, more features should be investigated. Errors of misusing one word into

References

R.C. de Amorim and M. Zampieri. 2013. "Effective Spell Checking Methods Using Clustering Algorithms," *Recent Advances in Natural Language Processing*, 7-13.

C. Blair. 1960. "A program for correcting spelling errors," *Information and Control*, 3:60-67.

A. Carlson, J. Rosen, and D. Roth. 2001. "Scaling up context-sensitive text correction," *Proceedings of the 13th Innovative Applications of Artificial Intelligence Conference*, 45-50.

A. Carlson and I. Fette. 2007. "Memory-Based Context-Sensitive Spelling Correction at Web Scale," *Proceedings of the 6th International Conference on Machine Learning and Applications*, 166-171.

C.H. Chang. 1994. "A pilot study on automatic chinese spelling error correction," *Journal of Chinese Language and Computing*, 4:143-149.

Q. Chen, M. Li, and M. Zhou. 2007. "Improving

Run	FAlarm	DetcAcc	DetcP	DetcR	DetcF	LocAcc	LocP	LocR	LocF
Dryrun1_NTOU	**0.475**	**0.600**	0.321	0.900	0.474	**0.440**	0.036	0.010	0.053
Dryrun2_NTOU	0.525	0.580	0.323	1.000	**0.488**	**0.440**	0.097	0.300	**0.146**
Dryrun3_NTOU	0.700	0.440	0.263	1.000	0417	0.280	0.053	0.200	0.083

Table 5. Dry run performance in Subtask 1

Run	LocAcc	CorrAcc	CorrP
Dryrun1_NTOU	0.320	0.220	0.225
Dryrun2_NTOU	0.500	0.380	0.388
Dryrun3_NTOU	---	---	---

Table 6. Dry run performance in Subtask 2

Run	FAlarm	DetcAcc	DetcP	DetcR	DetcF	LocAcc	LocP	LocR	LocF
Formalrun1_NTOU	**0.980**	**0.314**	0.304	**1.000**	0.467	0.109	0.096	0.317	0.148
Formalrun2_NTOU	0.943	0.338	0.311	0.993	0.474	**0.149**	**0.114**	**0.363**	**0.173**
Formalrun3_NTOU	0.926	0.350	**0.315**	0.993	**0.478**	0.135	0.088	0.277	0.133

Table 7. Formal run performance in Subtask 1

Run	LocAcc	CorrAcc	CorrP
Formalrun1_NTOU	0.324	0.279	0.279
Formalrun2_NTOU	**0.371**	**0.311**	**0.312**
Formalrun3_NTOU	0.318	0.268	0.269

Table 8. Formal run performance in Subtask 2

Query Spelling Correction Using Web Search Results", *Proceedings of the 2007 Conference on Empirical Methods in Natural Language (EMNLP-2007)*, 181-189.

Y.Z. Chen, S.H. Wu, P.C. Yang, T. Ku, and G.D. Chen. 2011. "Improve the detection of improperly used Chinese characters in students' essays with error model," *Int. J. Cont. Engineering Education and Life-Long Learning*, 21(1):103-116.

S. Cucerzan and E. Brill. 2004. "Spelling correction as an iterative process that exploits the collective knowledge of web users," *Proceedings of EMNLP*, 293-300.

F. Damerau. 1964. "A technique for computer detection and correction of spelling errors." *Communications of the ACM*, 7:171-176.

S. Deorowicz and M.G. Ciura. 2005. "Correcting Spelling Errors by Modelling Their Causes," *International Journal of Applied Mathematics and Computer Science*, 15(2):275-285.

A. Golding and D. Roth. 1999. "A winnow-based approach to context-sensitive spelling correction," *Machine Learning*, 34(1-3):107-130.

A. Islam and D. Inkpen. 2009. "Real-word spelling correction using googleweb 1t 3-grams," *Proceedings of Empirical Methods in Natural Language Processing (EMNLP-2009)*, 1241-1249.

M. Li, Y. Zhang, M.H. Zhu, and M. Zhou. 2006. "Exploring distributional similarity based models for query spelling correction," *Proceedings of the 21st International Conference on Computational Linguistics and 44th Annual Meeting of the ACL*, 1025-1032.

W. Liu, B. Allison, and L. Guthrie. 2008. "Professor or screaming beast? Detecting words misuse in Chinese," *The 6th edition of the Language Resources and Evaluation Conference.*

C.L. Liu, M.H. Lai, K.W. Tien, Y.H. Chuang, S.H. Wu, and C.Y. Lee. 2011. "Visually and phonologically similar characters in incorrect Chinese words: Analyses, identification, and applications," *ACM Transactions on Asian Language Information Processing*, 10(2), 10:1-39.

R. Mitton. 1996. *English Spelling and the Computer*, Harlow, Essex: Longman Group.

R. Mitton. 2008. "Ordering the Suggestions of a Spellchecker Without Using Context," *Natural Language Engineering*, 15(2):173-192.

T. Pirinen and K. Linden. 2010. "Creating and weighting hunspell dictionaries as finite-state automata," *Investigationes Linguisticae*, 21.

S. Verberne. 2002. *Context-sensitive spell checking based on word trigram probabilities*, Master thesis, University of Nijmegen.

C. Whitelaw, B. Hutchinson, G.Y. Chung, and G. Ellis. 2009. "Using the Web for Language Independent Spellchecking and Autocorrection," *Proceedings Of Conference On Empirical Methods In Natural Language Processing (EMNLP-2009)*, 890-899.

S.H. Wu, Y.Z. Chen, P.C. Yang, T. Ku, and C.L. Liu. 2010. "Reducing the False Alarm Rate of Chinese Character Error Detection and Correction," *Proceedings of CIPS-SIGHAN Joint Conference on Chinese Language Processing (CLP 2010)*, 54-61.

L. Zhang, M. Zhou, C.N. Huang, and H.H. Pan. 2000. "Automatic detecting/correcting errors in Chinese text by an approximate word-matching algorithm," *Proceedings of the 38th Annual Meeting on Association for Computational Linguistics*, 248-254.

Candidate Scoring Using Web-Based Measure for Chinese Spelling Error Correction

Liang-Chih Yu
Yuan Ze University
135 Yuan-Tung Road, Chung-Li City
Taoyuan County, Taiwan, 32003
lcyu@saturn.yzu.edu.tw

Chao-Hong Liu **Chung-Hsien Wu**
National Cheng Kung University
No. 1, University Road
Tainan City, Taiwan, 70101
chl,chwu@csie.ncku.edu.tw

Abstract

Chinese character correction involves two major steps: 1) Providing candidate corrections for all or partially identified characters in a sentence, and 2) Scoring all altered sentences and identifying which is the best corrected sentence. In this paper a web-based measure is used to score candidate sentences, in which there exists one continuous error character in a sentence in almost all sentences in the Bakeoff corpora. The approach of using a web-based measure can be applied directly to sentences with multiple error characters, either consecutive or not, and is not optimized for one-character error correction of Chinese sentences. The results show that the approach achieved a fair precision score whereas the recall is low compared to results reported in this Bakeoff.

1 Introduction

Errors existing in Chinese sentences can be classified into five categories: 1) Deletion, 2) Insertion, 3) Substitution, 4) Word-Order and 5) Non-Word errors (C.-H. Liu, Wu, & Harris, 2008; C.-L. Liu, Lai, Chuang, & Lee, 2010; C.-L. Liu, Tien, Lai, Chuang, & Wu, 2009; C.-H. Wu, Liu, Harris, & Yu, 2010). Deletion errors occur when there are missing Chinese characters/words in a sentence; Insertion errors occur when there are grammatically redundant characters/words; Substitution errors occur when characters/words are mis-typed by similar, either visually or phonologically, ones; Word-Order errors occur when the word order of a sentence does not conform to the language, which is a common error type exists in writings of second-language learners; Non-Word errors occur when a Chinese character is written incorrectly by hand, e.g., miss of a stroke.

Of the five error types, the Substitution errors is addressed in this SIGHAN-7 Chinese Spelling Check bakeoff and might be referred to as "Chinese spelling error" to emphasize its resemblance to counterparts in spelling-based languages such as English. It should be noted that Non-Word errors is also a kind of Chinese spelling errors. It is also a common error type in hand-writings of second-language learners. However, since it only exists in hand-writings of humans and because all characters used in computers are legal ones, it is not necessary to address this kind of spelling errors when given erroneous texts are of electronic forms.

The task addressed in SIGHAN-7 is a restricted type of Substitution errors, where there exists at most one continuous error (mis-spelled) character in its context within a sentence, with only one exception in which there is a two-character error (Chen, Wu, Yang, & Ku, 2011; C.-L. Liu et al., 2010; S.-H. Wu, Chen, Yang, Ku, & Liu, 2010). This allows the system to assume that when a character is to be corrected, its adjacent characters are correct. The correction procedure is comprised of two consecutive steps: 1) Providing candidate corrections for each character in the sentence, and 2) Scoring the altered correction sentences and identifying which is the best corrected sentence (C.-H. Liu et al., 2008; C.-H. Wu et al., 2010). In this paper, a web-based measure is employed in the second step to score and identify the best correction sentence (Macias, Wong, Thangarajah, & Cavedon, 2012).

This paper is organized as follows. Section 2 describes the system architecture for spelling error correction. Section 3 provides the details of the model using web-based measure to score candidate corrections. In Section 4 the experimental setup and results are detailed. The last section summarized the conclusions and future work of this paper.

2 System Overview

SIGHAN-7 bakeoff is comprised of two sub-tasks, 1) Error Detection and 2) Error correction. Each of the sub-tasks requires the system to report positions where the errors occur. The philosophy behind the separation of the two sub-tasks lies in the belief that it is easier to detect if there is an error than to locate that error and provide correction to it.

In this paper, we took a different philosophy to address spelling error correction problem, in which there is no separate error detection method to detect if there is an error character or where the error is in a sentence. In this paper there is the one error correction method for both sub-tasks. In our system, if a character is reported erroneous, there is always a correction to that character; the correction method itself serves as an error detection mechanism.

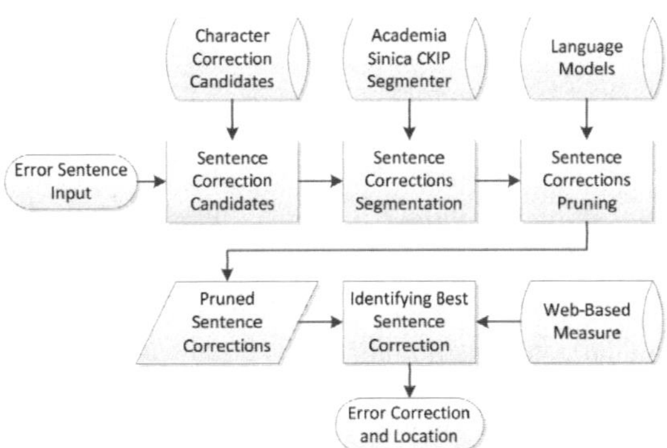

Fig. 1. System overview of the proposed spelling error correction using web-based measure.

The overview of our system is shown in Fig. 1. The input of the system is a sentence in which an erroneous character might occur. To recover the possible error, each character in the sentence is assumed to be an error one, and is given replacements (which are possible corrections to a character) using visually and phonologically similar sets provided by SIGHAN-7 bakeoff. For a character s_i in a sentence $S = (s_1, s_2, \dots, s_n)$ of n characters, there will be m possible corrections $S_i^1, S_i^2, \dots, S_i^m$ and the best correction sentence $\hat{S}_i$, concerning s_i, can be derived using equation 1.

$$\hat{S}_i = \operatorname*{argmax}_{j=1,\dots,m} LM\left(Seg(S_i^j)\right) \quad (1)$$

where $Seg(S_e)$ is the function returning Chinese segmentation results of sentence S_e, and $LM(S_g)$ returns the language model score of a segmented sentence S_g.

Therefore, sentence correction candidates $\hat{S}_1, \hat{S}_2, \dots, \hat{S}_n$ are derived, corresponding to the best correction characters, $\hat{s}_1, \hat{s}_2, \dots, \hat{s}_n$, respectively. Finally, Equation 2 is used to determine which candidate is the best correction, $\hat{S}$.

$$\hat{S} = \operatorname*{argmax}_{i=1,\dots,n} R(\hat{S}_i, \hat{s}_i) \quad (2)$$

where $R(S_c, s_c)$ returns the relatedness between a correction sentence S_c and its corresponding correction character s_c (Macias et al., 2012). The description of R is presented in Section 3.

In the proposed system, if the derived correction, $\hat{S}$, is identical to input sentence, S, it reports that there is no error in the sentence. On the contrary, if $\hat{S}$ is not identical to S, which indicates there is one character difference, the system then reports the sentence is detected erroneous along with the resulting correction character. Therefore there is no independent error detection module or procedure in our system; error detection itself depends on if the resulting corrections are identical to input sentences.

3 Web-Based Measure

There are two major directions to improve error correction system, 1) Finding correct and concise candidate sets for erroneous texts, and 2) Using measures such as language model scores to determine which correction sentence is the best result (C.-H. Liu et al., 2008; C.-H. Wu et al., 2010). In both directions, measures used to prune out unlikely candidates and determine the best correction are the fundamental technique. In SIGHAN-7 bakeoff, the visually and phonologically similar characters are provided as correction candidates. Therefore the focus of the proposed system lies in the second direction, i.e., to provide a measure that will rank correct candidates higher against other candidates.

To provide information about which of the candidates is a better correction, language models and pointwise mutual information (PMI) are commonly used (Chen et al., 2011; C.-L. Liu et al., 2010; C.-H. Wu et al., 2010). Although the information is usually trained with a large corpus such as Chinese Gigaword, they are still insufficient in general-domain applications.

To overcome this data insufficiency problem, web-based measures for estimating distances/similarities and relatedness have been proposed as alternative metric for several NLP applications (Cilibrasi & Vitanyi, 2009; Cilibrasi & Vitanyi, 2007; Gracia & Mena, 2008; Lovelyn Rose & Chandran, 2012). In this paper, we modified a web-based definition of semantic relatedness metric proposed by (Macias et al., 2012). Equation 2 is re-written as Equation 3.

$$\hat{S} = \underset{i=1,\dots,n}{\operatorname{argmax}} R(\hat{S}_i, \hat{s}_i) = \underset{i=1,\dots,n}{\operatorname{argmax}} \frac{\sum_{\forall k \in \hat{S}_i} W(k, \hat{s}_i)}{|\hat{S}_i|} \quad (3)$$

where W is the "normalized web relatedness" and k is a comprising character in the sentence correction candidate $\hat{S}_i$. $|\hat{S}_i|$ indicates the number of characters in $\hat{S}_i$. The definition of W is provded in Equation 4.

$$W(k, s) = e^{-0.6 \times D(k,s)} \quad (4)$$

where D is the "normalized web distance" and is defined in Equation 5.

$$D(k, s) = \frac{\log(\max(|k|, |s|)) - \log(|k \cap s|)}{\log(|G|) - \log(\min(|k|, |s|))} \quad (5)$$

where $|G|$ is the number of Wikipedia Chinese pages, which is 3,063,936 as of the time the system is implemented.

It should be noted that Macias-Galindo et al.'s original work is used in English texts. Currently we have not administered any preliminary experiment to find better setups of these equations.

4 Experiments and Discussions

In the proposed system, Academia Sinica's CKIP Chinese Segmenter is used to derive segmentation results (Ma & Chen, 2003) and the language model (trigrams using Chen and Goodman's modified Kneser-Ney discounting) is trained using SRILM with Chinese Gigaword (LDC *Catalog No.*: LDC2003T09) (Stolcke, 2002).

In a brief summary of the results, our system did not perform well in the final test of SIGHAN-7 bakeoff. The authors would like to defend the proposed method with a major problem in the runtime of the final test. In theory, the $\hat{S}_1, \hat{S}_2, \dots, \hat{S}_n$ as derived in Equation 1 should all be estimated using the web-based measure using Equation 2. However, since the number of sentences in the final test is huge (Sub-Tasks 1 and 2 each has 1,000 paragraphs and each paragraph contains about five Chinese sentences), the enormous number of queries sent to the search engine (Yahoo!) has caused our experiments being banned for several times. To solve this problem, two strategies were used to complete the final test, 1) only three of the candidates $\hat{S}_1, \hat{S}_2, \dots, \hat{S}_n$ (ranked the highest three using n-gram) are considered in the final test using web-based measure, and 2) three computers with different physical IP addresses were setup for the experiment. Therefore, the potential of the proposed method is far from fully exploited. A post-workshop experiment will be administered for further analysis of the method.

Table 1. Comparisons on Error Location Accuracy in SIGHAN-7 Sub-Tasks 1 and 2.

Sub-Task 1 (Detection)	**Error Location Accuracy**
NCKU&YZU-1	0.705
NTHU-3	**0.820**
SinicaCKIP-3	0.771
SJTU-3	0.809
NCYU-2	0.652
NCYU-3	0.748
Sub-Task 2 (Correction)	**Location Accuracy**
NCKU&YZU-1	0.117
NTHU-3	0.454
SinicaCKIP-3	0.559
SJTU-3	0.370
NCYU-2	**0.663**
NCYU-3	**0.663**

The comparisons of the proposed system and highly ranked systems in SIGHAN-7 are excerpted in this section. The first result that attracts our attention is error location accuracy as shown in Table 1. This is a common measure in both Sub-Tasks and is defined as "number of sentences error locations are correctly detected" over "number of all test sentences". The report of our system (NCKU&YZU-1) on error location accuracy in Sub-Task 1 (Detection) is 0.705, whereas it is only 0.117 in Sub-Task 2 (Correction). This result puzzled the authors because in our system, there is no error detection module. Similar results on both Sub-Tasks are expected since the same error correction method is used. A possible explanation is that the final test corpora of the two Sub-Tasks exhibited substantial differences in the composition of correct and erroneous sentences or in sentential characteristics. The results of other systems reported in both

Sub-Tasks seem to support this point of view. However, further analysis on the test corpora is still needed to clarify this problem.

Table 2. Comparisons on Error Location measures in SIGHAN-7 Sub-Task 1.

Error Location (Detection)	Accuracy	Precision	Recall
NCKU&YZU-1	0.705	0.410	0.137
NTHU-3	**0.820**	0.670	0.520
SinicaCKIP-3	0.771	0.500	**0.617**
SJTU-3	0.809	**0.710**	0.417

Table 3. Comparisons on Error Detection measures in SIGHAN-7 Sub-Task 1.

Error Detection	Accuracy	Precision	Recall
NCKU&YZU-1	0.729	0.650	0.217
NTHU-3	**0.861**	0.846	0.657
SinicaCKIP-3	0.842	0.692	0.853
SJTU-3	0.844	0.909	0.533
NTOU-1	0.314	0.304	**1.000**

Tables 2 and 3 show the results on error location detection and error detection in Sub-Task 1 (Detection). The difference between these two is that "error location detection" requires the detected location is correct while "error detection" will report correctly detected even the locations in sentences is not correct. Therefore it is expected that scores of Error Location Detection are a little bit higher than those of Error Detection. Our system exhibits a relative smaller difference between these two scores, 2.4%, compared to other systems.

The major weakness of our system is its low recall rate, which might be the result of not applying an error detection module. Therefore an error detection method using web-based measure will be examined in our future work.

Table 4. Comparisons on False-Alarm Rate and Detection Accuracy in SIGHAN-7 Sub-Task 1.

Error Detection	False-Alarm Rate	Accuracy
NCKU&YZU-1	0.050	0.729
NTHU-3	0.051	**0.861**
SinicaCKIP-3	0.163	0.842
SJTU-3	**0.023**	0.844

Table 5. Comparisons on Correction Accuracy and Precision in SIGHAN-7 Sub-Task 2.

Error Correction	Accuracy	Precision
NCKU&YZU-1	0.109	0.466
NTHU-3	0.443	0.700
SinicaCKIP-3	0.516	0.616
SJTU-3	0.356	**0.705**
NCYU-2	**0.625**	0.703
NCYU-3	**0.625**	0.703

Table 4 shows the error detection accuracy of our system is significantly lower although False-Alarm Rate is relatively small. The correction accuracy and precision are also much lower than high-ranked systems in the Bakeoff, as shown in Table 5. Further investigation is required to examine if more thoroughly exploiting web-based measures will provide useful additional information for the purpose of Chinese spelling error detection and correction.

5 Conclusions and Future Work

In this paper, a web-based measure is employed in addition to language models as a metric to score sentence correction candidates. The goal of this approach is to exploit as much texts (i.e., the web) as possible to provide useful information for error correction purposes.

The approach's major obstacle to participate in the Bakeoff's final test is our limited resources to access the results of search engines within two days. This has forced our final participating system to only take advantage of web-based measure in correction candidates' very last decisions. Further experiments administered on more thorough uses of web-based measure are required in the applications of Chinese spelling errors detection and correction.

The results of our system have confirmed the value of using a separate error detection module, i.e., detecting if there is an error in a sentence regardless where the error situated, such that sentences with no (detected) errors won't go through the error correction module.

Our direct future work would consist of 1) the inclusion of a separate error detection module, and 2) the administering of experiments exploiting web-based measure conforming to the method described in Section 3. A decomposition approach of web-based measure is also desirable to minimize runtime reliance on search engines.

Acknowledgments

This work was supported by National Science Council (NSC), Taiwan, under Contract number: 102-2221-E-155-029-MY3.

References

Chen, Y.-Z., Wu, S.-H., Yang, P.-C., & Ku, T. (2011). Improve the Detection of Improperly Used Chinese Characters in Students' Essays with Error Model. *International Journal of Continuing Engineering Education and Life Long Learning, 21*(1), 103-116.

Cilibrasi, R. L., & Vitanyi, P. (2009). Normalized Web Distance and Word Similarity. *arXiv preprint arXiv:0905.4039.*

Cilibrasi, R. L., & Vitanyi, P. M. (2007). The Google Similarity Distance. *IEEE Transactions on Knowledge and Data Engineering, 19*(3), 370-383.

Gracia, J., & Mena, E. (2008). Web-based Measure of Semantic Relatedness *Web Information Systems Engineering-WISE 2008* (pp. 136-150): Springer.

Liu, C.-H., Wu, C.-H., & Harris, M. (2008). *Word Order Correction for Language Transfer Using Relative Position Language Modeling.* Paper presented at the 6th International Symposium on Chinese Spoken Language Processing (ISCSLP'08).

Liu, C.-L., Lai, M.-H., Chuang, Y.-H., & Lee, C.-Y. (2010). *Visually and Phonologically Similar Characters in Incorrect Simplified Chinese Words.* Paper presented at the The 23rd International Conference on Computational Linguistics: Posters.

Liu, C.-L., Tien, K.-W., Lai, M.-H., Chuang, Y.-H., & Wu, S.-H. (2009). *Phonological and Logographic Influences on Errors in Written Chinese Words.* Paper presented at the The 7th Workshop on Asian Language Resources.

Lovelyn Rose, S., & Chandran, K. (2012). Normalized Web Distance Based Web Query Classification. *Journal of Computer Science, 8*(5), 804-808.

Ma, W.-Y., & Chen, K.-J. (2003). *Introduction to CKIP Chinese Word Segmentation System for the First International Chinese Word Segmentation Bakeoff.* Paper presented at the The Second SIGHAN Workshop on Chinese Language Processing.

Macias, D., Wong, W., Thangarajah, J., & Cavedon, L. (2012). *Coherent Topic Transition in a Conversational Agent.* Paper presented at the 13th Annual Conference of the International Speech Communication Association (INTERSPEECH).

Stolcke, A. (2002). *SRILM-an extensible language modeling toolkit.* Paper presented at the 7th International Conference on Spoken Language Processing, ICSLP2002 - INTERSPEECH 2002.

Wu, C.-H., Liu, C.-H., Harris, M., & Yu, L.-C. (2010). Sentence Correction Incorporating Relative Position and Parse Template Language Models. *IEEE Transactions on Audio, Speech, and Language Processing, 18*(6), 1170-1181.

Wu, S.-H., Chen, Y.-Z., Yang, P.-c., Ku, T., & Liu, C.-L. (2010). *Reducing the False Alarm Rate of Chinese Character Error Detection and Correction.* Paper presented at the The CIPS-SIGHAN Joint Conference on Chinese Language Processing.

Author Index

Association for Computational Linguistics
209 N. Eighth Street
Stroudsburg, Pennsylvania 18360

CURRAN ASSOCIATES INC
proceedings.com

11th International Workshop on Finite State Methods and Natural Language Processing

(FSMNLP 2013)

St. Andrews, Scotland
15-17 July 2013

ISBN: 978-1-62993-003-9